Television Dramatic Dialogue

OXFORD STUDIES IN SOCIOLINGUISTICS

General Editors:
Nikolas Coupland
Adam Jaworski
Cardiff University

Recently Published in the Series:

Talking About Treatment: Recommendations for Breast Cancer Adjuvant Treatment
Felicia D. Roberts

Language in Time: The Rhythm and Tempo of Spoken Interaction
Peter Auer, Elizabeth Couper-Kuhlen, and Frank Müller

Whales, Candlelight, and Stuff Like That: General Extenders in English Discourse
Maryann Overstreet

A Place to Stand: Politics and Persuasion in a Working-Class Bar
Julie Lindquist

Sociolinguistic Variation: Critical Reflections
Edited by Carmen Fought

Prescribing under Pressure: Parent-Physician Conversations and Antibiotics
Tanya Stivers

Discourse and Practice: New Tools for Critical Discourse Analysis
Theo van Leeuwen

Beyond Yellow English: Toward a Linguistic Anthropology of Asian Pacific America
Edited by Angela Reyes and Adrienne Lo

Stance: Sociolinguistic Perspectives
Edited by Alexandra Jaffe

Investigating Variation: The Effects of Social Organization and Social Setting
Nancy C. Dorian

Television Dramatic Dialogue: A Sociolinguistic Study
Kay Richardson

Television Dramatic Dialogue

A Sociolinguistic Study

Kay Richardson

OXFORD

UNIVERSITY PRESS

2010

OXFORD
UNIVERSITY PRESS

Oxford University Press, Inc., publishes works that further
Oxford University's objective of excellence
in research, scholarship, and education.

Oxford   New York
Auckland   Cape Town   Dar es Salaam   Hong Kong   Karachi
Kuala Lumpur   Madrid   Melbourne   Mexico City   Nairobi
New Delhi   Shanghai   Taipei   Toronto

With offices in
Argentina   Austria   Brazil   Chile   Czech Republic   France   Greece
Guatemala   Hungary   Italy   Japan   Poland   Portugal   Singapore
South Korea   Switzerland   Thailand   Turkey   Ukraine   Vietnam

Published by Oxford University Press, Inc.
198 Madison Avenue, New York, New York 10016

www.oup.com

Oxford is a registered trademark of Oxford University Press.

Library of Congress Cataloging-in-Publication Data
Richardson, Kay, 1955–
Television dramatic dialogue : a sociolinguistic study / Kay Richardson.
    p.   cm.—(Oxford studies in sociolinguistics)
Includes bibliographical references.
ISBN 978-0-19-537405-6; 978-0-19-537406-3 (pbk.)
1. Television broadcasting—Language.   2. Television series—Great Britain.
3. Television series—United States.   4. English language—Usage.
5. Dialogue analysis.   6. Sociolinguistics.   I. Title.
PN1992.8.L35R33 2010
302.2'345—dc22   2009024979

9 8 7 6 5 4 3 2 1
Printed in the United States of America
on acid-free paper

This book is dedicated
to the team in Combined Honours at Liverpool:
Jeanne, Becky, John, Helen, Kathy,
Debbie, Jim, Claire, and Janet

Acknowledgments

Most of all, I want to thank John Corner, who read the whole manuscript at a late stage and made important suggestions which improved the quality of the work. I also want to acknowledge all of the participants at the Ross Priory Broadcast Talk seminar of March 2008: they listened to an early version of chapter 2 and gave me valuable feedback. Some members of the Ross Priory group have provided intellectual stimulation and camaraderie over a longer period of time, especially Joanna Thornborrow, Stephanie Marriott, Martin Montgomery, Greg Myers, Andrew Tolson, Paddy Scannell, and Arnt Maasø (who provided me with a key reference at an early stage of the project). I am grateful to all of you.

Adam Jaworski and Nik Coupland, the series editors for Oxford Studies in Sociolinguistics, recommended this book for commissioning and helped to ensure that the proposal was a worthy one; the staff at Oxford University Press who contributed to its production include Peter Ohlin, the commissioning editor, as well as Molly Wagener, Stephanie Attia, Brian Hurley, Mary Anne Shahidi, and others behind the scenes whose names I do not know. Please accept my thanks for your support.

Contents

Television Dramatic Dialogue

1

Introduction

Television, as the dominant mass medium of the second half of the twentieth century and into the first decade of the twenty-first century, is responsible for bringing extensive amounts of drama into everyday life, from adaptations of classic novels and multiple episode serials to true story enactments and the scenarios played out in TV commercials. In doing so, it repeatedly displays *people talking*, showing audiences how characters behave in the varying circumstances of their narratives. These stories, and the talk they give rise to, mediate between the familiar and the extraordinary, and engage the imaginative powers of their receivers as well as their creators. This book offers a primarily sociolinguistic approach toward a better understanding of what the talking in these dramatic productions contributes to contemporary culture.[1]

THE SCOPE OF THE RESEARCH

Television drama dialogue can be defined as onscreen/on-mike talk delivered by characters as part of dramatic storytelling in a range of fictional and nonfictional TV genres. Television consumers are characteristically referred to as its *viewers* and described as *watching* programs on TV. But the experience of television is seriously incomplete unless viewers are also *listeners*, who engage with the various mixes of sound, speech, and music that the medium has to offer, in combination with its visual images. Most of television's product range offers us the sound of the human voice, and a considerable proportion of *that* involves the kind of talk that I have described above. When actors talk to one another on this basis, we in the audience are invited to hear *speech*, embodied and en-voiced. The *lines* crafted by writers in the confines of an office or other private space have been appropriated and transformed. Within the parameters of the representation, the on-screen bodies own their speech as the characters they purport to be. In television's favored realist modes, this embodiment accommodates well any inclination we may have to hear characters as people, and their talk as the kind of thing that such people could say, in the ordinary or extraordinary circumstances that the dramatized situations present them with.

Such speech is not authentic, if by *authentic* we mean unscripted, naturally occurring talk among human beings talking for themselves, as themselves; and as a mimetic copy of *real* conversation (cf. Quaglio 2009) it will always be found wanting, if only because of the functions it must perform over and above those of imitation. But even outside of drama, the line between *authentic* and *inauthentic* speech is a hard one to draw. Erving Goffman long ago demonstrated the extent to which performance was an essential part of everyday human interaction, and introduced a dramaturgical model into the analysis of such interaction (Goffman 1959). If, as he suggested, we stage-manage our routine encounters with others, then authenticity is itself a matter of negotiation in our social relationships. On the other hand, characters in drama (even, to a degree, those based on real people like Margaret Thatcher, former prime minister of the United Kingdom) are the product of imagination, so there can be no question of them producing speech "for themselves, as themselves"—they have no selves. But dramatists can write, actors can deliver, and directors can stage, lines that fit the character's design. They can, among them, offer plausibility, appropriacy and consistency, and they can even include some *re*staging of the stage management of everyday encounters. They are allowed, required even, to do so within the terms of larger narrative structures and thematic concerns—to realize just as much character depth and complexity in the characters' talk that the project, conceived holistically, requires.

In her groundbreaking study of dialogue in feature films, Kozloff had this to say:

> Although what the characters say, exactly how they say it, and how the dialogue is integrated with the rest of the cinematic techniques are crucial to our experience and understanding of every film since the coming of sound, for the most part analysts incorporate the information provided by a film's dialogue and overlook the dialogue as signifier. Canonical textbooks on film aesthetics devote pages and pages to editing and cinematography but barely mention dialogue. Visual analysis requires mastery of a recondite vocabulary and trained attentiveness; dialogue has been perceived as too transparent, too simple to need study. (Kozloff 2000: 6)

The image of dialogue as "transparent" is an interesting one in this context. It is a metaphor that fits the *visual* field much more readily than it fits the aural (including verbal) field. In the visual field it relates to the well-known practices of continuity editing, designed to efface all evidence of the work required to achieve the pictures on screen and to create narrative continuity between them (Bordwell and Thompson 2006). The metaphor invites us to think of substances like glass or water. These substances allow us to look *through* them rather than *at* them, seeing only what is on the other side. The point of continuity editing is to invite that kind of viewing by audiences, though many viewers, including critics, want to resist the invitation and to understand the mediation itself.

How can *transparency* also be a property of *talk?* Talk is something we listen to, not something we look at (or through). Sight and hearing are equivalent in this sense—that in both cases one basic interpretation strategy is the one that tries to efface the form and substance of the text in order to retrieve the content—the *meaning.* For the specific purposes of analyzing television dialogue, it is helpful to think of that dialogue as talk designed to create the impression that it has delivered up its meaning *without effort on the hearer's part.* Film and TV critics have learned to resist the visual transparency effect (which anyway does not apply to *all* screen fictions). The next lesson is resistance to its verbal equivalent, the "easy listening" effect. This book will help develop such resistance, by focusing on such matters as the following:

- How other effects, as well as, or instead of, those of easy listening—humor, for example—are created through television drama dialogue. This also includes the use of dialogue for narrative exposition and for the creation of believable characters.
- How the craft skills of writers and performers contribute to the easy listening effect of television dialogue—and how these skills depend upon the same kinds of resources that are deployed in the construction of intelligible interaction more generally.
- How audiences make use of dialogue in their own appropriations of television's dramatic texts.
- How the cultural significance of television dialogue goes beyond the specific effects it sets out to achieve.
- What can be learned about the social conditions of linguistic creativity with reference to this particular kind of language use.

In mainstream television and film, there is a preference for realistic rather than stylized or poetic modes of talk in many genres. This approximate, and conventionalized, verisimilitude encourages audiences to take the easy road and hear *drama talk* as they hear everyday talk. But as all sociolinguists know, even everyday, unscripted talk *categorically does not* give up meaning without effort on the hearer's part. Much research in the fields of pragmatics (including politeness theory), interactional sociolinguistics, and conversation analysis is dedicated to understanding the work involved in conversational sense making (for an introduction to pragmatics research, see, e.g., Verschueren 1999). Although that effort can be idealized out of existence in the routine practices of listening and talking, it becomes evident when communication gets problematic for participants. Then, they might query one another's choice of words, self-correct, ask for repetition, object to offensive or racist and sexist phrasings, protest against being interrupted, or engage in any number of metacommunicative practices. These practices, too, are a normal part of everyday talk (Cameron

2004). As far as realist drama dialogue is concerned, they, too, can be brought under the regime of its easy listening protocol.

When easy listening in dramatic dialogue is a design goal (on the production side) and a default interpretation preference (on the reception side), the result should indeed correspond to its counterpart in daily life, with audience in the role of eavesdroppers (cf. Bubel 2008). This kind of easy listening (which will be reinforced by the visual transparency effect) allows audiences to hear that the dialogue belongs to the characters, and that the characters are people getting on with their lives. It discourages audiences from hearing other things in the dialogue—for example, it discourages them from hearing characters as channels of narrative exposition. Characters are not there to tell the story: they are there to act, to have experiences and to talk.

WHAT IS TELEVISION DRAMATIC DIALOGUE?

The object of study has some very clear prototypical forms, but fuzzy boundaries, for example, where *television* ends and *film* begins, where *drama* meets *documentary*, and where *dialogue*, typically pre-scripted, becomes improvised. The purpose of this section is first to illustrate the nature of dramatic dialogue in its prototypical form, and then to establish the limits of its distribution on television, moving outward from the core cases toward the periphery. This chapter, and the two that follow, are the most expansive chapters in the book, and reference will be made to the following kinds of screen production using dialogue: situation comedy, sketch shows, dramatized documentary; TV commercials; legal dramas; political dramas, "dramedy"; fantasy drama, soap opera; monologues; historical dramas; improvisation game shows; and current affairs using dramatization.[2] In the remaining chapters, 4 to 10, there will be a narrower focus on programming at the more prototypical end.

Transcribed orthographically from the broadcast original, standard dramatic dialogue in TV can be made to look like this (lines here have been numbered for ease of reference):

1 TONY: Carmela, something I gotta confess.
   [*Carmela moves her wine glass*].
2 What are you doing?
3 CARMELA: Getting my wine in position to throw in your damn face!
4 TONY: You're always with the drama, you.
5 CARMELA: Go ahead and confess already, please! Get it over with!
6 TONY: [*covering his face*] I'm on Prozac.
7 CARMELA: Oh—Oh my God!
8 TONY: I've been seeing a therapist.

9 CARMELA: Oh my God! I think that's great! I think that's so wonderful! I think that's
   so gutsy!

(*The Sopranos*, HBO 1999–2007, episode 1, written by David Chase)[3]

The Sopranos is perhaps the most significant Anglophone television drama series of the first half of the 2000s. "Tony" is Anthony Soprano (James Gandolfini), head of a New Jersey mob family, and thus one in a long line of Italian-American crime family "godfathers" on film and television. "Carmela" (Edie Falco) is his wife. An informal account of the interaction in these few lines might look something like this:

The extract comes from two-thirds of the way through the first episode. Viewers have seen Tony's first and second meetings with his therapist, as well as flashbacks depicting events that led to the original therapy session. Carmela is about to become the first person to learn that he has sought professional help for his state of mind. The narrative business of the scene is "Tony tells Carmela" and "Carmela reacts to the news." The psychological context is the costs and benefits of disclosure for Tony. Because of his precarious position as de facto head of the mafia operation in New Jersey, Carmela is a less risky confidante than a "capo" if he must tell someone, and in terms of family politics there are other risks if she is kept in the dark. The dialogue here shows that Carmela already has a script/schema in place for "Tony's confessions"—adultery being the most likely, though wrong in this instance; it also displays the chronic state of tension that characterizes their relationship. Note the linguistic markers of informality appropriate to this relationship—*gonna, gutsy*—and of emotional content appropriate to the business at hand: *damn, Oh my God!* The distribution of such markers in television dialogue will not be explored in this book, but has been usefully examined elsewhere (Quaglio 2009).

Structurally Tony's disclosure is a drawn-out one. There is a presequence consisting of an announcement soliciting Carmela's assent to hear the confession (line 1), which is satisfied when the assent is granted (line 5). This exchange is broken up by an insertion sequence initiated by Tony in line 2 but provoked by Carmela's nonverbal action after line 1. The insertion sequence is collaborative linguistically (question-response-feedback in lines 2, 3, and 4, respectively) but interpersonally confrontational. The question is straightforward; the answer, though true, relevant, sincere, and (arguably) informationally satisfactory,[4] promises violence. The feedback to this undercuts Carmela's threat. She gives ground and engages on his original terms, though the wording of line 5 is styled to convey that her assent is grudgingly given—that for her it can only be bad to hear this news. Falco's performance realizes this "grudging consent" interpretation of the line through her intonation, voice quality, and body language. The actual information, divided by Tony into two parts, is handled by Carmela as a genuine surprise (line 7), and subsequently by her as *good* news (line 8).

According to Nelson (2007: 27), *The Sopranos* mixes the conventions of the mafia movie with those of soap opera and psychological drama. Most drama could claim to be *psychological* in some sense, but not all of it sets out to explore the complex inner lives of characters, and certainly not the traditional gangster films and TV shows. Husband-and-wife confrontations based on infidelity are common enough in any of these three genres—the twist here is that Tony is *not* confessing to adultery and Carmela's expectations are thwarted, though the audience's are not because they know the secret already. Akass and McCabe (2002) are interested in the introduction of strong women into a traditionally masculine genre. Tony's therapist is one of those strong women, and Carmela is another. The dialogue here starts to point the audience away from a simple "wronged wife" schema, particularly in Carmela's enthusiastic response to Tony's admission. His own hesitancy (the presequence, the face-covering) display him as a weaker brand of godfather—at least in his wife's presence, though with a more assertive alternate repertoire also available to him, as displayed in line 4. Aspects of the show's discourse that are apparent at the broad level of its narrative structure can also be recognized in microcosm at the level of the dialogic exchange.

But this kind of drama is just the start. Some TV stories claim to be *true*—based on real life. The characters in these are, or were, real people. Tony Blair, Britain's former prime minister, was constructed as "Tony Blair" in *The Deal* (Granada Television 2003) in a performance by Michael Sheen—which Sheen then reproduced for the feature film *The Queen*. A "Julius Caesar" character was constructed, with much more creative latitude than in the case of Blair, for *Rome* (HBO/BBC 2005). There is no guarantee that the lines spoken by these dramatic characters were ever spoken by the corresponding individuals in real life—usually "their" words come from the imagination of a writer, just as much as those in *The Sopranos*. Nonfictional TV dramatization falls within the scope of the definition. So, too, does advertising. Not all TV commercials take a drama-tized form, but some do, and some of those use dialogue. The definition also includes sketches in TV shows, as well as soap operas and situation comedies that, although fictional and dramatized, sometimes fall inside, and sometimes outside, the scope of the genre term *TV drama*, depending on the context. Most television dramatic dialogue is pre-scripted, but this is not essential. Game shows like *Whose Line Is It Anyway?* (UK Channel Four, 1988–1998; USA ABC 1998–present) require comedy actors and stand-up comedians to create characters on the spot and improvise dialogue, playing out scenarios to order (partly from audience suggestions). The talk in *Whose Line* sketches is not only improvised but proudly so, because it is the quick-wittedness of the contest-ants in responding to one another, to the show's host, and to the audience that is the show's raison d'être. Elsewhere, improvisation may be disguised in postproduction for the sake of fluency in the finished work, as it was in the British comedy *Outnumbered* (BBC 2007–2009), about the routines of family life.

Up to this point, the focus has been on forms of production in which storytelling and dramatization coincide, and dramatization that has included dialogue. But not all storytelling on television takes a dramatic form,[5] and not all dramatization involves dialogue (multiparty talk among characters). Mime is obviously excluded by my definition, and so is nondramatized storytelling (including all those stories that form the daily news diet—the outcome of a court hearing, a bad drop in the stock market, an important bill being voted down) has no place for dialogue.

Also excluded are series like *Jackanory* (BBC 1965–1996, 2006)—a long-running children's TV series in the United Kingdom that used celebrities to read aloud from storybooks, and produced imaginative visual illustration to watch while listening to the tale. Reading aloud is, for obvious reasons, more common on radio than on television. The celebrity could perform the dialogue "in character"—as well as narrating the expositional elements. This kind of production certainly shares with *The Sopranos* an element of dialogue performance. But it is a special case: not only are the character roles and the narrator role given to the same performer, mitigating the normal arrangement in drama in which the performer is identified with his or her character, but also the prose narrative modality dominates over that of performed talk.

Dramatic monologues, such as the *Talking Heads* plays of Alan Bennett, are another interesting marginal case, for a different reason:

It's a funny time, three o'clock. Too late for lunch, but a bit early for tea.

This is what "Muriel" (played by Stephanie Cole) says at the start of "Soldiering On," (*Talking Heads*, series 1, BBC 1987). She is reflecting on her experience at the end of the day of her husband's funeral. She is the only one on camera throughout the production: she speaks "to camera." The performance calls for a kind of "diary" voice, or an address to a nonparticipating interlocutor—a sympathetic, interested "pen pal" for instance. Although there is no linguistic or nonlinguistic input from this correspondent, Muriel speaks to him/her as if they had a shared history: "I thought of Jessie Marchant," she says at one point, using a memory of this "Jessie" as part of an interpersonal common ground. "Jessie" has not been referred to previously and will not be referred to again. Such usages construct the *monologue* as a kind of *dialogue*. Unlike the *Jackanory* characters, the speaker produces lines appropriate only to her character of Muriel. Nevertheless, it is a marginal case because its dialogic character is covert rather than overt, and begins to remind us of the Bakhtinian argument that *all* speech and writing is engaged in conversation with other voices.

One final observation is necessary in this section. For some years now in Britain, and no doubt other countries too, closed-captioning (optional written subtitles) has been variably available for broadcast programming, for the benefit of hard-of-hearing viewers. Those who prefer sign language are accommodated less well: a few shows are repeated with an inset screen signing dialogue and commentary. Visual challenges are not overlooked either: some digital services provide optional audio commentary. In Britain broadcasters are legally obliged to attempt to meet the needs of all viewers over a variable 10-year timeframe, subject to some exclusions.[6] The arrival of the digital age has not made television drama instantly more accessible. My interest here, though, is not in the politics, economics, and technology of access, but in the variability of reception. Even at this basic level, different modes of delivery and reception are currently possible, and being used by audiences. Throughout the rest of this book, generalizations about how TV audiences receive information will continue to be normative ones referring to the majority audience, but it is important to acknowledge that this is an analytic convenience. There are signs that these services, provided with particular subgroups of the audience in mind, are also used more widely. Non-American audiences have come to appreciate that it can be easier to follow the dialogue and plot of some of the more "artful" American dramas with the subtitles turned on. (see chapter 10).

THE PLACE OF DIALOGUE IN TELEVISION DRAMATIZATION

Although this book is about language in TV dramatization, it is important not to put language at the center of the study of dramatic form and meaning. When drama is a way of delivering a particular kind of narrative, it falls within the scope of Seymour Chatman's view that narrative is a substratum of expressive form and thus not essentially linguistic:

> Literary critics tend to think too exclusively of the verbal medium, even though they consume stories daily through films, comic strips, paintings, sculptures, dance movements, and music. Common to these artifacts must be some substratum; otherwise we could not explain the transformation of "Sleeping Beauty" into a movie, a ballet, a mime show. (Chatman 1978)[7]

The substratum of narrative is supposed to involve some kind of cognitive construct. Researchers such as Emmott (1997) have argued that the comprehension of narrative requires the construction of mental models of the fictional world. Although Emmott writes about linguistic narratives, the points she makes apply, *mutatis mutandis*, to all narrative texts.

The distinctiveness of dramatic narratives has to do with the role of showing and the shown. Drama requires, among other things, *performed narrative actions*. These performances need not be linguistic ones, as the example of ballet clearly shows. Even dramas that do make use of language will need to do much more besides—especially in films and TV drama, of which so much is expected in the visual dimension. The nonlinguistic aspects of film and TV drama are so preeminent that in film studies it is necessary to *argue* for some attention to dialogue—the tradition here is to ignore, downplay, and disparage talk in favor of nonlinguistic form, structure, and meaning, as Kozloff (2000) has persuasively argued. One kind of narrative action in a screen drama, on TV or at the cinema, may involve an actor pulling a gun on another, or running from an assailant as in the best James Bond tradition. Another kind of narrative action is the linguistic kind, such as a threat, a declaration of love, an apology—or a confession, as in the extract from *The Sopranos* at the start of this chapter. Of course the conduct of *real life* also includes linguistic performances, as linguistic anthropology, ordinary language philosophy, and sociolinguistics have long recognized. The balance between linguistic and nonlinguistic actions will vary according to genre, but very little contemporary screen drama is entirely dialogue-free—the *Mr. Bean* series (ITV 1990–1995), and some film/TV commercials, are about as close as we get to this in the past few decades. To eliminate dialogue entirely is to eliminate not only actual speech acts, but also the possibility of using speech for exposition, helping viewers to understand what has happened or is happening at the level of plot, or as a contribution to the creation of plot expectations.[8]

Even when actors are required to talk, the vocal delivery of the words (timing, pitch, melody, voice quality, volume, etc.) already takes us out of the sphere of language and into that of the semiotics of sound (Van Leeuwen 1999), and nonvocal aspects of delivery (gaze, gesture, bodily orientation) take us further still (Naremore 1988). Language has a contribution to make to dramatic expression, but it is neither a necessary nor a sufficient element of its construction. Its most basic contribution is to assist in the realization of the underlying narrative form and characterization, though there are other less basic contributions too.

At the same time, not all language in dramatic texts takes the form of dialogue. Those linguists who study *literary* drama, in its written form, are interested, for instance, in stage directions (McIntyre 2006). Performed dramas may include *voiceover* components in many productions involving dramatization—common in dramatized documentary and TV commercials, but not unknown in popular drama too: it is deployed in both *Heroes* (NBC 2006–present) and *Desperate Housewives* (ABC 2004–present), among others:

> Where does it come from, this quest, this need to solve life's mysteries, when the simplest of questions can never be answered? "Why are we here?" "What is the

soul?" "Why do we dream?" Perhaps we'd be better off not looking at all, not yearning, not delving. That's not human nature, not the human heart. That is not why we are here.

(*Heroes*, season 1, episode 1, written by Tim Kring)

SHOWING AND TELLING

Dramatic dialogue exists within a storytelling frame. Stories can be shown, they can be told, or they can use a combination of showing (mimesis) and telling (diegesis). Drama aligns itself more with showing, and prose narrative more with telling, but neither alignment is exclusive, and there are different kinds of *showing*. Prose narrative and drama in its written form try to *show* using letters and words—conventional codings of sounds and meanings, whereas prose narrative, when read aloud, and drama, when performed and produced, appear to offer more directness in their representations. It is important to understand that writings and performances strive to show to the *ear*, as well as to the eye. The distinction between *showing* and *telling* is not the same as the one between audio and visual modes in TV and film drama. To understand this point, a good place to start is with a minimalist written *story* already familiar in language studies (Sacks 1972):

1. The baby cried. The mommy picked it up.

In this story we are not shown the crying—we are told about it. A writer who wanted his reader to hear the cry in her "mind's ear" might prefer the following:

2. The baby went: "Waaaagh!" The mommy picked it up.

"Waaaagh!" in version 2 is closer to the aural experience of hearing a baby cry than the verb "to cry" in version 1, but it is still an approximation of sound, made possible by the conventions of a writing system. The multiple repetition of the letter "a" between a "w" and a "gh" corresponds to no English word, but literate Anglophones can be relied on to get the point.

A *raconteur* (a term I will use to avoid confusion with a silent reader), reading aloud the second story, can use this approximation as a clue to guide her imitation of a baby's cry at this point. Though true verisimilitude may be missing, due to physiological differences if nothing else, we will at least hear the imitation as a *showing* of what the baby did, and not as a telling about the baby's act. Version 3 takes the point further:

3. The child went: "It huuuuurts!" The mommy picked him up.

A crying infant may be capable of verbalizing distress as well as emitting distress cries. Our prose narrative is able to represent this, and our raconteur may be as capable of doing vocal justice to the delivery of these words as she was capable of imitating the cry. The introduction of verbalization into the narrative changes nothing from a theoretical point of view. Nor does the elimination of written textual clues regarding the vocal qualities of the speech, except to create opportunity for someone other than the writer to take responsibility for those qualities:

4. The child went: "Kiss it better." The mommy picked him up.

The child in examples 1–3 is obviously being vocally expressive: the writer has indicated this, and the raconteur will want to do it justice. The writer of 4 makes life harder for the raconteur, by eliminating expressive clues from the text. Any vocal expressiveness in the words of the child then becomes the raconteur's contribution, in the absence of any other clues to build upon.

In a dramatization, showing is foregrounded and telling is backgrounded. A dramatized version of the above story would take away the responsibility to imitate speech/sound from the raconteur and give it to actors who, for story-showing purposes, embody and en-voice the characters in the story. *Telling* is linguistically manifest in the written and read-aloud versions: the sequencing and cohesion of the sentences made it into the telling of a *story*, of sorts. In a dramatization, including screen dramatization, sequencing of *actions* makes this a story. The sequenced actions must be visually displayed. This requires decisions about camerawork and other matters. Should there be one shot or two for this scene? Should the "mommy" be in shot all along, or enter the shot following the cry? Should the camera move to follow the mommy's movements? Should the mise-en-scène exclude or include other people in addition to the two protagonists? How fast should the sequence progress? Should the mommy's comforting action seem to be successful or unsuccessful in pacifying the child?

On television, it is in drama proper that aural and visual showing goes furthest. In other genres using dialogue—dramatic reconstructions in current affairs shows, TV commercials—there is likely to be a greater proportion of explicit telling in the mix, in the form of voiceover narration and/or on-screen written information (scrolling *tickers*, intertitles, captions, legends, etc.). In commercials we are likely to learn from a voiceover narration the point of what we have just been shown. A recent pharmaceutical product commercial features a performance of suffering, taking the product, and recovering, accompanied by this voiceover:

Isn't it annoying when things aren't complete? Especially when you've got all the symptoms of colds and flu. That's why we've created new [product], our most complete remedy ever. So, when you're suffering from a chesty cough, headache, fever, blocked nose, or sore throat, [product] gives you all the help you need.

The soundtrack is a mixed compilation of voiceover, music, and a background dialogue track in which only the fact of speaking matters and not the words spoken, which are indecipherable.

In factually based dramatized stories, an emphasis on telling can inhibit viewers from too readily transferring the show's claims from the told to the shown component. But the formal and conventionally permissible possibilities are broad, so that a recent dramatized documentary about the life of the legendary Spartacus is able to make the storyteller into a character in Spartacus' world, retrospectively pulling together what he knew of the hero:

> *Scene*: a cell full of chained prisoners: pan from cell window down and across to pick up one prisoner—Spartacus. Voiceover begins:
> No one even knows where he came from. Some say he was from Thrace, in Greece. But he never said.
> Dramatized sound as Spartacus and a female prisoner are unfastened from the wall, and escorted away by guards.
> All I know for sure is he had once been in the army. And then he and his wife were seized, and taken to the slave market in Rome. And that's where the story of Spartacus really began.
> Fade down voiceover: fade up character speech:
> . . . a woman and a child. We'll start at three thousand sesterces. What am I bid? *[auctioneer selling other slaves]*.

> (*Heroes and Villains: Spartacus*, BBC 2008, written by Colin Heber-Percy and Lyall B. Watson)

In this voiceover, the commentary is that of an *implied narrator*—a character with a fictional identity of his own. Later the narrator tells that Spartacus was his friend, and we learn that he, too, was a slave, and ran away as part of the rebellion, though we never learn how he comes to tell us the story. As for Spartacus's origins—the narrator is required to convey the fact that historians have no information on this. He is made to say that no one in Spartacus's own acquaintance knew where he was from either, because Spartacus "never said," but such a speculative proposition is more acceptable from the mouth of a character from the (hi)story world than from a more authoritative, "voice-of-God" narrator.

HOW TO STUDY DIALOGUE ON TELEVISION

As indicated at the start of the chapter, this is not a well-trodden research path. There are contextual reasons to explain the lack of attention paid to television dramatic dialogue in academic research. In those branches of language studies in which *conversation* is of interest, naturally occurring unmediated talk takes precedence over other kinds because of its greater claim to authenticity.

Stylistics is canonically interested in the language of literary texts, including plays (see, e.g., McIntyre, 2006, Culpeper 2001, Herman 1995), but most TV drama seems insufficiently literary to be included in this enterprise. Broadcast talk has its own literature, but this focuses on unscripted talk in chat shows, interviews, phone-ins, and reality television—the agenda here is with the social relations of broadcasting—including radio (Tolson 2006, Hutchby 2006). In textually oriented studies of TV drama, shows are regarded as a source of narratives and social themes that merit analysis, often with an interest in the visual form through which such meanings are delivered, but, as we have already seen, and as Geraghty (2003) also notes, they show little interest in the contribution of the dialogue. In each of these areas, the *relevance* of TV dramatic dialogue is problematic—not authentic, not literary, not special to the medium, and not visual. The limited amount of published work (see chapter 2) is evidence that there is no single research agenda in this area.

I have tried to achieve a mixture of breadth and depth in the following chapters. Breadth is important because, as indicated earlier, television dramatization comes in many forms. The forms and functions of talk in a drama series like *Heroes* are very different from those found in a TV commercial. Among those productions that fall under the narrower designation of *drama* rather than the broader *dramatization*, there are differences that seem to have something to do with genre, as, for example, between *The West Wing* (NBC 1999–2006) and *CSI* (CBS 2000–present). Both of these are American dramas, though they use speech in different ways. Generic categorization is no guarantee of similar language use either. Medical dramas, for instance, vary in the proportion of talk that is technical/professional.

Breadth here also means thinking about the dialogue from different points of view. Sociolinguists are inclined to see the meaning of a text as a *given*, so that their job is to explain what makes that meaning possible—including meaning that can be reasonably designated *indirect*. Other critics may be in the business of proposing interpretations of particular works—as with Akass and McCabe's (2002) suggestion regarding the contribution of strong women in the narrative discourse of *The Sopranos*. Typically in these cases they will require evidence to support their interpretations: so that dialogue, along with image, editing, structure, and so forth, will all, variously, be called upon in that capacity. But criticism is not a methodology, in the social-scientific sense, and is thus not necessarily bound to specific evidential protocols. The next chapter has more discussion of how television dramatic dialogue has been treated in different approaches in work already published. Subsequent chapters try to move on from this point in different ways: by trying to specify what kind of language this is (chapter 3), by considering the writers' point of view (chapter 4) and the audience's point of view (chapter 5), as well as a textual approach informed by sociolinguistics (chapter 6) and another informed by cognitive stylistics (chapter 7). Between them, these five chapters cover a wide range of perspectives; within each of them, reference is made to an extensive range of examples.

Depth of analysis will be offered primarily in chapters 8 and 9 (the two case studies), though I have also found it useful to focus on one particular extract in one particular series for chapter 5.

The research is based on extensive viewing of contemporary work on television, from dramatized TV commercials through to high concept drama such as *Heroes*, and some consultation of secondary sources. A principle adopted for the purposes of citation and analysis were that the works in question should for the most part be produced in the decade 2000–2009, during which the research was undertaken—this includes works that may have commenced broadcasting in the previous decade but that continued thereafter (e.g., *Law and Order*, NBC 1990–present). Some of this work was no longer being produced when the research began (e.g., *The West Wing*). Occasional mention is made to work from earlier periods (e.g., *Mission: Impossible*, CBS 1966–1973). The non-U.K. shows mentioned here are known to have been made available as broadcasts beyond the country of origin, and also in DVD and electronic download format. Most of the U.K. programs discussed have likewise been internationally distributed. The general principles about the nature of dramatized dialogue transcend national origins, and should be applicable to television dramas in all countries and languages, even if there are significant national differences in how those principles are applied. DVDs provide the bulk of these reference materials, a few have been recorded off-air, and when I have referenced the research of other scholars, I have occasionally had access only to their transcripts. A full index of all the television material referred to throughout this book is provided as an appendix.

WHY DIALOGUE?

Many years ago John Ellis observed of television that, although an audiovisual medium similar to film in many respects, the medium's conditions of reception led it to rely more on the audio than on the visual track to hold its audience:

> The role played by sound stems from the fact that it radiates in all directions, whereas view of the TV image is sometimes restricted. Direct contact is needed with the TV screen. Sound can be heard where the screen can not be seen. So sound is used to ensure a certain level of attention, to drag viewers back to looking at the set. Hence the importance of programme announcements and signature tunes and, to a certain extent, of music in various kinds of series.... Sound carries the fiction or the documentary; the image has a more illustrative function. (Ellis 1992: 128–129)

At home, attention could be more easily distracted than in the cinema, and the space-filling property of sound made it less escapable than the television set's restricted visual field. The feeling seemed to be that to be out of sight of the TV could be accommodated, up to a point, but to be out of earshot was really to miss it. Voices, sound effects, and music can be heard by domestic audiences within range of the TV set when they cannot see the picture or are aware of the picture only as a flickering image in peripheral vision. To hear is not necessarily to understand, and Ellis himself talks of TV sound causing viewers to reengage with the image too, rather than being a self-sufficient source of meaning or pleasure for audiences.

The three components listed here—sound effects, music, and voice—function in a variety of ways across television's varying generic forms, as well as constitute a common ground between the two forms of broadcasting, radio and television. Where drama is concerned, sound effects can be understood in part as by-products of the dramatic business, not necessarily of narrative interest in their own right. A chair's legs scrape across the floor; a fire crackles in the grate. The noises contribute to the realism, even when they are added in post-production by Foley artists and their broadcasting counterparts. The spoken voice itself can be a sound effect in that sense, the paid extras required to contribute to a background "hubbub" of some kind. Or a sound effect can be foregrounded for communicative purposes, as when in drama it is necessary to hear the creaking door to "feel the fear." Music's mood-enhancing (and attention-calling) functions are ubiquitous in television, and it is perhaps the extra-diegetic role of music, as used in the delivery of television drama specifically (as also in feature films), that most readily comes to mind. The human voice can be part of this extra-diegetic discourse too. The accompanying music may use songs that have pertinent lyrics, or a singer's voice quality may contribute to a feeling.

But speaking voices have a potential hold on viewers' attention that is qualitatively different from that of either sound effects or music. What viewers hear, when they listen to the speaking voice using a language that they share, is a unified combination of vocal and verbal meaning in which it is interpretatively impossible to separate the one from the other. The *vocal* meaning is the delivery—voice quality, volume, pitch, timing, rhythm—its prosodic and para-linguistic features. These are all deployed in the service of *verbal* meanings—wordings that are understood to carry particular significance at the place they occupy in the developing text. So much is true of speech wherever it occurs in television. The physical body as the visualized source of that speech is also semiotically important, and I have no wish to downplay its contribution to the construction of meaning in television texts. Nevertheless, Ellis's argument concerning the significance of the audio track in television broadcasting generally, and my own argument about the particular salience of speech as part of that track, suggests that the interpretation of television's heard speech will be central to most people's encounters with the medium.

In the case of drama dialogue, the speech in question is standardly of a particular kind: pre-scripted and interactive. Not all talk on TV is interactive in the sense I have in mind. A political interview is interactive, because interviewer and interviewee are obliged to respond to one another's contributions, even if both parties have separately prepared for the event ahead of time, even down to rehearsing particular lines that they intend to use if they have a chance. A dramatic encounter, such as that between Carmela and Tony in the *Sopranos*, cited earlier, is also interactive between the two characters: more accurately it is *displayed as* an interaction between them. A newsreader's bulletin is not interactive in that sense: it is a monologue to a remote audience. The oddness of talk that is both pre-scripted and yet displayed as interactive is a point that I will return to several times in the coming pages. At this point, all I want to say is that with pre-scripted talk the achieved unity of vocal and verbal contributions as transmitted to the audience belies the origins of that talk in which vocal and verbal properties have come together from the *separate* contributions of a performer and a writer. In standard cases, we are dealing, in Goffman's (1979) terms, with distinct authors and animators, and the contributions of the latter are dependent on those of the former.

Television's voices in Britain now speak with many different forms of pronunciation and in the performance of many different identities and relationships. But the variety being offered is not limitless or without structure. Mainstream television is probably as monolingual as it ever was: speakers of other languages are relegated to the margins to find, via the paying services, channels that broadcast material they can relate to. There is also a bias toward the more intimate end of the interpersonal spectrum. Even public discourse, from the leaders to the citizenry, has had to come to terms with television's preference for the informal, interactive, and domestic. Viewers in the United Kingdom can, if they choose, use TV to witness daily proceedings from the floor of the House of Commons, politically the country's foremost debating chamber. But such events, by design "theatrical" and "spectacular," at least in potential, have lost much of their power over the collective imaginations except on certain key occasions that viewers learn of in advance from the broadcast media. Rarely are parliamentary debates staged as part of dramatic representations on TV. The cost of realistically replicating the Commons chamber as a studio set is a factor in this. But the money would be found, if there were good dramatic reasons to display this kind of interaction and evidence suggests that this is not common. Nationally, viewers seem to be more engaged by exchanges conducted in kitchens, living rooms, bedrooms, and bathrooms, especially if there is a chance that such exchanges are *real*—not just the product of a writer's imagination or self-consciously staged for the camera's benefit. This preference is a factor not just in the success of *reality* television, but also in the dramatized *biopics* of actual public figures, in which satisfaction can also be had from exploring the space between private and public realms. Public discourse is frequently staged in the form of courtroom drama (*Judge John Deed*, BBC 2001–present, *Law and Order*). But even in *Law and Order*, a series that largely seeks to exclude the *personal* from its narratives of crime investigation and prosecution, there is always behind-the-scenes contextualization as well, so that audiences can understand the strategies lying behind the words spoken in the courtroom by one or more of the parties in the case. *Judge John Deed* is more typical in allowing itself also to explore the domestic dramas of its central participants.

The marriage of vocal and verbal meaning in the speaking voice is utilized by TV drama for the purposes of displaying identities and relationships from the intimate end of the range, and for accessing the personal meanings behind more public identity displays. Voices are technologically (re)produced so that they come across as congruent in respect to social distance with the faces and bodies on the screen. Viewers expect more of the grain of the voice when the shot is a close-up than when the shot is from farther away. Not all TV dramatization is intimate in the sense of deploying mainly close-up shots and their audio equivalent. Close-ups offer the greatest proximity of viewer to speaker, but the lens and the microphone can draw back from this intensity and still show a preference for the personal and interpersonal significance of talk exchanges. Studio-based drama, for example, offers the acoustic of a room as a closed space, and makes the talk appropriate to such a space in terms of either its verbal or its vocal characteristics, or both in combination. Location filming deletes, then reintroduces, background sound for the sake of dialogue that is clean—every word can be heard. To hear every word is also to hear every beat, every stressed syllable, and every filled or unfilled pause. To hear these is to have access to the personal and interpersonal meanings they may carry. Even TV drama that is perceived as covertly or overtly thematically purposeful or didactic has to work with the grain of dramatic fiction's preference for issues personalized, and with television's preference for the more domestic and private versions of the personal.

This orientation toward intimacy cannot be sustained by vocality alone. It is in the combination of the vocal and the verbal that the work is accomplished. Actors do not *deliver* lines in the way that postmen deliver packages, with vocality just the wrapping paper to be discarded on receipt. But neither can performers constitute vocality as the only basis of exchanged meaning. The writer's material counts for something, and may preempt some of the decisions regarding vocal expression. Nor is the conduct of personal relationships the only function of drama on television, however prominent it may be. Such conduct is itself a vehicle for other layers of meaning, contextualizing personal relationships within contemporary or historical social institutions such as law enforcement, marriage, schooling, government, and so forth. Relationships mediate the plot details of the stories that TV drama tells—who wins, who loses, what are the consequences?

The chapters that follow represent an attempt to construct an account of television drama dialogue that is general enough to do justice to all of the contexts in which this can appear, as well as examine the phenomenon from a number of related perspectives. To begin, in chapter 2, I examine previous research that has focused on dialogue in television texts and show that the variety of work here is very small and diverse: different scholars, with different purposes, have treated TV drama as a source of language-based interactive material relevant to their disparate concerns. Chapter 3 sets up some points of comparison to determine the place that this kind of *talk* occupies in sociolinguistic space—specifically, with naturally occurring unscripted talk in comparable social situations, with other kinds of mediated talk on television, and with dialogue in other representational genres. Chapters 4, 5, and 6 collectively set out to examine how different perspectives—those of writers, audiences (including critics), and sociolinguists—differ in their understandings of what dialogue is and the kinds of meanings it can carry. Chapter 7 picks up a particular interest from cognitive stylistics in the dialogic construction of *character* in plays, and develops this in its particular relation to television drama. Chapters 8 and 9 each present a case study, one British (*Life on Mars*, BBC 2006–2007) and one American (*House*, 2004–present), the former emphasizing the functions of the dialogue in respect of the production, and the latter emphasizing particular interactional characteristics. The shortest chapter in the book is its conclusion, chapter 10, which returns to some of the themes of this introduction, to offer an overview of what the book has accomplished, and considers how future research might take that forward. It steps back from the details of particular TV shows and their compositional elements to consider how these contribute to a "dramatized society" (Williams 1975) with specific reference to current research on language creativity in everyday contexts (Maybin and Swann 2007).

2

Previous Research

Who else has written about dialogue in TV drama/dramatization, and why have they done so? Are their interests sociolinguistic, aesthetic, or cultural? Are they theoretical or substantive? The following survey of the available research demonstrates that there is no unitary project behind them, that what exists focuses on fictional drama more than on dramatization in factual television, and that there is considerable tension (as well as scope for cross-referral) between an "arts" discourse, concerned with formal characteristics of particular texts and text types (and sometimes, despite the difficulties, with the value/quality of such texts), and a "social science" discourse, concerned with shared meanings and social influence. This tension cuts across the disciplinary lines that separate sociolinguistic research from media research.

The first section of this chapter focuses on references to dialogue from the perspective of TV drama studies (a subbranch of media research) to provide a context for the subsequent sociolinguistic account, with a digression on dialogue in factual television programming. The second section surveys existing substantive research on dialogue in TV drama, along with an account of some theoretical contributions. On the basis of its interest in language-in-use, this section incorporates contributions from stylistics, usually positioned as an arts discipline, along with contributions with a stronger social-scientific/sociolinguistic heritage.

TELEVISION STUDIES, DRAMA, AND DIALOGUE

The first point to make is that although television drama research is now an established field, dialogue is not yet a topic in its own right within that field. Geraghty (2003) proposed that scholars working in this area should give greater attention to formal aspects of TV's dramatic texts, as part of a move to take more seriously the aesthetic contribution of television to contemporary culture, along with its ideological/representational contribution. She recognized in this context the relative neglect of dialogue: "it is surprising in a medium that is

strongly associated in a variety of ways with talk, with "overheard conversations"
[...] that the tone and delivery of dialogue is often overlooked in favour of
narrative progression" (Geraghty 2003: 34). Since 2003, researchers have begun
to respond to Geraghty's wider challenge.[1] But dialogue is still neglected. In
the two most recent publications of this field, Nelson (2007) and McCabe and
Akass (2007a) the term *dialogue* does not warrant an index entry, and neither
does *language*. Dialogue does, however, come in for some attention in both of
these works. There are two ways in which it makes an appearance. It is used as
one marker among others for a particular kind of dramatic production—*quality
drama* (here *quality* refers to its descriptive, rather than evaluative, use), and it
is recognized as offering scope for the articulation of thematically relevant
content. In both cases dialogue may be quoted, by way of illustration for the
points being made.

Dialogue and Quality

Writing about quality drama, using *quality* as a genre classification (cf. Thompson 1996), and trying to understand how quality in the genre sense relates to
judgments of worth and value (i.e., "quality" in its evaluative sense), Cardwell
offers *The West Wing* (NBC 1999–2007) as a member of the quality drama genre,
on the following grounds: "Other aspects [besides its high production values,
weighty themes, and strong characterization/acting] encourage an intense level
of audience appreciation and engagement, such as the complex narrative structure, its intricate themes, its use of erudite, technical, oratorical and even poetic
language, and its fast-paced style" (2007: 26).

Language use is treated here as a sign of *West Wing*'s membership status.
Cardwell is also indicating that the clever dialogue is not an *arbitrary* sign of that
status, but is a functional device in the communication between dramatist and
audience, because its cleverness encourages "appreciation and engagement."
What is missing from this kind of account is any attempt to prove or demonstrate
that the dialogue does indeed have the characteristics ascribed to it. The
meanings—erudite, technical, and so forth—are taken for granted; it is the
value of these meanings that is argued for.[2]

Where space permits, some commentators are able to go into more detail:

> The dialogue itself [in *The Sopranos*] is as sharp and streetwise as the camera style,
> arguably introducing a greater level of realism than hitherto [...] it is low key and
> oblique, with the characters unable to articulate that understanding of themselves
> and their predicament which marks more regular, formulaic drama which feels the
> need to be explanatory [...] A particular feature [...] is *The Sopranos*' demotic use
> of expletives in New Jersey speech patterns which the constraints of broadcast
> television have previously kept from the small screen [...] the dialogue is on
> occasion overtly witty and by no means politically correct, with Tony Soprano

afforded some of the sharpest lines. When Richie Aprile takes up again with Janice [Parvati] Soprano, having served time in jail, he tells a sceptical Tony that he and Janice "got history together," to which Tony quips, "Yeah, Israel and fuckin' Palestine." (Nelson 2007: 32)

Nelson evaluates Sopranos dialogue positively on the basis of three main criteria—realism, including the use of expletives; obliqueness in character revelation; and wit. He gives examples, some of which have been omitted in this citation, to explain and illustrate these points. He does not examine the logic of the Israel and Palestine joke—it is offered as a piece of textual evidence supporting two claims: one, that the drama displays wordplay for its own sake, and two, that witty use of language is a character point for Tony Soprano.

Here and elsewhere in this literature, where there are dialogue quotations, they are frequently offered as self-evidently manifesting the qualities they are said to possess. Contrast Nelson's account with my description, in the previous chapter, of the conversation between Tony and Carmela Soprano in which he tells her for the first time about his recourse to psychotherapy. That description or analysis was developed in sufficient detail to support a broader interpretation about gender relations in this series, while recognizing that the exchange in question was just one moment in Tony and Carmela's relationship. The dominant approach to dialogue in television drama studies, although recognizing that dialogue makes a contribution to dramatic meaning and value, perpetuates a different version of the easy listening effect from the one discussed in the introduction to the present volume. Basic *easy listening* involves hearing characters as people and their talk as everyday talk. Advanced easy listening hears dramatic qualities in that talk, but can't or won't say much about how those qualities got there.

When dialogue is used as a marker of quality drama status, it may be the vice of profanity rather than the virtue of wit that qualifies it for membership. There is merit, it seems, for some audiences, and for some broadcasters (notably America's HBO subscription channel), in breaking with mainstream television's prescriptive language taboos. This, along with taboos related to sex and violence, is the subject of discussion in McCabe and Akass (2007c), who point to the way that HBO's excesses, enabled by the economic basis of its restricted access (which it shares with ordinary pornography) are legitimated by its metadiscourse of *quality* and thus respectability, which intentionally restrict access along sociocultural lines.

Dialogue and Politics

Critics of the "aesthetic turn" in television drama research worry that this distracts attention from more important questions of how television engages its audiences' thoughts and sensibilities on particular topics—the subject matter of drama: "What was perhaps most troubling about the conference [on American quality TV in 2004] to me was the emphasis in many papers on the aesthetic and formal qualities of the programmes discussed, often at the expense of any consideration of their content, and the ways they might play into real-life relations of power and politics" (Fricker 2007: 14). TV drama can be political with a small *p* or a big one, without abandoning the appeal of intimacy. In either case, characters are likely to produce dialogue that speaks to the political thematics of the production and scholars such as Nelson respond to this as they do to its formal aspects. Nelson uses the British series *Spooks* (BBC 2002–present) to show how it sets in play two different arguments about Western interventions in the affairs of other countries. A sympathetic guest character puts forward one view, and a principal character from the main ensemble cast puts forward an alternative:

> We don't want to see our country blown to bits like Iraq. The parallels between us and Iraq are frightening. But it doesn't seem to bother the Barthist [sic] hardliners who are running the country.
>
> I want you to help me get rid of the current regime . . . and replace it with a real government . . . a government for the people but one which can keep the Mullahs at bay (Episode 7, written by Raymond Khoury and David Wolstencroft). (Nelson 2007: 145)

> This will end up just like Iraq. We [the Brits] keep doing this. We keep getting sucked up into these foreign nightmares and for what? Our job is to protect the country. (Nelson 2007: 145)

The narrative plays out in such a way that the Syrian who favors intervention is eliminated at the hands of his own government—but the wife of the principal character also dies, and MI-5 does not come out of the mix as unequivocally victorious and in control. Nelson says, "The political theme of conflict is used to raise the stakes and crank up the tension of the narrative, but here questions are articulated and left open in ways which invite thinking and, perhaps, debate amongst viewers" (2007: 146). It is not the quoted dialogue on its own that raises the issues, but interaction between dialogue and specific narrative contingencies. There are questions to be asked on the back of this account that textual analysis alone cannot answer, about the extent to which actual audiences do in fact use this material for their own reflections on the politics of intervention in foreign affairs, but this need not detract from the work involved in recognizing how this theme is formally addressed in the production.

A distinctive thing about the television drama research reviewed in this section is that all of it is grounded in an "arts" rather than a "social science" epistemology, even when it seems to touch on questions of television's effects on its audience. The effects agenda is very muted, and there is no empirical research in pursuit of hypotheses concerning influence and effect. Because of the emphasis on *quality* in the two books chosen for attention, their dominant discourse is either one of positive approval for the form and/or the content of particular shows like *The Sopranos* (HBO 1999–2007), *The West Wing*, and *Spooks*, or else more or less detached regarding value judgment. Explicit *disapproval* is not very evident here. Elsewhere, when specific quality shows have been subjected to negative criticism, it is generally in respect to their content, as with the series *24* (Fox 2001–present), which has been attacked because of its reactionary politics (see, e.g., Broe 2004). Later in this chapter, I will introduce some research on dialogue in TV drama that, although retaining a focus on the text rather than the audience, puts its approach on to a strongly social-scientific foundation in order to support a negative assessment of a particular show's possible influence on its audience.

Factual Television and Dialogue

Published research specifically focused on *dialogue* in factual television is virtually nonexistent. This contrasts with *unscripted* talk on TV in which there is a considerable literature. The fact that dialogue in fictional drama can be improvised, and that supposedly unscripted talk, in interviews and so forth, can be partially prepared in advance, complicates the picture here but does not compromise the argument regarding prototypical forms. Almost by definition, *dialogue* indexes "drama," so any factually based programming that includes dialogue is, at least to that extent, dramatic. The kind of programming that falls within this description is variously referred to as *dramadoc, docudrama*, or *dramatized documentary*, among other terms (Paget 1998). The functions of dialogue in such documentary modes will be very similar to its functions in fictional drama:

> [Documentary drama] is usually carefully constructed to develop character, sustain narrative and reveal context and circumstances [. . .] In drama-documentary, where there is often a requirement to use dialogue to convey information to the viewer that might otherwise have been conveyed by commentary, the conversational plausibility of the speech is sometimes in tension with its descriptive, explanatory functions. (Corner 2006: 758)

Corner goes on to draw attention to one additional point of concern for documentarists that writers of dramatic fiction do not have to worry about: "The further issue, of how far it might approximate to what was really said in the situation being reconstructed, is a long standing point of contention in the discussion of films and programmes using this approach" (2006: 755).

Behind this specific point lies the general issue of documentary's truth claims. Being faithful to what was said is sometimes less important than being *safe*. The mother of a child suffering from leukemia believed, and said, that contamination from the Sellafield nuclear reprocessing plant caused her daughter's illness. Her character could not, for legal reasons, be allowed to say this in the show *Fighting for Gemma* (ITV 1993), because legal liability had not been proven in court (Paget 1998: 41). The original script gave "Stella D'Arcy" the stronger, more controversial, line—but, on legal advice, it was modified before production.

Corner (1991b) focuses on dialogue in a selection of Associated-Rediffusion (ITV) shows from 1956, broadcast under the series title *Look in on London*, that center on ordinary people's lives in the capital city. Corner's interest is a historical one, in the emergence of the location interview as a staple form of *dramatized exposition*. One sequence (from the "Streetcleaners" episode) starts like this:

INTERVIEWER: Good afternoon.
RESPONDENT: Good afternoon.
INTERVIEWER: You ever get tired doing this all day long?
RESPONDENT: No, I don't get tired at all.
INTERVIEWER: Don't you?
RESPONDENT: No.
INTERVIEWER: Don't you . . . doesn't it get a bit monotonous sweeping the same gutters?
RESPONDENT: No, I got so used to it now.
INTERVIEWER: How long have you been doing it?
RESPONDENT: Seven years.
INTERVIEWER: Oh, what were you doing before then?
RESPONDENT: I was working for the Kensington Borough Council.

(Corner 1991b: 37)

Clearly this has nothing to do with reconstructing a prior, real encounter between this interviewee and this respondent. But neither are the two having a spontaneous conversation, having just chanced to meet, though there are markers here that some such spontaneous encounter is a model for what has actually been written and performed. The interviewer knows the answers to his own questions, and the interviewee knows that he knows them. The significance of the extract is its creation of an interactive frame for expositional discourse. Its awkwardness has to do with what the technique suggests about the social identities and relationships of the various participants in this exchange—the interviewer, the respondent, and the television audience—positioning the respondent as working class and exotic, and the middle-class interviewer and audience as sympathetically curious. The styling of the dialogue keeps it in limbo between different realities. Contemporary equivalents of this program would not use pre-scripted dialogue at all. In the interests of greater authenticity, any interviewing now would allow more spontaneity in its question-and-response sequences, and comparable shows would also create opportunity for audiences to overhear the naturally occurring talk produced in the course of the subject's working life.

SOCIOLINGUISTICS AND TV DRAMA DIALOGUE

Because the media scholarship is short on analysis, it is necessary to look elsewhere for research efforts that do pay analytic attention to the formal details of conversational exchanges in television drama. However, in contrast with the research described above, these efforts do not derive from a shared perception of what their accounts should be trying to achieve—instead, there are three distinct trends or groupings, with different intellectual starting points.

One of these trends is an approach that derives from the stylistic study of drama dialogue in general, which very occasionally includes television drama. This stylistic approach includes studies of, for example, *Fawlty Towers* (BBC 1995–1997), *Monty Python's Flying Circus* (BBC 1969–1974), *One Foot in the Grave* (BBC 1990–2000) and *Little Britain* (BBC 2003–present). These works are analyzed as drama, but not particularly as *television* drama (Simpson 1998, Short 1998, Culpeper 2001, Snell 2006). That is to say, in formal terms the focus is entirely on language and only in passing to the multimodal character of the texts, or the particular circumstances of their production and reception. *Monty Python* and *Little Britain* are sketch shows; the other two are situation comedies. It is no accident that comedy, rather than straight TV drama, attracts the attention of these scholars, because comedy is more likely to involve a playful relationship with language and thus provide more for stylisticians to notice and comment on.

In the second place, there are some studies that use dramatic dialogue in TV shows to stand in for comparable sociolinguistic phenomena in unmediated, face-to-face settings. Tannen and Lakoff (1984), for example, are interested in "couples talk." In the absence of any recordings from actual couple relationships, they make use of a surrogate: dialogue from Ingmar Bergman's *Scenes from a Marriage* (originally made for Swedish television in 1973; English language theatrical release, Cinema 5, USA 1974) as their data. Coupland (2004) discusses "stylized deception" using an episode of *Sergeant Bilko/The Phil Silvers Show* (CBS 1955–1959). *Scenes from a Marriage* was a miniseries that became a movie; *Sergeant Bilko* is a situation comedy. One book-length study (namely, Quaglio 2009), uses corpus linguistic techniques and a theoretical approach derived from Biber (1988) to compare the grammar of television dialogue (in *Friends*, NBC 1994–2004) with that of naturally occurring American conversation. Quaglio finds the two corpora to be essentially similar, and distinct from other English language genres as established in the earlier research. The dialogue is thus for him a credible surrogate of the "real thing." He also uses grammatical evidence to demonstrate that, by comparison with the naturally occurring conversation, *Friends* dialogue is both narrower and more intense in its usage of conversation's distinctive forms in general and specifically those which index emotional expressiveness and informality. The dialogue is *less* inclined to deploy strategic vagueness and more focused on immediate context at the expense of narrativising past or imaginary events.

In addition to these two ways of engaging with dialogue in TV drama, there is a third approach that shares some of the goals of the media research and that can therefore usefully be termed *applied sociolinguistics*. A distinguishing characteristic of this work is that it is concerned with dialogue in TV drama for the sake of the wider social and cultural issues that the particular shows in question seem to raise—mostly focused on the representation of social identities and relationships. Harwood (2000) and Harwood and Giles (1992) are interested in negative representations of aging in *The Golden Girls* (NBC 1985–1992) and *Frasier* (NBC 1993–2004); Richardson (2006) is interested in positive representations of political spin doctors in *The West Wing*; Bubel (2005) and Bubel and Spitz (2006) are interested in negative and positive representations of gender relations in *Ally McBeal* (Fox 1997–2002), and Mandala (2007a) is interested in representations of youth social networks in *Buffy the Vampire Slayer* (WB 1997–2003). *The Golden Girls* and *Frasier* are standard 30-minute situation comedies; *The West Wing* and *Ally McBeal* could be considered "dramedies" on account of their mixture of serious and comic elements in a 1-hour broadcast slot. *Buffy the Vampire Slayer* is fantasy drama, with some comic interest.

Most of this work draws upon relevant sociolinguistic as well as media studies literature. Fine (1981) points out some interesting interactional characteristics of the conversation in daytime soaps such as *All My Children* (ABC 1977–present). But Fine's research was too far ahead of its time, and was unable to benefit from, on the one hand, the later media studies research on the (gendered) cultural significance of soap opera,[3] or, on the other, the various areas of work that can now be collected together under the umbrella of "spoken discourse studies" (Cameron 2001; see also chapter 4).

Dialogue Stylistics

By the late 1990s, the usefulness of pragmatics, interactional sociolinguistics, and conversation analysis in the analysis of literary drama was well established, thanks to works by Burton (1980), Herman (1995), and Culpeper, Short, and Verdonk (1998). This interactional approach formed part of textbook introductions to the subject, for example, in Thornborrow and Wareing (1998). Drama, of course, is traditionally recognized as one of three major subdivisions in literary discourse, along with poetry and prose narrative; the language of drama had never been a neglected topic. What was new, in this branch of stylistics, was the emphasis on dialogue as *talk*, rather than on its use of metaphor and other tropes that it shared with poetry. The emphasis on interactive properties of dramatic dialogue contributed to a conceptual realignment of generic forms. The affiliation of drama with poetry became weaker, and its affiliation with prose fiction became stronger, because drama and prose fiction both depend on underlying narrative structures and both characteristically incorporate dialogue. This realignment was also broadened: narrative as such was recognized as including nonliterary (multimodal) texts such as feature films (Chatman 1978), and *literary* drama itself was reconceived in terms of performance as well as of text (Swann 2006; McIntyre 2008).

In terms of the new alignments, and without prejudice to questions of aesthetic and/or social value, it is possible to identify three major representational forms that depend heavily on performed dialogue: stage plays (prototypically encountered in theaters), films (in cinemas), and TV dramatizations (at home).

Discussions of dialogue in drama stylistics have been able to provide a literary-critical rationale for their approach. In relation to the stage play, for instance, along with the preference among stylisticians to focus on the written play rather than the performance, there is often a sense that the analysis is intended to *illuminate* textual meaning—a characteristic visual trope in the discourses of literary criticism beyond the specific territory of stylistics: "As the studies in this book clearly demonstrate, applying methods and findings from linguistics to the study of language in drama allows us to *shed new light* on the plays investigated" (Mandala 2007: xiii; emphasis added). Mandala uses sociolinguistic tools to explore plays by Pinter and Stoppard, among others, treating them in the first instance as producers of written English literature. There is a point of connection here with a tendency in television drama studies that now wants to develop a better understanding of the aesthetics of TV drama (see discussion in the previous section of this chapter). Mandala's standpoint is an aesthetic one, in which language use is of the essence. That standpoint does not need to be argued for in respect of Pinter and Stoppard: it is the *kind* of analysis she proposes that has to be defended. The aesthetic standpoint in respect of television is not language-centered, though, as discussed previously, it could take more account of language than it does in practice. Without wanting to downplay its particularity and generic variety, from a historical perspective, the trajectory of TV drama has been away from language/theater and toward image/film as its primary models (Jacobs 2000).

Before the advent of postmodernism and the questioning of the literary canon, there were attempts to recognize the aesthetic value of movie screenplays, too, on a par with the scripts of stage plays, though not without considerable conceptual difficulty (see Maras 2009: chapter 3), bearing in mind that screenplays are written to be a step in a process that culminates with a production. Even if we reject this suggestion, the discourse of film studies has certainly incorporated a range of critical idioms comparable to those deployed in the study of literary texts—an aesthetic perspective (or range of perspectives) interested, like Mandala, in the project of *illumination*. This perspective extends to the study of dialogue in film. In the following quotation from Kozloff (2000), her initial deployment of a functional frame—"'why are these lines here?'"—suggests a primarily analytic standpoint. A functional analysis does not assume any prior evaluation of the text's merits. But the quotation ends with the very suggestive keyword "reverberation"—an aural metaphor that, coupled with the author's own reference to unpredictable factors of production and reception, potentially extends the scope of dialogue's functionality beyond the range of categoric analytic schemes.

> The first questions to be asked when analyzing a segment of film dialogue may be: "Why are these lines here?" or "What purpose do they serve in the text as a whole?" Such inquiries might imply that one is attempting to uncover the *intentions* of the screenwriters and director, and, indeed, a large degree of overlap might be anticipated between what the filmmakers consciously had in mind and the ultimate effects of dialogue. Some overlap, but not total; for through "accidents" (psychological or practical) and through the unpredictable nuances of performance, filming, editing, scoring, exhibition, reception, and so on, the reverberations of a segment of dialogue may exceed or confound the intentions of its authors. (Kozloff 2000: 33)

Kozloff believes that dialogue is interesting for what it contributes to the artwork as a whole, whether or not the effects it helps create are supposed to be under the conscious control of authors. Leaving to one side the vexed question in textual criticism of intentionality, an aesthetic perspective is also invoked via the assumption that the *whole* work is the object on which the study should ultimately focus. The implication here is that this object has an integrity and essence that must be acknowledged in the analysis. To encounter just a part of it shows disrespect and risks misunderstanding.

The stylistic criticism of dialogue in television dramatization has a comparable interest in explaining the effects of that dialogue, and its own struggles in setting limits on the extent of the meaning that it can be concerned with. This struggle is apparent, for example, in Paul Simpson's account of the well-known "nudge, nudge" sketch from *Monty Python's Flying Circus*, which I reproduce here:

FIRST SPEAKER: Evening, squire!
SECOND SPEAKER: Good evening.
FIRST SPEAKER: Is, uh, . . . Is your wife a goer, eh? Know what I mean, know what I mean, nudge nudge, know what I mean, say no more?
SECOND SPEAKER: I, uh, I beg your pardon?
FIRST SPEAKER: Your, uh, your wife, does she go, eh, does she go, eh?
SECOND SPEAKER: Well, she sometimes "goes," yes.

FIRST SPEAKER: Aaaaaaaah bet she does, I bet she does, say no more, say no more,
know what I mean, nudge nudge?

SECOND SPEAKER: I'm afraid I don't quite follow you.

FIRST SPEAKER: Follow me. Follow me. That's good, that's good! A nod's as
good as a wink to a blind bat!

(Sketch written by Eric Idle)

Simpson's paper is concerned with *absurdity* and its functions in different kinds
of dialogue. *Monty Python* produces one kind, whereas the (stage) dramatist
Ionesco provides another. The equation of the two can either be taken as an
attempt to elevate the Python sketch to the level of the *literary*, where Ionesco
already sits, or else implies that for the analyst-as-technician, questions of value
are less important than questions of form and function. It is interesting that
Simpson seeks not only to analyze the *Python* material so as to explain the
incongruity effect, but also to indicate a way of reading the purpose of the
incongruity. As regards analysis, Simpson's general claim is that incongruity is
often the result of a mismatch between the expectations deriving from a particular embedded discourse context and the interactive strategies that the participants actually deploy. In the case of this particular sketch, there is a mismatch
between the context (two middle class males, strangers to one another, sharing
a table in a British pub) and the talk (sexual innuendo, very pronounced, on
the part of one of the men, repeatedly and incredibly misunderstood by the
other). Simpson's analysis goes into considerable detail in making this point, and
he goes on:

> Foregrounding odd talk implicitly draws attention to the canonical and the everyday
> in interaction and it is possible to read this text as a skit on the repressively
> mundane trivia that often passes for conversation. Both interactants are white,
> male and middle class and both speak with southern English accents, yet...the
> interactive diffidence that might be anticipated in social interaction between (par-
> ticularly English?) middle class strangers is shattered. To the extent that this
> fracture is engendered by a fracture in discourse strategies, the sketch becomes
> language about language—a kind of "meta-discourse." It constitutes a form of
> humor where language itself becomes the subject matter...and which relies for
> its decoding on the cultural competence and cultural attitudes of the interpreter;
> those very decoding strategies, in fact, which are brought into play in the interpre-
> tation of absurd drama dialogue. (Simpson 1998: 47–48)

One telling aspect of Simpson's account here is its attempt to find some
kind of thematic relevance in the properties of the sketch, through the invitation
for audiences to hear it as satire. This view, tentatively offered ("it is possible to
read..."), without any commitment as to whether Eric Idle intended this kind
of effect, is a critical, interpretative move, appealing to aspects of context
that Simpson and his readership share, such as their knowledge of suburban

middle-class masculinity in Britain in the post–World War II world. This level of interpretation is held in tension with the more analytic discourse cultivated within stylistics more generally, by means of which Simpson can focus on the metadiscursive characteristics of the talk. The specific characterization of the sketch as *satire* in this account (I take Simpson's term *skit* to be indicative of this characterization) is also worthy of note. If we regard the meaning of satire as essentially concerned with social criticism, then Simpson's interpretation can also be read as a validation of this particular material in terms of its social purpose. The dialogue is *interesting* because of its oddness, it is *pleasurable* because its metadiscursive characteristics appeal to a certain sensibility, and it is, arguably, *good* dialogue because of its specific derived propositional content, which is critical of contemporary manners. There is a point of connection here with that strand in television drama studies that is interested in the content and themes of dramatic production. The mix of social and formal criteria in Simpson's commentary is significant, and provides a marker for some of the discussion to follow later in this book, notably in chapter 8, "Dialogue and Dramatic Meaning: *Life on Mars*."

The tension between interpretative and analytic frames is less pronounced within the approach known as *cognitive stylistics*, adopted, for example, in the recent work of Jonathan Culpeper, in which the function of contextual assumptions is built more explicitly into the analytic apparatus, and in which there is a focus on normative levels of meaning. Culpeper (2001) adopts this perspective in his work on the interpretation of character in plays and other works of fiction. He discriminates between *top-down* and *bottom-up* comprehension. In top-down strategies, familiar, general character schemata (e.g., American detective, hospital nurse, hapless middle-class parents) exist as mental constructs prior to the readers' encounters with the particularized versions of those constructs in the text. Readers make sense of the specific cases by drawing on their general, cognitive schemata. (These are my examples rather than Culpeper's, supplied for the sake of their specific relevance to the television experience.) Readers then make use of textual information to allocate characters to those schemata. Bottom-up comprehension occurs when characters are assembled from a range of textual clues. This of course is a theoretical distinction because in practice readers will make use of both top-down and bottom-up strategies as they engage with texts. Most of Culpeper's own examples are drawn from the works of Shakespeare, texts which he can assume his readers will be familiar with, but the theory is a general one, and there is a short discussion of an extract from *One Foot in the Grave* (BBC 1990–2000)—a humorous *mistaken identity* sequence. Viewers, as well as Victor Meldrew, the main character (played by Richard Wilson), are led to suspect that two unannounced visitors at his house are policemen following up a complaint about indecent exposure on his part; they are actually Jehovah's Witnesses:

1 VISITOR: Victor Meldrew?

2 MELDREW: Yes.

3 VISITOR: Wondered if we might have a little word with you sir.

4 MELDREW: Oh God.

5 VISITOR: On the subject of obscene behavior.

6 MELDREW: Look . . . it's all very simple really.

7 VISITOR: Rather a lot of it going on these days wouldn't you say? Acts of
unbridled filth perpetrated by perverts and sexual deviants who should know
better at their age.

8 MELDREW: Look . . . I . . . I just got out of the bath and I was just rubbing,
I was rubbing . . .

9 VISITOR: How do you think God feels about all this?

10 MELDREW: What?

11 VISITOR: How do you think the Lord feels about so much sin and wickedness
in his holy Kingdom on Earth? If we look at Proverbs 6 verse 12 I think we can
find the answer . . . a naughty person a wicked man walketh with a . . .

12 MELDREW: You're Jehovah's Witnesses! You're bloody Jehovah's Witnesses,
I thought you were policemen!

(Series written by David Renwick)

Culpeper's account of the mechanism behind the humor here references
schema theory:

> Given that the audience has fairly recently heard that Victor was reported to the
> police for indecency, a police-related schema is readily activated . . . research sug-
> gests that schemata that have been recently activated are more likely to spring to
> mind . . . the opening turns, checking the identity of the interviewee and request-
> ing permission to commence the interview (with lip service to politeness) are
> strongly associated with the police interview activity type. . . . The recategorization
> of the police detectives as Jehovah's Witnesses is brought about by a switch in
> activity types. [The question] *How do you think God feels about all this* clashes
> with the police interview activity type, and this is clear from Victor's response,
> *What.* . . . After the question *How do you think the Lord feels about so much sin
> and wickedness in his holy kingdom on earth* and the quotations from the Bible,
> Victor realizes that the activity type is actually one of religious proselytizing,
> and, consequently, that these are Jehovah's Witnesses, a religious group that is
> well known for making door to door visits. (2001: 99)

This example is used in the context of a discussion of character categories in
drama. Culpeper has argued that in top-down character processing, the basic way
of enhancing character understanding is to move from an initial categorization
into a subcategory, with a greater or lesser accumulation of attributes. The *One
Foot in the Grave* (OFITG) example illustrates an alternative to this—recategorization. When there is recategorization it occurs, as here, because the dramatists have
deliberately encouraged an incorrect schema to be activated in the first instance.

Culpeper's approach, which I have made more systematic use of in chapter 7, "Dialogue, Character, and Social Cognition," could be described as *process* research: more interested in the *how* than in the *what* of textual meaning. Meanings are regarded as given, obvious, and the goal of the research is to spell out what resources and efforts are required to realize those meanings. (This brand of research is therefore different from traditional literary criticism, which seeks to penetrate more deeply into layers of meaning that are less obvious). Culpeper's example involves some very specific assumptions about the resources necessary to get the proposed meaning of the OFITG passage. Audiences must be able to understand English spoken in both a standard and an (arguably) nonstandard accent, and they must possess schemas for handling both police interviews and doorstep visits by evangelists. They must also recognize the form and degree of politeness here to be within an acceptable range for suburban British middle-class culture in the 1990s: on this basis, they will be able to hear motivated *im*politeness at line 12. My own personal cultural horizons are such that I find it easy to accede to Culpeper's assumptions. I hear the meanings he proposes, I recognize that my repertoire does include the resources he has specified for producing those meanings, and I believe in the widespread availability of those resources in the wider audience. The analysis is a normative one, but acceptably so, not just because I can relate to its principles but also because of my confidence that those principles are fairly widely shared. But it would be presumptuous to assume that they are *universally* shared. Some viewers will not have had first- or secondhand encounters with Jehovah's Witnesses, and will lack a schema for this part of the exchange. Empirical research through interview, questionnaire, and focus group methods is the only reasonable way to pursue the question of what this dialogue means for them, or for any audiences who cannot or choose not to contribute context on normative terms.

Also of interest in Culpeper's book is his mention of certain TV shows (*Neighbours*, 7 Network 1985–present, *Holby City*, BBC 1999–present) as the domain of *flat characters*: "... these soaps are phenomenally successful: viewers come back day after day for more. It may be the case that some viewers positively value the schema-reinforcing nature of flat characters" (2001: 96). Culpeper offers a theoretically grounded account of the traditional concept of a flat character in literature: "The attributes and features of a flat character are organized according to a preformed category or schema to form a category-based impression" (2001: 94).

He contrasts a top-down *category-based impression* with a bottom-up *person based impression*, which can lead to rounded characters. Whatever the truth of his claim regarding soap opera characters, this passing observation on what viewers value in their TV dramas opens up another possible avenue in the exploration of dialogue on TV.

Dialogue as Talk

The stylistic research reviewed above has involved attention to comprehension and/or interpretation of dialogue within the narrative frame, and has been attentive to the dramatic purposes of the language, including aesthetic and social-critical purposes. There is another tendency, in which the focus is more on how the language in a show exemplifies a particular kind of data or sociolinguistic phenomenon. Coupland (2004) approaches an episode of *Sergeant Bilko/ The Phil Silvers Show* (CBS 1955–1959) as a researcher who is more interested in the general phenomenon of *stylized deception* than he is in the fact that this phenomenon is apparent in a particular television series. Whereas the writers who employ a stylistic perspective mostly believe that analysts need only examine written texts, Coupland shows that it is possible, and in this particular case necessary, to engage with the performed material.

The theoretical point of departure here is the concept of *stylization*, referring to "bounded moments when others' voices are . . . displayed and framed for local, creative, sociolinguistic effect" (Coupland 2004: 247). Such moments are very common in this series, and they are usually the work of the main character. Within the dramatic frame, Bilko's performances are not in fact intended as stylizations, but rather as attempted deceptions of others, notably his commanding officer, Colonel Hall. Silvers/Bilko produces outrageous lies when he speaks to the colonel, to protect his face and his freedom of action as an unscrupulous but lovable schemer. Sometimes he succeeds in deceiving the gullible colonel, and sometimes he fails. But he never deceives us, the audience, for a number of reasons. First, we are always well prepared by previous scenes to expect these deception attempts. Second, the delivery of speech in deception attempts is always markedly in contrast with that of the *offstage*, strategizing Bilko. Third, part of the marking involves adopting characteristics that supposedly (though wrongly) can be expected in the speech of willful deceivers (e.g., lexical repetition, distancing from message content, implausibility of utterance, and some exaggeration of vocal and kinetic mannerisms). It is because of this *marking* that they count as stylizations. Coupland argues that "familiar stereotypes of deceptive communication constitute a repertoire of creative possibilities for Bilko's projections to fail as deceptions . . . and succeed as stylizations" (2004: 268).

From a production perspective, we might want to say that Bilko, the character, owns the failed deceptions, and Silvers, the performer, owns the successful stylizations. The concept of stylization, and its articulation with the related concept of deception, allows Coupland a theoretical perspective in which the content, the wording, and, crucially, the *delivery* of wording (pitch, speed, voice quality, etc., as well as management of gaze and facial expression) are essential to the communicative effect. This is in contrast with the school of thought in linguistic criticism (Short 1998) that written play texts are the appropriate object of study. A written version of the script for this episode would give the talented Silvers ideas as to which aspects of his delivery repertoire would best service that script. It could not be predictive, let alone prescriptive, in the absence of a codified metadiscourse around delivery. That said, there is an evident tension in Coupland's study between attention to Bilko as a character with goals and strategies, and attention to the context of those goals and strategies as fictional creations.

On the question of what 'text' to study, it should also be noted in this section that Quaglio's (2009) data comprises transcriptions of *Friends* episodes written by fans and posted online, such transcriptions then being grammatically tagged so that key features could be retrieved and counted. In this research too the focus is on the verbal not the paralinguistic and kinesic elements of performance, though in principle some of these elements (e.g., intonation contours) could be tagged in a similar way to the grammatical features.

Applying Sociolinguistics to TV Drama Dialogue

In one particular published article from 1992, long before television drama studies had a secure academic base, there is an unequivocal commitment to a mainstream social science agenda for the study of such drama. Harwood and Giles have questions about the effects of a particular show on its audience (or a section of that audience); they undertake an analysis to establish that the effects are likely to be bad, and they do so with an approach that focuses specifically on the dialogue.

This publication was concerned with ageist stereotyping in representations of older people and the potential effect one particular TV show might have on public attitudes toward such people. Harwood and Giles focus on *The Golden Girls*—another comedy—and lay their groundwork carefully. First, they demonstrate that the show has a public reputation for being counterstereotypical—for representing older women as physically and sexually active as well as mentally alert. Second, they establish that the age of the characters is very pertinent to its discourse, by analyzing the numbers and types of age markers in the dialogue in a representative number of episodes.[4] There is a separate analysis of the moments of humor in the production, as signaled via the laugh track on the tape. Third, the authors put their analysis into the context of a particular kind of relationship between text and audience—an *intergroup* context, in other words, a situation in which one party to the interaction belongs to a particular social group (the elderly) and the other party is not of that group. This is important because there are certain conditions to be met in intergroup contact situations if any positive or negative responses to the encounter are to have cognitive effects. Harwood and Giles demonstrate the extent of the overlap between age markers and humor markers is extremely high. They conclude that the counterstereotypical elements of the dialogue are also the laughter-provoking elements, effectively showing, repeatedly, that older women are ridiculous when they go against cultural expectations—for example, by expecting to enjoy a sex life. Although Harwood and Giles do employ quantification techniques, it is particular discursive phenomena, not *content* that they quantify (unlike Fine 1981), and they also provide a number of transcribed extracts from the show in order to show in greater depth the nature of its humor (Harwood and Giles 1992: 426):

> *Sophia is being taken to hospital by Dorothy, her daughter.*
> DOROTHY: Ma, I know you're frightened, but do you really think I'd be pushing for this operation if I believed there was any risk?
> SOPHIA: I don't know, my little beneficiary.

(Season 6, episode 2, "Once in St. Olaf," written by Harold Apter)

The reliance on a laugh track as guide to the comic moments in the drama is somewhat problematic: these will be the moments that the producers have *designed* as "funny," which may include some instances that home viewers may not find funny—perhaps they do not understand the humor or do not appreciate it. The extension of the concepts of *intergroup research* beyond the sphere of face-to-face interaction in which they were originally developed and into the study of mediated communication is another aspect of the approach that might require further thought if this kind of research were to be further developed. Copresence may make intergroup identities more salient for face-to-face interlocutors than for audiences remote from the voices to which they are listening. The "us" and "them" viewing relationship will not hold good for all parts of the audience.

Harwood and Giles are clearly not suggesting that it is part of the *purpose* of *The Golden Girls* to make older women look ridiculous whenever they step out of line. Rather, their point is that this stereotypical way of thinking about the older generation is so culturally ingrained that it is hard to resist, that the goal of attracting audiences through humor is such a nonnegotiable industrial imperative, even in a series that wants to paint a sympathetic picture of life as an older person. They do not provide any empirical audience research to support their claims about its likely negative effects, and they also consider some arguments against their position. From a methodological point of view, their research provides support for the suggestion that social scientists researching effects should pay more attention to textual form:

> ...it has been demonstrated that the examination of texts within the mass media is a crucial counterpart to more conventional effects research. A sophisticated study of mass media effects can only benefit from a fuller understanding of the nature of what is causing the effects. Indeed, attempts to understand "effects" processes are inadequately informed without commentary and discussion on the nature of the "independent variable"—the show itself. It is argued that a socially grounded

discourse analysis is a productive and informative way of approaching such texts.
(Harwood and Giles 1992: 469)

As far as drama dialogue is concerned, this is another road not (yet) taken. Arts
perspectives have been stronger than social science ones, and even they have
been sparse, as my account has shown.

Theoretical Perspectives

The foregoing review examined the published work in TV dramatic dialogue
studies from a substantive rather than a theoretical perspective. In this section
I will focus on two contributions that have theoretical significance for the present
enterprise. One of these is by Short (1998), a piece which has already been
mentioned above; the other is by Bubel (2008).

Short writes a spirited defense, regularly cited in subsequent work in drama
stylistics (Culpeper 2001; McIntyre 2006; Mandala 2007b), of the value of studying the literary dramatic text—the written Shakespeare or Stoppard *play*—when
drama critics had been arguing that only a performed version of the play was
worth studying.

With *Fawlty Towers*, what Short wants to establish is that the performance is,
to a very large extent, implicit in the written text:

> I hope to have demonstrated that if you pay close attention to the linguistic form of
> (parts of) dramatic texts you can infer a huge amount of information about an
> appropriate way to perform them. This comes about because we carry with us a
> large amount of information about how to interpret utterances, and hence how they
> will be said, what gestures and actions will be appropriate, and so on. Not every-
> thing is predictable, and there is plenty of room for the director and actor to make
> their contributions to performance. But the range of appropriate behavior is con-
> siderably more restricted than many critics would have us believe. (1998: 16)

Short claims to see in the printed dialogue plus stage directions such matters
as the general layout of the set (it has to be congruent with our preformed ideas
of a hotel lobby, as specified in the script), right down to the appropriate intonation patterns for particular utterances: "The fact that Sybil's utterance assigns the
word "Goodbye" to a sentence of its own suggests that it will have to have its own
intonation group; and to receive that kind of weighting it will need to be said
fairly loudly and with quite a wide range of pitch movement" (1998: 11).

From here we move into a summary of the brought-to: the kinds of linguistic
and extralinguistic knowledge that Short's "sensitive and experienced readers"
already have, and use, when they engage with play texts:

> Background information about the world and how it works, often
>   arranged into pre-packaged schemata

Understanding of implicature/inference
Understanding of politeness requirements
Turn taking conventions
Speech acts
Sociolinguistic conventions
Graphological information
Sound structure
Grammatical structure
Lexical patterning (1998: 13)

These areas and possibly others all help with the interpretation of the text: world knowledge is what helps us in relation to picturing the right kind of studio set, whereas knowledge of grammar and of sound structure is what we need to hear Sybil say "Goodbye" appropriately in our mind's ear.

Fawlty Towers is an odd choice of *case study* text with which to make this point, because in ontological terms it is undoubtedly more like film than plays and their theatrical productions, and Short himself acknowledges that films are ontologically distinct from plays. He comments parenthetically (1998: 8) that films are different from plays because in films the director is more important than the writer and because most films have only one performance. *Fawlty Towers* exists in a canonical, performed version (the 1970s broadcasts, canned and made available since through repeat broadcasting, VHS, DVD, and even electronic download format). The actress who played Sybil (Prunella Scales) brought to the part a voice quality all of her own. All voices are different, of course, but some vocal performances (think of Martin Luther King or Churchill) are distinctive (it helps if the performances are frequently recycled, of course), and Scales's Sybil is one of those. Short is right, up to a point, because the contribution of voice quality (note that the term *quality* has yet another sense in this collocation) must be consistent with the shrewish persona prefigured in the wording of the script, before any actress was selected for the part. A light, whispery voice would not have served, for instance. But Scales's *specific* voice quality is not anticipated by the script. Here is the space that the script offers for performers and directors to make their contribution to meaning, and it seems appropriate, when the production rather than the written script is the canonical text, for analysts to focus on the former rather than the latter. There is some recent work in drama stylistics which has moved in this direction (McIntyre 2008).

Bubel's (2008) piece was not mentioned in the previous section because it is presented as an account of film discourse, not television, and does not feature any TV extracts. Nevertheless, the author indicates that it is applicable as well to small-screen drama. Bubel's work is also different from the one and only book-length study devoted to dialogue in movies (Kozloff 2000) in that it is interested not so much in the details of the talk, but in the discourse structure of interaction in this context. Bubel uses fragments from Mike Lee's *Secrets and Lies* (Channel Four Films 1996) to improve upon existing models of *film discourse,* in an attempt to understand the relationships among various kinds of participants from actor, to film editor, to cinemagoer, as well as the *conversations* witnessed (in her term, *overheard*) on screen, as the outcome of a layering process. Bubel's account points us toward asking how audiences might make sense of what "Maurice" and "Stuart" (characters in *Secrets and Lies,* played respectively by Timothy Spall and Ron Cook) say to one another: how we "follow" their dialogue when there are things they mutually know that we in the audience do not know, and so have to construct. Bubel is also interested such matters as the fact that the actors have to perform so that audiences can hear (audience design) even though from a Maurice-and-Stuart point of view, there is no one else to hear them, and that this "conspiracy" to include the excluded (the viewing audience) implicates the entire production crew. Some of her commentary points toward the existence of an underlying narration—for example, some comments on how audiences make character inferences to guide their interpretation of subsequent behavior by those characters—but this is underdeveloped in her account. Nevertheless it is the most in-depth account available of the participation framework (Goffman 1979) relevant to fiction-film interaction (and by extension to social interaction via TV drama).

DISCUSSION

The various studies reviewed over the course of this chapter approach the topic from different angles. Despite differences of disciplinary orientation among media research (e.g., Nelson, Corner), linguistic criticism (e.g., Culpeper), sociolinguistics (e.g., Harwood and Giles), and film studies (e.g., Kozloff), it is possible to situate each contribution within an overall picture, as follows. General attempts to understand the communicative basis of screen dialogue (Short, Kozloff, Culpeper, Bubel) are complemented by efforts to make sense of particular kinds of dialogue (Simpson) or of particular communicative forms that can be found in dialogue as well as elsewhere (Coupland), whereas some specific texts are claimed to be intrinsically interesting/important for their time and place of production and distribution (Howard and Giles, Corner, Richardson). Audience research informed by these particular textual studies would be likely to produce valuable results, though in some cases the moment has passed when such research would have been possible and its findings of current relevance.

An interest in communicative form does not preclude an interest in the social meanings mediated through dialogue, though some researchers are clearly more interested in this than others. Although Simpson gestures only tentatively toward the idea that the Monty Python sketch might be *saying* something to its audience about their society, Corner is clear that the presumptions about the social relations of the two speakers, mediated through innovative use of dialogue on commercial television in the United Kingdom, are of particular significance in the specific context of 1950s social change. The cognitive approach favored by Culpeper is interesting here. Any analysis on these terms is compelled to *spell out* the content of the schemata that it claims to be necessary to derive the required meanings, and these can be fairly general ones (the police interview schema is likely to be quite widespread in those English-speaking cultures that also have a developed television culture) or more specific (the doorstep evangelist schema, arguably). As long as the analysis requires this degree of explicitness, it serves the useful function of drawing attention to social meanings brought *to* the text *by* the audience, as well as those that might be taken away from the text by them.

3

What Is TV Dialogue Like?

The starting point for this chapter is a set of questions about the specificity of this particular form of talk. Does dialogue on television do different things from other kinds of talk? What, if anything, makes it distinctive? In order to answer these questions, what should TV dialogue be compared with?

TV dialogue is talk that is both *mediated* and *representational*. It can therefore be compared not only with the kinds of talk it claims to represent, but also with other representations of talk found in other media and other genres. In addition, it can be compared with mediated talk that does not have a representational function. This, then, gives us three other points of reference. First, TV dialogue relates to naturally occurring spoken interaction in real life (cf. Quaglio 2009). Second, it relates to other depictions of talk, such as those in novels and written drama, as well as in other kinds of performed drama on stage, screen, and radio. And third, it relates to television's other kinds of mediated talk, those that do not involve any attempt at representation. This chapter will make use of these three reference points in order to clarify, with examples, the particular nature of dialogue on television.

Naturally occurring face-to-face talk (or voice-to-voice if the talk involves telephone calls) is sometimes called *ordinary conversation*. Tannen (1989) uses this term, even while she is demonstrating the poetic qualities that such talk possesses. Others have reservations about using this expression. Cameron (2001) points out that talk can take many different forms, and observes that the use of the term *ordinary* here contentiously suggests that this is talk at its most basic. It is certainly true that an interview is very different from an informal chat between friends. But it is inappropriate to regard the chat as *ordinary* and the interview as extraordinary, or indeed vice versa. Each has its own specific configuration of participant relations, and each involves strategies that have to be learned. However, for the purposes of analyzing TV dialogue, any comparisons will always relate like with like. Dramatized job interviews are comparable to job interviews in the real world. Dramatized informal chats are likewise comparable to their unmediated, nonrepresentational equivalents. The important principle is the real-time coconstruction of spoken interaction, shared by both the job interview and the chat. It takes two to tango, and it takes at least two to create conversation—making it up as they go along.

If there is a first-order world, constituted by action and interaction, then one characteristic of this world is that it can be transformed into tales, accounts, plays, novels, gists, summaries, and other representational versions of what happened. Versions can also encompass depictions of what might happen, or what can be imagined, such versions being anchored to the presumed real world at different points and in different ways depending on the nature of the representational project. The anchoring of a fantasy drama such as *Pushing Daisies* (ABC 2007) is distinct from that of a newspaper report on a United Nations conference.

TV dialogue can also be compared with other kinds of represented talk. This would include not only other forms of drama and dramatization, whether made for radio, theater, or film production, but also prose fiction. Fictional talk differs from real-life conversation because it is usually composed by someone other than the performers (i.e., not jointly constructed by them) and the writing takes place before the speaking (i.e., the composition does not take place in real time). Occasionally, dialogue in performed fictions may be improvised by performers, but this is the exception, and noteworthy when it does occur. On the very comprehensive *Internet Movie Database*, the entry for the recent U.K. comedy series *Outnumbered* (BBC 2007—present) specifically notes that the dialogue is "part-improvised." The speech in *Outnumbered*, however, is *canned* (the show was not broadcast live), which means that the shots of people could be edited prior to transmission, with some thought as to the management of the improvised material for best effect—not at all the same as what happens in corresponding real-life situations. Of course, one of the things that fictional talk has to imitate is the real-time, joint construction effect of nonfictional talk. A *revelation* by one character must be met by a reaction of *surprise* by another, if that is what would have happened in the corresponding real-world situation.

When dialogue on TV is compared with other kinds of represented talk, the comparison has to be respectful of the different media and generic forms. Speech in novels and short stories raises issues about the grammaticization of the words spoken: direct versus indirect speech, use or omission of verbs of reportage, and so forth. The option of studying drama as written, literary text is attractive to some researchers. This might involve, for instance, attention to written stage directions prefacing and contextualizing speech (McIntyre 2006). It is *performed* speech in other dramatic media (theater, radio, and cinema) that compares most directly with dramatized speech on TV. Of these three, cinema has the greatest potential for overlap. Television and cinema are both in the business of delivering *screen fictions*. The *grammar* of cinema as a visual discourse is similar across these media: many practitioners, behind the camera and in front of it, move readily between the worlds of TV and film production. Television drama production, at least at the "high" end (see previous chapter) has become more film-like in recent years.

Finally, TV dialogue can be compared with *broadcast talk/media talk* (Scannell 1991; Tolson 2006). This kind of spoken interaction, such as an encounter on *The Jerry Springer Show* (NBC 1991–present) is like naturally occurring speech in some respects and like fictional speech in other respects. It is jointly constructed in real time, and can even go out live. In the era of 24-hour news, the *live two-way* between a studio anchor and a location reporter is a well known instance of this (see Montgomery 2006). Media talk of this kind shares with dramatized fictional talk a complex discourse structure. On one level, participants are talking to one another: the anchorperson and the reporter in the news report, and the accuser and the betrayer in a *Springer* episode. On another level, the participants themselves, or someone puppeteering them, are communicating with an audience or readership. The talk carries the effects of both communicative relationships.

Represented talk can, in principle, be transferred among media. Television drama includes numerous adaptations (for some relevant research, see, e.g., Cardwell 2002) along with its original works. *Pride and Prejudice* was originally a novel with embedded character dialogue. It has also been a theater production, a radio play (in an adaptation by Arthur Miller in 1944), a television broadcast (more than once, including BBC 1995), a feature film (more than once), and an audiobook. The dialogue of the original novel, despite being cut, reworded, and supplemented on every occasion, along with aspects of plot, characters, and elements of description, remains an important point of reference in the mediation of the earlier text.

The media talk literature, by contrast, is clear that unscripted interactive speech production on radio and television is somehow distinctive. The genres developed here—radio phone-ins, reality television arguments, formal political interviews, celebrity chat shows—do not and could not have equivalents outside of broadcasting, and they are constitutive of the social relations between broadcasters and audiences. The oft-quoted phrase intended to differentiate broadcast talk from unmediated face-to-face talk, that it is "designed for an overhearing audience" is not helpful here, because drama dialogue (and not just on television) is also talk designed to be overheard. Below are some more extended discussions of these comparisons, drawing on a range of television dramatic productions by way of illustration.

TV DRAMA DIALOGUE AND UNMEDIATED FIRST-ORDER TALK

All dramatic dialogue occurs in a context of representation, to which it makes a contribution. Plenty of previous commentary on dialogue in literature has made the descriptive point that it is not appropriate to expect, even from *realistic* drama and novels, full fidelity to the characteristics of spontaneous talk (Abercrombie 1963, Page 1973, Burton 1980). Drama outside of the realist tradition may be more interested in aesthetic than in realistic effects. Books for students often introduce this topic by presenting transcripts of naturally occurring talk, complete with false starts, repetitions, overlaps, filled pauses, hesitations, and self-corrections, for comparative purposes. Sanger (2001) and Thornborrow and Wareing (1998) both take this approach. Burton observes that some dramatic dialogue gives a better *impression* of verisimilitude than others, and that it is important to try to account for that impression. Most writers on drama dialogue make only minimal comments on *why* true verisimilitude is not achievable. Comprehensibility is certainly a factor (when there is too much overlap, audiences can't hear the lines), as is the obligation to convey meaning at different levels (dramatists use character dialogue to get across information about place, time, and action that the characters themselves could probably have taken for granted). Less often mentioned is the fact that real-time interaction leads to multiple possibilities of uptake at all points, and that dramatic versions of talk have to foreclose on all but the most relevant to the ongoing narrative. There may also be, on the part of some linguists, a suspicion that dramatists themselves don't fully understand what naturally occurring talk is *really* like. As ordinary language users, they, like the rest of us, mentally edit out disfluency and other complications in the everyday business of making sense—and carry this deafness over to their representational work.

But some dramatists and directors certainly do have an awareness of the ways dialogue can be fashioned that move it away from standard-issue, one-speaker-at-a-time fluency. Harold Pinter's pauses, Woody Allen's repetitiveness and disfluency, and Robert Altman's use of multiple voices are all well-known examples of divergence from the standard model. Nor is such divergence unknown on television. A current British forensic crime series, *Waking the Dead* (BBC 2000–present), is very keen on the use of overlapping speech, as in the following example from a 2008 episode.

The police officers and scientists are investigating a death. The corpse is headless and handless, but one of the hands has been found. The chief scientist suspects that the murder weapon is a sword, and knows the age of its construction. The crime is linked to an army base, and swords are found there. A particular sword is tested:

(*Brackets and indentation indicate overlapping speech*)

Is this our murder weapon?

No. Because even though it's the same age, it's been re-shaped and re-sharpened, the metal fragments contained in this sword are markedly different to the ones in the hand as you can see there (*indicating computer screen images*).

So how does this help us?

Because each and every sword is unique in its [metallurgic composition].
                              [But that's fantastic, I mean] Mallam would've
got rid of the sword wouldn't [he? I mean, it's incriminating evidence so . . .
                    [No I don't believe he would have got rid of it because if it was
a hundred and fifty years old it's historical significance wouldn't [let him] dispose of it.
                                        [No].
Also, if you go some way towards matching up the fragments you go some way towards
    finding out who the killer might be.
That's right because he's initiated a lockdown so whatever sword he uses . . . We can't get into
    the barracks so it could be anywhere by now.

(Season 7, episode 5, "Duty and Honour," written by Adrian Mead)

The overlapping speech here is not just in the service of realism. Its use under-
writes a sense of urgency and frustration, as well as of competition among the
characters to hold the floor and have their views prevail. Audibility suffers: the
line that begins "I don't believe he would have got rid of it . . ." is inaudible after
"historical significance," when two other voices join in. However, the key points
in each contribution (not entirely coherent) are allowed to stand proud of the
hubbub—"it's not the right sword," says the scientist, "the right one has been
disposed of by now," says the senior detective (played by Trevor Eve); "probably
not," says the forensic psychologist (played by Tara Fitzgerald), "if it is has
historical significance"; "but we've been prevented from looking for it, and it
could be anywhere now," the detective concludes.

The most useful comments in this area of study are those of Herman (1995),
who is aware that the "language of drama" is hardly a neglected topic (e.g., in
relation to the plays of Shakespeare) but recognizes that this scholarship has
focused primarily on such matters as textual imagery, thus valuing drama
insofar as it can be seen as a type of poetry, and having little to say about realist
drama (i.e., most contemporary drama) in which poetically styled eloquence is
not a high priority:

> Conversational language, apparently, reveals us to be tongue-tied, incoherent
> when our passions are aroused; we splutter with rage or are stunned with grief.
> Playwrights who use a realistic mode are hampered by the mismatch between the
> force of felt emotion and the threadbare possibilities for expression of them
> afforded by everyday speech. (1995: 4)

Herman here is not presenting her own view but giving an account of traditional
prejudices in some literary critical discourse against realism as a dramatic mode,
with particular reference to the implications of this for the description and
analysis of language in dramas that adopt this mode. (That a dramatization's
nonlinguistic ways of conveying emotion, as in film and television, might be
aesthetically interesting, is beside the point in this context.) As Herman points

out, what gets neglected in the poetic approach to drama language is precisely its character as *dialogue*, as the interactive exchange of utterances between speakers. Her own contribution is to take this character on board, exploring the language of plays from Shakespeare to Beckett as they exploit the resources of spontaneous conversation and turn these to expressive effect. Her aim is to do this without falling into the trap of treating (fictive) dialogue as simply a copy of nonfictive talk:

> It is not therefore a question of whether dramatic dialogue is seen to mirror faithfully some real life correlate or not, even assuming that some such exists to be mirrored. Even the most naturalistic forms of dramatic speech do not quite reproduce the real life product. The mirror is not the point of reference between the two forms. Rather, it is a question of mechanics, in the exploitation by dramatists of underlying speech conventions, principles and "rules" of use, operative in speech exchanges in the many sorts, conditions and contexts of society which members are assumed to share and use in their interactions in day-to-day exchanges. (Herman 1995: 6)

Herman can be seen as on a mission to find the everyday basis of drama dialogue, inasmuch as her approach involves exploring such dialogue using the tools developed for studying talk in naturally occurring social interaction, from speech act theory, to conversation analysis, to the pragmatics of implicature and politeness. Other linguists, notably Tannen (1989), have put forward the idea that strategies (repetition, quotation, and imagery) traditionally viewed as literary or poetic not only have their source in spontaneous talk, but also have a specific social function there as *involvement strategies*. From Herman we learn that literary drama dialogue may do its work by virtue of what it shares with everyday talk; from Tannen we conversely learn that everyday talk is interestingly "literary." Note that Tannen's approach does not involve a view of literary language as more *original* (novel, inventive, creative) than everyday forms of talk. As she says herself, *repetition* is the key feature, in different guises.

Where does *television* drama dialogue fit into this picture? Dialogue in stage plays became primarily *realistic* in the twentieth century. The practice of particular dramatists (notably Harold Pinter) opened scholarly eyes to the possibility of recognizing purposeful aesthetic craft in materials perceived as ordinary (Quigley 1975, Burton 1980). Three consequences flowed from this recognition. First, a particular kind of *ordinariness* became recognized as a possible design feature. Second, it became clear that not all *ordinary-sounding* talk in plays, films, and TV shows has the expressive value of Pinteresque dialogue. Third, stylisticians came to appreciate that the recognition of the particular expressive qualities of dialogue in realist drama generally required an analytic apparatus different from the one traditionally brought to bear on the language of plays. Attention to imagery, rhythm, rhyme, and so forth might work well for Shakespeare, but would be of much less help with John Osborne, let alone Harold Pinter. *Realistic* drama dialogue would reveal its particular kind of creativity only through the use of approaches drawn from the study of naturally occurring talk, as argued by Burton in the 1980s (Burton 1980), Herman in the 1990s (Herman 1995), and Mandala in the present decade (Mandala 2007b).

Realism, broadly defined, has always dominated in television drama, and departures from it have attracted attention. A notable example of this (chosen here because its nonrealist dramaturgy affected the dialogue) would be Dennis Potter's *Pennies from Heaven* (BBC 1978), a narrative about a frustrated sheet music salesman in the 1930s. This miniseries took the form of a musical and it had actors miming to 1930s popular songs—the main character's principal source of imaginative release. The show was a critical success, and a popular production.

Even more popular was the comedy *The Royle Family* (BBC 1998–2006). But whereas the dialogue in *Pennies from Heaven* eschewed realism by becoming more obviously artificial, *The Royle Family* follows a more Pinteresque formula, engaging in what might be called "foregrounded banality." Banal talk in drama can be construed as talk that is not *about* anything that matters and is inconsequential in relation to plot developments. The inconsequentiality of the talk, as when Barbara, wife and mother (played by Sheila Johnston), regularly asks every visitor to the house what they have had for their tea, is a trademark feature of this show, frequently mentioned in reviews and critical treatments.[1] *Tea* is understood as a reference to the main evening meal in this working-class environment. The inconsequentiality of the exchanges teaches viewers what to expect in this world. It also does character/relationship work. Some of the banal dialogue has the effect of displaying how all family members from time to time ask the younger child Antony to make cups of tea for them, or pop out to buy cigarettes, and how Antony does their bidding—mostly without complaint.

The series does not deny audiences the pleasure of story. Things happen over the course of the seasons but they are not melodramatic events, just the same kinds of high points (births, marriages, new jobs, deaths) that all families experience. (A 'season' in the United States is a finite run of 20–24 episodes, generally broadcast consecutively from late autumn to the following late spring/ early summer. Throughout this book, I have expanded the term to refer to consecutive episode runs of any series irrespective of national origin or scheduling). These high points are planned for, and talked about, more than they are shown. They do not absorb the attention of the characters to the exclusion of all other topics of talk, such as whether or not to buy a new jacket. In the majority of television drama, dialogue exists to service the narrative: in *The Royle Family*, the priorities are reversed. The levels of intimacy the characters enjoy with one another allow the routine exchange of nonperturbing insults (insults that are part of the relationship and that therefore leave relationships unchanged). In episode 1 alone, there are 26 face-to-face exchanges of epithets and insults. These range from the innocent, teasing, "you lemon," through the more forceful/masculine "knobhead," to conversational insults that require more than a single line to bring about:

> DENISE: Cheryl, that'd look good on you.
> ANTONY: What is it, a tent?

(Denise is played by Caroline Aherne, who also cowrote the scripts with Craig Cash; Antony by Ralf Little; and Cheryl by Jessica Hynes). The mutual intimacy of the dramatis personae also allows the talk to focus frequently on the vulgar body and bodily processes (defecation and flatulence the application of makeup and cosmetics, the inspection of bodies for wounds and blemishes). The first episode begins with a shot of Denise's feet: she is painting her toenails—not in the privacy of a bedroom or bathroom, but in the living room and in the presence of Barbara and Jim (played by Ricky Tomlinson), her parents. The absence of any talk about this is significant in depicting Denise's actions as normal behavior. Later discussions fix on hairstyles, clothing, weight, going to the bathroom, other people's makeovers (including TV celebrities), foot massages, and verrucas (warts).

It is important to point out that *The Royle Family* does not rely exclusively on the audience's sensibility to hear the dialogue as banal. There are textual cues, verbal and visual, that invite us to hear it in that way. Jim, for example, picks on Barbara when he thinks she has gone too far in this direction, thus introducing a reflexive element:

1 BARBARA: Have you had your tea, Dave?
2 DAVE: Yeah.
3 BARBARA: What'd you have?
4 DAVE: Corned beef hash.
5 BARBARA: Ooh. We should have that one day. Hey, Jim, Dave's had corned beef hash.
6 JIM: Funny, they never mentioned it on the news.

(Season 1, episode 1, "Bills, Bills, Bills," written by Caroline Aherne, Craig Cash, and Henry Normal)

The sarcastic wit in Jim's response to Barbara, characteristic of his persona in the series, is certainly there to add to the show's comedic value. From a critical perspective, it also raises questions of audience alignment: do we hear Barbara as Jim does, and share with him the very mild joke at her expense, or do we align with Barbara as the victim of a put-down, albeit one verbalized humorously? The banality of Barbara's talk about food is of the foregrounded kind, but the banality of the *joke* is something else.

Given the realist basis of most TV drama, it would be surprising if dramatic dialogue in television was not *formulaic* to a considerable degree, because research suggests that large proportions of naturally occurring language, both in speech and in writing, is itself formulaic. Estimates vary, but even the lowest gives a figure of around one-third (Schmitt and Carter 2004: 1). The research in the present book is not quantitative, and cannot therefore assess the extent of the phenomenon in televisual contexts. In any event, the estimates in the *formulaic speech* literature come with a health warning, because the scope of *formulaic* is troublesome, as Schmitt and Carter indicate. It is another category that has clear central members but many borderline cases. Strings of words that repeatedly occur together, and without any grammatical modification, such as the idiomatic "beat around the bush" are certainly regarded as formulaic. But so are sentence frames with slots in which speakers can place a word or phrase of their choice, appropriate to the situation. "I'm sorry to keep you waiting" is formulaic in this sense even though the "I" could be "we," or it could be the name of a third party. If intensifiers, adverbials, or other optional elements are added, this still does not compromise the essentially formulaic character of the sentence frame here: "Mr. Jones is very sorry that he had to keep you waiting again." But there are limits, and it seems to me that "Mr. Jones is mortified to realize that he's had to keep you kicking your heels in here for so long" has virtually abandoned the formulaicity of the original version. ("Kicking one's heels" is a different formula, and its use here does not impinge on the argument.) Beyond this, Wray and Perkins (2000), citing Bouton (1998), point out that there are formulae of language use that are based on semantic-pragmatic factors rather than formal ones at word and sentence levels: "In response to the question *Did you enjoy the party?* a person might answer *Is the Pope a Catholic? Does a one-legged duck swim round in circles? Does the sun rise in the morning?* Etc. [This formula] allows the use of any question to which the answer is both obvious and is the same as the answer to the original question" (Wray and Perkins 2000: 12). All kinds of predictable language use occur in drama as they do in real life. However, comparing real life to drama in respect of formulaicity is a complex business. Schmitt and Carter (2004: 9) argue that recurring situations in the social world may call for conventionalized language to realize such functions as apologizing, making requests, giving directions, and complaining. One important function is "maintaining social interaction" (2004: 10), in which the content of the talk is less important than the fact of talking. Formulaic expressions produced in such contexts are less likely to occur in (realist) dramatic dialogue than in real life, because the contexts themselves are less likely to be dramatized than more *weighty* encounters between speakers. It is therefore possible that TV drama dialogue—especially in comedy—features more *defective* and reflexive uses of such speech than it does of straightforward instances, contributing displays of irony (dramatic or otherwise), mistrust, hostility, and communicational trouble, to give point to otherwise bland material. Prodromou (2007: 20) cites an example from *Fawlty Towers* in which one character introduces formulaic speech, and another makes creative play with the formula for sarcastic purpose—instantiating a conversational display that is characteristic of the relationship between the two characters—Basil Fawlty, hotel proprietor (played by John Cleese), and his wife Sybil (played by Prunella Scales):

SYBIL: No Polly doesn't forget things.
BASIL: Doesn't she?
SYBIL: Can you remember the last time she did?
BASIL: No, I can't but then my memory isn't very good
SYBIL: You can say that again.
BASIL: Can I, dear? Oh, thank you . . . I've forgotten what it was.

(Series written by John Cleese and Connie Booth)

"You can say that again" is a conventionalized way of agreeing, emphatically, with what the previous speaker has said. It is playful, albeit in a rather predictable way, to respond by actually repeating the previous utterance. Basil's creativity goes a step beyond this: there is semantic and pragmatic relevance in his claiming forgetfulness as a reason for not repeating what he said, because the observation that is not repeated is precisely his forgetfulness. He does make the point "my memory isn't very good" for a second time, but in the second occurrence the point is implied rather than stated explicitly. As we shall see in the next section, when television dramatists do display routine encounters using routine dialogue, they often have ulterior, that is to say, narrative, purposes for doing so. And chapter 5 will return to the question of banality in its discussion of TV drama and catch phrases.

TELEVISION DRAMA DIALOGUE AND REPRESENTED TALK

A very large proportion of all represented talk is deployed in the context of narrative. Both prose fiction and drama, as narrative modes, make use of represented talk. Because prose fiction makes it possible to separate narration from character speech, the speech does not have to service the narrative to the same extent that it does in drama. Some novels and short stories may make no use of dialogue at all. We should not forget that narrators in fiction can be characters too, and their discourse can be a kind of speech, with its own point of view or "slant," in Chatman's (1990) terms.

Drama itself may provide space for a narratorial voice and for direct address to the audience, in the tradition of the Greek chorus. Such narrators have varying degrees of dominance over the textual discourse: a production may take the form of a narrative recitation, with occasional dramatized inserts, or there may be little more than an introductory scene-setting remark before the drama "takes off" in its own internal time and space. Television dramatization spans all these possibilities, as well as the more usually preferred option in which there is no narrator at all. A crime reconstruction on *Crimewatch* (BBC 1984–present) will give the narrating voice prime control.[2] A largely wordless reenactment will be witnessed while events are recounted in voiceover. The voiceover soundtrack will provide occasional gaps for the audience to listen to the voices of participants, real people, but played by actors—especially if there is some kind of firsthand record of what they actually said to one another at the time. If a physical recording exists, for example, of a phone call to the emergency services, then this may be used in the broadcast in the interests of authenticity.

In TV drama proper, uses of narrator speech are much more restricted though some recent shows have introduced it. Both *Heroes* (NBC 2006–present) and *Desperate Housewives* (ABC 2004–present) use voiceover speech at the start of episodes and occasionally elsewhere. In both cases the speaker is one of the characters in the fictional world. In *Desperate Housewives* the voiceover is that of a character who is already dead by the time the story events begin, and she seems thereafter to have an omniscient view of the story world. In *Heroes* the "narrator" (an inappropriate label here, because he does not recount narrative events) steers clear of story events, and articulates quasi-philosophical musings (see chapter 1) that purport to be relevant to those events. The connection between these musings and the narrator's on-screen character are very tenuous. In TV and film drama, audiences may be given verbal help with story information visually rather than aurally, via subtitles, keeping alive a tradition that began with the early silent films.

Relevant information may also be provided visually in nonlinguistic ways: iconic shots of particular locations can be included to show where the action is meant to take place; once the action is under way, it is always possible to return to locations that have been established earlier. *The Amazing Mrs. Pritchard* (BBC 2006) opens with a close-up shot, from neck to chest only, of a besuited female pinning a name badge to her lapel that reads, "MANAGER: ROS PRITCHARD." Immediately we know that this is the eponymous Mrs. Pritchard (played by Jane Horrocks), and that she is a manager. Before a word is spoken we learn, again visually, that she is the manager of Greengages Supermarket: a subsequent shot includes a poster reading, "*Greengages: This is how the customers see you.*" These possibilities raise the issue of *being* versus *showing*. It is one thing for characters to "be" in a flat, in London, in the 1960s. It is another thing for productions to *show* that this is where and when they are, providing audiences with sufficient visual and verbal clues to come to the right conclusions.

Dialogue, therefore, is one of the means that dramas use to provide story information, alongside or instead of direct narration and subtitles, and alongside mise-en-scène. Such provision accounts for two out of nine functions in a useful typology developed by Kozloff (2000) with reference to dialogue in feature films. The nine functions in Kozloff's account are divided into two groups. Her claim is that the first group relates to functions that are "fundamental because they are centrally involved in the communication of narrative"—such as the anchorage of the diegetic world, characterization, and the enactment of narrative events—whereas the second group "involves functions that go beyond narrative communication into the realms of aesthetic effect, ideological persuasion and commercial appeal" (2000: 2).

Is this typology relevant only to feature films? In practice, there are certainly differences among media. In theater, the expositional responsibilities of dialogue (encompassing functions 1 and 2 below) may be greater than they are in cinema, because of the limitations of the physical space. In radio, they may be either fewer or greater. They will be fewer when a narrator is given most of the expositional work. Otherwise, they will be greater, because there is no physical space that can be shown to audiences. Notwithstanding these differences in realization, the typology itself may be generalizable, and it is certainly a useful starting point in relation to television drama, fiction film's closest analogue.

It is worthwhile to take a closer look at Kozloff's schema. In the first, basic group, she gives us the following:

1. Anchorage of the diegesis and characters
2. Communication of narrative causality
3. Enactment of narrative events
4. Character revelation
5. Adherence to the code of realism
6. Control of viewer evaluation and emotions (2000: 33)

There is no suggestion here that dialogue is necessary or sufficient to fulfill these functions, only that if dialogue is present, then it *must* discharge some or all of these functions. No indication is given as to any order of priority, and it is acknowledged that any given stretch of actual dialogue is likely to be multifunctional in these terms. The two functions that are of particular interest here are the first two: anchorage and causality. I have already dealt with realism (Kozloff's function 5) in the previous section, discussing the relations between performed, scripted dialogue and everyday forms of talk, and I will be discussing character revelation (function 4) at length in chapter 7. The other two functions in this group deserve a brief comment, if only to indicate what is meant.

Enactment of narrative events (function 3) is distinct from communication of narrative causality (function 2), inasmuch as, in the first case, audiences see and hear narrative events as they happen to the characters, whereas in the second, characters learn from one another about what has happened, what might have happened, and what might happen in their future—and audiences, thereby, learn this too. None of this is peculiar to feature film dramatization, though screen fictions can and do tend to show more action than other dramatic media. This conception of action treats sex, fights, and car chases on a par with confessions, declarations of love, and threats: those that are linguistically "lite" with those that are linguistically full. The difference between a car chase and a confession is roughly as follows: a car chase is an event in which talk may occur as an adjunct feature: "Go, go!" "That way, quick!" "Lost him!" A confession, by contrast, is an interpersonal event in which talk is likely to take a lead role: "I've been seeing other men." However, the distinction between talk and action in this context is a scale, not an opposition, because the car chase undoubtedly requires some talk, and the confession exists as much in exchanges of gaze and body language as it does in its wording. Different narrative events will call for more or less verbalization according to context.

Function 6, "control of viewer evaluation and emotions," is harder to pin down because it is so often developed alongside other functions. It refers to dialogue that exists to direct the viewer's attention to specific aspects of the mise-en-scène or plot, but also to manage the nature of that attention. An example from the world of television drama will help to clarify this. In season 5 of *24* (Fox 2001–present), one pivotal character is the president's wife, Martha Logan (played by Jean Smart). Before the audience sees or hears Martha, we are guided in what to expect by the following exchange between the president (played by Gregory Itzin) and an aide (John Allen Nelson as Walt Cummings):

1 LOGAN: Have you checked on my wife?
2 CUMMINGS: She's still getting ready. She'll be fine, sir.
3 LOGAN: Hmm.
4 CUMMINGS: I'm in contact with Dr. Hill.
5 LOGAN: I'd feel better if you would check on her yourself. She cannot have one of
    her meltdowns today. Look, you're the only one she listens to, Walt.

(Season 5, episode 1, "7:00–8:00 A.M.," written by Howard Gordon)

Here we not only learn that the president's wife is the sort of person who has "meltdowns," but get a pretty good clue that the drama to unfold will certainly include at least one such meltdown. When she appears on screen in her first scene, we are ready to read her behavior in light of this prior warning.

In addition to the six basic functions in Kozloff's account, there are three "value-added" ones—to use an economic metaphor. I will briefly introduce and comment on these, before returning to the subject of dialogue and exposition:

1. Opportunities for star turns
2. Exploiting the resources of language
3. Thematic messages/authorial commentary/allegory

The three functions that come into this second grouping all offer meanings that are essentially nonnarrational, in other words, which do not require to be delivered in the form of narrative texts. Two of them (opportunities for star turns and exploiting the resources of language) are indicative of meaning as *display*.

This idea of verbal display can be related to an interest in the cognate idea of *spectacle* and the *spectacular* in some of the film studies literature. The label *spectacular* suggests a primarily *visual* experience but *aural* display is also included. The musical numbers in musicals are simultaneously visually and aurally spectacular in this sense. Films, notwithstanding the general preference for the prosaic over the poetic, do provide opportunities in which language *itself* is put on display ("exploitation of the resources of language" in the schema refers to this kind of formal foregrounding). They also provide moments of performance display, the spoken equivalent of the operatic aria—this is what Kozloff has in mind when she refers to "opportunities for star turns."

In television dramatization, too, display of the former kind certainly occurs from time to time. Star turns, in which the performance is more noteworthy than either the narrative context that houses it, or the words that are being performed, may also occur. In January 2008, an entire 30-minute episode of the popular British soap opera *EastEnders* (BBC 1985–present) was given over to a single character, Dot Cotton (June Brown). The pretext for Dot's talk was that she was speaking into a tape recorder for the benefit of her sick husband—also, as the monologue progressed, she was meant to discover her true feelings about the prospect of having him back to live with her as an invalid, should he ever come out of hospital. This episode required considerable acting stamina and skill from June Brown; the unusual nature of this episode was extensively trailed beforehand, and the actress was subsequently nominated for a BAFTA award (the episode was written by Tony Jordan).

The third of the value-added functions in Kozloff"s scheme she labels "thematic messages/authorial commentary/allegory." Within the scope of this conception come ideas about texts as *arguments*: bits of discourse with a point to make. Argumentation and point making can take many forms: stories can illustrate and provide evidence for the case being made. If all stories have a point (as some, e.g., Labov and Waletzky 1967, have claimed), then perhaps this function belongs in the first and not the second group of Kozloff's schema. Yet it still seems to me to fit better in the second group, because first, argumentation can be carried out without the use of narrative, and second, because within a narrative context, the argumentative/thematic meanings are typically implied rather than made explicit.

Returning to the first two functions that together can be called the *expositional* functions, it is clear that in television, as in the cinema, dialogue is indeed one of the ways of conveying story information. It can result in rather bland talk, as in this example from the British/American thriller, *The State Within* (BBC 2006):

1 CAROLINE: Mark.
2 MARK: Caroline, hi. How are you?

3 CAROLINE: Good. This is my dad, Anthony. Dad, Sir Mark Brydon.
4 MARK: Mark. How do you do?
5 ANTHONY: Delighted to meet you.

(Series written by Lizzie Mickery and Daniel Percival)

On one level, this kind of dramatic dialogue is as banal as it gets. But it does its job: the main character now has a name as well as a body. The cited lines do not constitute the whole scene, which does other things besides giving Brydon (Jason Isaacs) a name. Anthony (Jonathan Whittaker), father of Caroline (Genevieve O'Reilly), will be one of the passengers to die in a plane explosion, caused by a suicide bomber, shortly following this scene. One strand of narrative development will focus on his involvement in events that led up to the atrocity, so it is significant that he is the father of Mark's former lover (as we learn here) and dramatic irony in the meeting taking place so very soon before the fatal crash.

Kozloff believes that dialogue in many movies is confined to the functions of her first grouping, with no interest in either thematic content or display. Outside of comedy, drama on television may have similarly restricted productions. The thriller series *24*, excerpted earlier in this chapter, is a case in point. In this series, each episode depicts an extraordinary day in the life of the Counter Terrorism Unit and of one of its key members, Jack Bauer (Kiefer Sutherland). As an action-adventure thriller series, we shouldn't be surprised to find that much screen time is devoted to showing bodies in action rather than speech. However, some acts and events must be realized verbally; on top of that, our characters need to talk, so that we know who they are, what they are like as people in these dramatically momentous circumstances, and what is happening to them.

Toward the start of season 5, with Jack Bauer supposedly dead but in reality living under an assumed name as a casual laborer in the Mojave Desert, the production contrives to display him in "off-work" mode by including some otherwise irrelevant dialogue (a possible illustration of function 5 in the narrative-related function group) between himself as Frank Flynn and his new girlfriend Diane (Connie Britton):

1 JACK/FRANK: Since I don't have to go to work today, I can take care of the fence out back if you want?
2 DIANE: Oh, that'd be great. I can't thank you enough for all the work you've done around here.

(Season 5, episode 1, "7:00–8:00 A.M.," written by Howard Gordon)

This is the last we ever hear of Diane's fence, or "Frank's" work commitments. These topics are quickly set aside by the demands of the plot. Nevertheless, the dialogue here has narrative-related functions besides that of constituting normality through realism. It is also helping to display the current state of their relationship. They are intimate enough for him to take on this kind of work for her, but not so intimate that she can demand it or take it for granted.

Within seconds of this exchange, Bauer will be caught up in the aftermath of a former president's assassination, because he has been set up as the perpetrator of the crime. From then on, his style of dialogue is better illustrated by the following:

1 DEREK: Don't shoot me!
2 JACK: What the hell are you doing here?
3 DEREK: I'm sorry I followed you, I'm just—I'm just worried about my mother.
4 JACK: Get up. Get up. Get up. Dammit! Come here. You're going with me.
5 DEREK: This is none of my business. This is none of my business. I won't tell anyone. Just let me go, okay?
6 JACK: I really wish I could, kid, but I can't. You're going with me. Now, get in the helicopter.

Derek (Brady Corbet), Diane's son, has become suspicious of "Frank" and followed him. Jack needs to get to Los Angeles, where he has arranged to meet another regular character, Chloe O'Brian (Mary Lynn Rajskub), who has narrowly escaped her own murder and is now on the run. Jack can't afford to postpone his trip, for which he hijacks a helicopter, nor can he afford to let Derek betray his whereabouts. Hence the abduction of the scared and confused young man, and the brutality of its verbal and nonverbal management, with unmitigated directives backed up by the threat of further force. Jack's only concession to their prior relationship is in line 6, in which he acknowledges Derek's request and "apologizes" that he can't accede to it. *Uncompromising* is a good description of the persona that emerges from dialogue such as this and much more of a similar kind throughout the several seasons of this series.

Functionally basic dialogue in television, as illustrated here, need not be uninteresting or poorly written. In particular, the use of dialogue for characterization, function 3, is crucial for dramatization in all media—perhaps especially so in television drama where, because of the long-form possibilities, there are opportunities for audiences to develop attachments to particular characters as well as in-depth knowledge of their histories and backstories. Dialogue for characterization is the topic of chapter 7.

Television comedy is where we might expect to find examples of dialogue that extend beyond functional basics, with particular reference to function 8: exploitation of the resources of language. Not all comedy is in the business of language display, but some of it certainly is. *The Royle Family*, with its foregrounded banality, is a good example (see above), but, in a very different way, so is *The Thick of It* (BBC 2005–2007), another British comedy. This behind-the-scenes sitcom about British politics has been described as offering "a masterclass in creative swearing" ("Today's TV," *Daily Mirror*, July 3, 2007), on the basis of

scenes such as "the iPod rant," composed by the series' "swearing consultant,"
Ian Martin (video available on YouTube at the time of writing):

> JAMIE (PAUL HIGGINS): You take the piss out of Al Jolson again and I will remove your
> iPod from its tiny nano-sheath and push it up your cock. Then I'll put some
> speakers up your arse and put it on to shuffle with my fucking fist. Then, every
> time I hear something that I don't like—which will be every time that something
> comes on—I will skip to the next track by crushing your balls.

> (Season 2, episode 1, "Special: The Rise of the Nutters," written by Jesse Armstrong,
> Simon Blackwell, Armando Iannucci, Tony Roche, and Ian Martin)

Television dialogue can be seen, therefore, to have the same functions in respect
of dramatized narration as feature film does. However, across the range of
television dramatization (i.e., including dramatized documentary and factual
shows like *Crimewatch*, involving reconstructions), much wider than that of
feature film, it exploits those functions differently. In television drama proper,
the similarity with cinematic dialogue will be extensive. But even here there are
differences. British television drama has not always sought to distance itself from
theater to the extent that film has. In the earliest period, before 1955, stage drama
was the principal resource for live on-screen performance. Even after 1955
the words *play* and *theater* were used as names of anthology series, for identification and promotional purposes: *Armchair Theatre* (ABC Weekend Television,
1956–1973), *Play for Today* (BBC 1970–1981), *The Wednesday Play* (BBC 1964–
1970)—though television by then had certainly emancipated itself from more
established forms of dramatic production, whether in theater, cinema, or on
radio. This suggests that the rejection of dialogue, familiar in cinema, as "too
theatrical" need not apply here. Jason Jacobs (2000) argues with the too-easy
characterization of early British television drama as displaced theater, but his
emphasis is upon the development of new modes of visualization and has little to
say about the implications of this for dialogue in such work.

Media theorists such as Ellis (1983) and Altman (1986) have emphasized
the significance of the sound track in television generally. Dialogue is not especially significant in this elevation; music and announcements may be more
important. But talk is nevertheless part of the sound track and may benefit in
terms of audience attention from the relative priority given to sound in general.

In radio drama, talk is its essence, whatever augmentation is supplied via
sound effects, music, and narration. Television dramatization in the area of
comedy has an extremely strong radio heritage, with many popular shows
(*Dead Ringers*, BBC 2002–present, *The League of Gentlemen*, BBC 1999–2002)
making a transition from one to the other. Nor should the connection between
television soap opera and radio be forgotten. *Guiding Light* (CBS 1952–2009), the
longest running *soap opera* in the world, started on radio in 1937 and made the
transition to television in 1952, before being finally cancelled in 2009.

The role of dialogue may be significantly different in a medium that has increasingly adopted the *long-form series* as exemplified by *The Sopranos* (HBO 1999–2007), *Desperate Housewives*, and many more (see Creeber 2004) with both episode-level and running storylines (story arcs) as its characteristic drama form, in contrast to a medium in which narrative closure over a number of acts is the standard model.

TELEVISION DRAMATIC DIALOGUE
AND BROADCAST TALK

The study of broadcast talk has developed a small but focused literature, including two recent works with the identical title, "Media Talk" (Hutchby 2006, Tolson 2006). Despite differences of emphasis, especially regarding conversation-analytic methods and other approaches, the one thing both authors agree on is that simulated talk (i.e., drama dialogue) is excluded from the scope of the research:

> [Media talk] often appears to be "live" (even when the programme has been recorded) and relatively unscripted (though usually some sort of pre-planning is apparent). This book is not concerned therefore with the overtly scripted dialogue of fictional programming such as forms of drama, including soap opera and situation comedy. (Tolson 2006: 3)

> Much of the talk that radio and television audiences encounter is pre-scripted: for instance in news bulletins, in documentaries, in drama or in situation comedy. But in phone-ins, talk shows, interviews and the like, while there may well have been some planning and preparation prior to the broadcast, the talk as it unfolds in the real time of the show is not scripted, meaning that the participants have to be creative in reacting and responding to one another's talk in the course of its production. (Hutchby 2006: 1)

In Hutchby's account, three characteristics of media talk are specifically mentioned: it is prototypically scripted, it is "as-if" live, and it involves participants who are not professional broadcasters (politicians, celebrities, "ordinary" people), as well as, or instead of, professionals. Drama, by contrast, is prototypically scripted, scarcely ever live, or even "as-if" live (performers can not be allowed to be heard fluffing their lines), and is performed and produced by professionals. These professionals strive to conceal, as much as possible, that the "conversations" in drama are designed by writers, producers, and actors with an audience in mind, rather than by characters, for other characters. They strive to maintain the imaginary fourth wall of classical realist dramaturgy, and keep viewers on the other side of it.

However, most of these criteria can be questioned. It is not a necessary condition of drama dialogue that it be scripted: it can be improvised and, to that extent, coconstructed. Although modern TV drama is not broadcast live, it certainly used to be (see Jacobs 2000). It is not true that only media talk, and not drama dialogue, is designed for an overhearing audience—it is usually constructed without overlap between turns, for example, in the interest of audibility. Media talk is much more likely to be directly addressed to an audience, though such talk constructs the audience as ratified listeners, not overhearers, in Goffman's (1979) terms. Recipients of drama can be ratified listeners too, in productions such as *Desperate Housewives*, which allow for a narrator role. Breaches in the fourth wall are not unknown. A TV play from the 1960s by Dennis Potter, *Vote, Vote, Vote for Nigel Barton* (BBC 1965) had one of the characters, a cynical political agent, speak directly to the camera, in other words, the audience, about the candidate's strengths and weaknesses in politics.

We are accustomed to using the idea of the filmgoer as a voyeur, surreptitiously spying on the actions of the on-screen characters. What has often been overlooked is that *viewers* are also *listeners*; in fact they are *eavesdroppers*, listening in on conversations purportedly addressed to others, but conversations that—in reality—are designed to communicate certain information to the audience (Kozloff 2000: 14; see also Bubel 2008).

Another potential point of contrast is that in media talk, performers are being "themselves" and in drama dialogue they are being "other people"—characters. This can be challenged, too, as an absolute means of discrimination. In media talk, performers (especially the professionals) are being *versions* of themselves. The concept of *persona* is often used here (Horton and Wohl 1956, Tolson 1996, Tolson 1991). Sometimes they are being other, fictional people. Fictional interviewers in that sense include "Dame Edna Everage," aka Barry Humphries (Tolson 1991), and Mrs. Merton, aka Caroline Aherne (Montgomery 1999).[3] Sometimes, in dramatizations, performers play themselves—Kirsty Wark, a professional news presenter and interviewer on British television played herself in the TV drama *The Amazing Mrs. Pritchard* (Corner and Richardson 2008).

It is necessary, then, to imagine the marginal case of a live production, with improvised dialogue, respectful of its audience's needs, with all performers playing themselves and no opportunity to edit out or conceal production errors. This would be an unusual, nonprototypical example of the category, but it could still be TV drama, not media talk, even though it ticks all the boxes in Hutchby's characterization. It would be drama, as long as it understood and displayed itself as *representation*. This would involve the use of displaced deictic coordinates of time and space: *here* would have to mean "somewhere else," not the place of production and not necessarily real—it could be an imaginary setting. *Now* could mean concurrent with the time of production but it could also mean "some other time"—past or future.

Among the possible events that TV drama can set out to represent, we can include events that are themselves televisual. Television can be reflexive about its own forms and practices, not only in journalistic treatments but also in its fictionalized, dramatic modes. Thus, many TV dramas set out to display, along-side the "private" discourse of characters, moments from television news reports, TV interviews, celebrity talk shows, and confessional TV chat shows, when it is topically appropriate to do so. It is not surprising to find extensive use of this particular kind of metacommunication in political series such as *The Amazing Mrs. Pritchard*, *The West Wing* (NBC 1999–2007), and *The Thick of It*. In the real world of professional politics and government, engagement with the mass media plays a crucial part in both institutional and personal terms, and displays of political performance on TV are amongst the ways that dramatists can address this aspect of political life.

The potential for communicative *layering* in TV drama is considerable and various. *Jerry Springer: The Opera* (BBC 2005) is a particularly complex example. *The Jerry Springer Show* is a notorious American confessional TV chat show. Its basic character was reinterpreted in 2005 in the terms of a theatrical musical that provided scripted dialogue and song lyrics where the actual series featured spontaneous unscripted talk. A single performance of this production was, in its turn, treated as a pro-filmic event for the purposes of a national broadcast transmission in the United Kingdom, which went out amid much complaint regarding blasphemy and bad language. So far away was this broadcast produc-tion from the prototypical characteristics of TV drama that it is arguable whether or not it should be included under that designation.

The West Wing (see Richardson 2006) and *Jerry Springer: The Opera* have very different relations to the fourth wall. *West Wing*'s drama takes place on the other side of the fourth wall as a *classic realist text* (McCabe 1974). The generic conven-tions of mainstream television drama are here respected and its representations of media talk (e.g., when the president is interviewed about his energy plans) are given a clearly defined place within a coherent diegetic world, "behind the scenes" of political life.

By contrast, in *Jerry Springer: The Opera* the diegetic world is a front-of-stage event—the event being an imaginary, fantastic, episode of *The Jerry Spring-er Show* ("Jesus Christ" is one of the characters). This world is represented nonrealistically, deploying the conventions of an opera, so that participants sing rather than speak their lines. The third lamination (the TV broadcast), preserves the generic condition of the second (the musical). A staged production, not a made-for-television dramatization, is shown to the audience. In relation to the theater experience, the broadcast has an as-if live status. The theater production does not have, and could not have, an as-if live status in relation to Jerry Springer's actual series. *West Wing*–style representations of media talk are more common than those of the Jerry Springer musical, though of course all we ever get are fragments of imaginary broadcasts, not complete events.

IS TV DIALOGUE DISTINCTIVE?

Because of its representational character, television dialogue is different from both primary, face-to-face interaction and from media talk in Tolson's (2006) sense. There is some common ground, however. Of these two forms of nonrepresentational talk, TV dialogue shares with everyday talk the goal of mediating social relationships in a wide range of interactive situations, whereas it shares with media talk its public quality, its obligation to have regard for an audience.

In comparing TV dialogue with representational talk in other fiction and nonfiction contexts, its closest relation would seem to be dialogue in feature films, because both work with essentially the same visual/aural resources, whereas the resources available to prose fiction, stage drama, printed drama texts, and radio each make for very different *affordances*, to use the term in its social semiotic sense (van Leeuwen 2004). Despite the similarity, film and television drama do not produce identical results in all cases as far as dialogue is concerned. Long-form drama, for instance, may present greater opportunities to use language for characterization (see chapters 4 and 8) than feature film does. When television drama was ephemeral, it tended not to produce memorable quotes as the movies did ("Frankly, my dear, I don't give a damn"), but, like radio, it did produce catchphrases, by virtue of extensive repetition ("You may think that, I couldn't possibly comment"—*House of Cards*, BBC 1990). Conditions of television distribution are very different in the twenty-first century, though catchphrase repetition may still be significant ("Save the cheerleader, save the world"—*Heroes*, NBC 2006–present). The social significance of the television catchphrase is the subject of further attention in chapter 5, in the context of an analysis of what television audiences know about dialogue.

4

What TV Screenwriters Know about Dialogue

Chapters 2 and 3 have prepared the ground for the next stage of this book's project by showing, with particular reference to dialogue, how questions of textual form are repeatedly referred back to the sociocultural contexts that make television's dramatic texts possible, meaningful, and satisfying—or unsatisfying. TV dramatizations, as imaginative transformations of the sociocultural world, are accountable in that world for their choices. On one side of the social relationship between dramatist and audience, those choices are constrained by industrial and cultural conditions of production. On the other side, they are subject in interpretation to the operation of other intellects and other imaginations—those of the audience, whose understanding, skills, values, tastes, and beliefs dramatists must anticipate without being able to control. Dialogue is one of the elements that mediate the relationship, and so it is appropriate to not only ask how dramatists themselves (specifically, screenwriters, who take primary responsibility for dialogue) understand its semiotic affordances (the topic of the present chapter), but also to examine how audiences make use of dialogue from the productions they encounter (the topic of the next chapter). These two inquiries are consistent with a broadly ethnographic approach to the study of creativity in communication generally and language use in particular, a theme that is revisited in the book's conclusion.[1]

SCREENWRITING IN CONTEXT

Television dramatic dialogue is a particular kind of speech, one that has origins as a form of *written* language. The design of this written-spoken language takes place under particular social conditions of production within an industry. This chapter shows that these conditions influence not only what is crafted by writers, spoken by actors and displayed by directors, but also the kind of understanding that its writers develop as to what is required of them.

There is a traditional belief that holds that writers become good at what they do by practicing the craft, building on and developing innate talent, which cannot be taught. In this view, very little of writers' craft knowledge is explicitly formulated. The distinction is one between tacit understanding, *knowing how*, and explicit knowledge, *knowing that*. If this is true, then, there is, for writers, nothing practical to be gained by acquiring explicit understanding of the language they and other writers use in the exercise of that craft. It will not make them any better at what they do, and may make them worse. Such understanding will make them worse writers if it *interferes* with their writerly instincts, introducing a smoke screen of cognitive-rational discourse in which success depends on keeping rationality in check. Along with this gap between different kinds of knowledge, there is a related but different gap between the activities of *writing* and of *criticism*, when writers feel that critics are "reading into" their work meanings they never intended and were not themselves conscious of. From either perspective, there is an issue as to what the writer consciously contributes to the creation of meaning.

The above account relates primarily to the Romantic theory of authorship, in an ideal-typical form. "The death of the author" in this Romantic, source-of-meaning sense was announced many years ago (Barthes 1977) and has become widely accepted, even in relation to such individualist forms of writing as poetry and prose fiction. There is even less reason to subscribe to such a theory in respect of texts that are designed and built by teams, such as those that are under investigation in this book. Challenging the Romantic view of authorship has involved, for example, looking carefully at all forms of intertextuality on which supposedly "new" written works depend. It also involves interrogating the basis of the walls that have separated writing from criticism and analysis. This is enough to justify trying to find out whether, and to what extent, screenwriters themselves as a professional community had already worked out everything they needed consciously to know about the forms and functions of dialogue in TV drama. It would be a mistake to expect that this professional community would use the same metalinguistic terms that sociolinguists use, but interesting nonetheless to be alert for signs that screenwriters were aware of interactional forms and devices that have also been the subject of scholarly investigation.

Interactional sociolinguistic approaches to dialogue-as-talk (the subject of chapter 6) would only ever be of partial value to screenwriters because, where dialogue is concerned, they impose a naive reading position—one that treats the characters as people rather than constructs. A character stumbles and hesitates; a listener infers from the awkwardness that he-the-character is embarrassed. The sociolinguistic account takes its point of departure from this inference and is to that extent naive, indifferent to the fact that the hesitation has been put there *in order to* convey embarrassment. The meaning is *given* by the dramatist but *given off* by the character. The naivety of the sociolinguist analyzing a conversation in a TV drama is *strategic*, of course, adopted as part of an analytic protocol, but for writers (and also for critics) its value is limited.

The knowledge of screenwriters does incorporate, in general terms, understanding of what filled and unfilled pauses and nonfluent pronunciations can achieve in a performance. However, the industrial conditions of textual production are such that a written version of a *hesitant* line may well not include any such forms, or at least rather fewer than the actor eventually produces, and differently managed. Within the industry, other things being equal, such departures from fluency are regarded as matters of *delivery* (the province of the actor) not as matters of *script* (the province of the writer): "Don't try to force things by putting in 'uh' and 'er,' or telling them when to laugh or cry. Let your basic words be their guide, and sit back and enjoy the actors' ride" (Brody 2003: 215; see also Jane Espenson, *Jane in Progress*, http://www.janeespenson.com, blog entry for July 18, 2007). In practice, scripted disfluency is only partially excised from television screenplays. Writers cannot bring themselves completely to repress it. The searchable script for the first episode of *Ashes to Ashes* (BBC 2008–present; script available online at http://www.twiztv.com) has no "um," "er," or "uh" forms. It does, however, use sequences of dots for short pauses, and occasional disfluent repetition, as when detective inspector Alex Drake, who has time-traveled from 2008 to 1981, is meant to be nonplussed when she recognizes Gene Hunt and his colleagues from Sam Tyler's descriptions of them in her own world.

The interest of this advice is the indication it gives that screenwriting culture constructs its division of labor between writers and actors through a practical implementation of the general folk-linguistic understanding that expressions of disfluency are not part of *the (verbal) meaning* but instead are performance *errors*. Writers are meant to manage meaning only up to this particular water's edge. The fact that they cannot completely remain behind their lines shows that the distinction is a difficult one to maintain in which this kind of communication is at stake. As far as the finished production is concerned, no one doubts that the *errors* are meaningful. But phenomenologically speaking, hesitation phenomena belong to speech, not writing. The industry understands that professional *writers* are likely to be less successful than professional *speakers* (actors) in creating and integrating such phenomena convincingly.

RESEARCHING SCREENWRITING

The starting point for these inquiries was with the textbooks, websites, online forums, and blogs designed for novice and apprentice writers, along with participant observation in a U.K. television writers' workshop in autumn 2008.

There are no manuals or websites devoted specifically and exclusively to dialogue in television, though there are some instructional books about dialogue in novels (Chiarella 1998, Kempton 2004) and one (Davis 2008) about dialogue in scripts for theater, cinema, radio, and television, which I will discuss further below. There are plenty of resources about screenwriting in general, though in some of the books (e.g., Keane 1998, Field 2005) television scripts are an afterthought—the main focus is on feature films. Dialogue is one of the topics that is mentioned (often rather briefly) in such general works on TV writing as McKee (1999), Brody (2003), Epstein (2006), Smethurst (2007) and Batty and Waldeback (2008). The dominance of American perspectives here (Batty and Waldeback wrote the only British book in this collection) is to be expected, given the quantity of drama production coming out of Hollywood. Scriptwriting blogs and forums also discuss dialogue from time to time. *Jane in Progress* (http://www.janeespenson.com) is particularly valuable, along with TVwriter.com, and, in the United Kingdom, the BBC's writersroom blog (http://www.bbc.co.uk/blogs/writersroom/) is a useful starting point. Batty and Waldeback also wrote the only book in the list above that tries to integrate *critical* and *creative* approaches to screenwriting, in other words, relating academic perspectives with more vocationally oriented advice. However, its chapters on dialogue focus more on the latter than on the former, and they do not use any sociolinguistic references in their exploration of this area.

These resources provided a way in to the professional folk theories (no condescension intended) of dialogue in TV drama, developed as part of the practicalities of producing it. It provided substantial evidence of television's work culture, which includes screenwriting, in which the *theories* developed take the form of a discourse developed by writers themselves, in order to talk to one another about their work, as well as to the other professionals involved in the making of television shows. Before discussing the findings of this inquiry, it is worthwhile to spend a little time talking about the work culture itself.

The processes of screenwriting encourage reflexivity, to the extent that screenwriters have to engage in conversations with others about the effectiveness of their scripts and how the scripts can be improved. *Auteur* screenwriters such as Steven Poliakoff, Aaron Sorkin, and Lynda LaPlante may suffer the pressure to revise, or be revised, less than others do, but for TV drama in general the picture is clear—TV production starts with an idea, which becomes an outline (which may have references to speech, but no dialogue as such), which becomes a script (in which dialogue is first introduced), which goes through several passes and several drafts before entering production. Production may then require further written drafts on the way to becoming an audiovisual product. The original writer is usually asked to rewrite his or her own work on the basis of *notes* (practical criticism) from others; some rewriting may also be undertaken by script editors and/or executive producers (*showrunners*). This is different from the world of cinema, in which drafts may often be passed to other writers for revision, and different again from theater, in which an authorized version of text remains much more sacrosanct in the hands of the director and actors.

This account shows some different ways in which the individuality of *creative* writing is sacrificed in television. There may be some collective "writing by committee," some serial rewriting (one writer redrafts the work of another and may not consult the first), and a lot of self-revision (writers take notes from other people—editors, executives, actors, directors—and change their work to suit the requirements of those who own and control the show). In Goffman's (1979) terms it is not just "authorship" that is shared in the world of TV drama but "principalhood" as well. The *vision* of the show as a whole does not come from the freelance or even the staff writer, but from the showrunner (Messenger Davies, 2007, discusses this in relation to Gene Roddenberry's role on *Star Trek Enterprise*). The blurring of boundaries between these different blends of authorship is inevitable, so within the business the crucial decision has to do with official, public *credit*. Because it is impossible to credit everyone who has influenced actual wordings used in the production, there have to be conventions of attribution. Very often, the convention is that the person who wrote the first draft gets the credit, however much the text was subsequently adjusted and by whom (Epstein 2006: 231). Television writers in Britain may get a more individualized experience than writers in the United States, but they are certainly just as aware of how writing for television is not a matter of personal expression, particularly on continuing serials:

> My *Eastenders* episode was finally great to watch after the 3rd viewing. After I'd got over the shock of cut scenes and changed dialogue, which is what happens when somebody else interprets your story. It's a "cog in the machine" scenario—my humble little episode is only part of a bigger picture. A goody bag with various different elements thrown into the mix, elements such as budget, casting, choice of director, rehearsal time, etc. (Abi, "Cog in the Machine," writersroom blog, October 22, 2007)[2]

In the United States, and specifically Los Angeles, the craft discourse of TV writing is developed partly "in the room" to facilitate cooperation among teams of writers. "The Room" is the heart of the writing process for a majority of TV dramatic series productions. For noncomedic drama it is where episode stories are normally constructed, and possibly series' arcs as well, and for comedy it is where jokes are created, tested, and revised:[3]

> You want to keep the conversation moving and the ideas flowing, but you can't just blurt out everything that pops into your head because you need to respect the direction that the story is already moving in (unless you have an unbelievably genius idea). And even if you have a genius idea and it gets shot down, you have to let it go right away and not take it personally. Some of the worst things you can do in a room are: (a) stay immovably fixed on a single idea; (b) not come up with any ideas at all; and (c) fail to keep up with the discussion—e.g., forget discarded ideas

that have already been raised, not follow the twists of the story that the other writers are proposing, not think fast enough and have to have things repeated and reexplained for your benefit. (Melinda Hsu, quoted in Epstein 2006: 226–227)

"Room" conditions are favorable to the creation of specialized terminology, and this includes terminology that refers to dialogue. For example, it seems that American TV writers have their own term for what nonprofessionals simply describe as a "stale joke." Writers, more than others, need to be able to *name* this concept, for the practical reason that they need to be able to quickly identify instances of it and move (if necessary) into dealing with the problem it represents. On the cultural level, they may also value its contribution to their group solidarity, sharing language that is opaque to outsiders in a way that "stale joke" is not. Hence the term *clam*:

> HOW do jokes age? Like a bottle of fine red wine left on the kitchen counter a few days, without a cork. Yet as the most casual watcher of TV sitcoms knows, jokes can live well beyond their natural life span, losing more of their punch with each retelling. Just think about how many times you have heard these lines:
> "Don't go there."
> "Too much information."
> "Don't talk to me. Talk to the hand."
> Or the time-honored, "That's why (I/he/you/she/they) gets paid the big bucks."
> Concerned sitcom writers have come to call these jokes "clams." These clams are not to be confused with the jazz term that has come to mean "bad note," or with the popular shellfish. Comedy clams are jokes that you've heard once too often, that make you groan instead of laugh. (Blum 2001; see also http://www.janeespenson.com, *passim*)

The professional argot of screenwriters contains many terms of this kind— employed more informally and without the rigorous, technicized, meaning enforcement that sociolinguists would associate with terms like *implicature* or *presupposition*. Technical vocabulary of this latter sort is unlikely to emerge in the world of TV writers because there is no *formal* theory to which they are, or seek to be, accountable in their use of specialized terms. There is, however, another strand of specialized vocabulary, which includes terms like *spec script*, *slug line*, and *parenthetical*.[4] These are words that have come to have more enforceable meanings, perhaps because they are not confined to the writers' community itself but are used within the wider discourse of the entertainment industry, in conversations that cross the boundaries of professional expertise.

TOWARD A THEORY OF DIALOGUE FOR SCREENWRITERS

With the exception of Kozloff (2000), whose work has been mentioned elsewhere in this book, the nearest thing to an *explicit* theory for dialogue is Davis (2008). It is appropriate to discuss Davis in this chapter because his book is designed as a practical manual for writers rather than an academic account. Unlike Kozloff, it includes an account (with examples) of naturally occurring talk, facilitating comparison of this with the scripted kind. Davis also proffers a typology of different types of dialogue, which merits some discussion. It should be noted, however, that the book is concerned with all dramatic scripted dialogue, not just television. The typology he comes up with emerges from this broader perspective. His three main stylistic categories are *naturalistic, heightened naturalistic,* and *nonnaturalistic.* He rejects the label *realistic* because of its ambiguity: *naturalism* as Davis uses it refers unambiguously to mimetic intentions. Naturalistic dialogue comes in two subtypes: *selective naturalism* and *extreme naturalism.* The rationale for this division will be easy to explain in the light of how he characterizes naturalistic dialogue in general. This is dialogue that displays the following:

> ...a consciousness of the class, gender, geographical origins and upbringing of each speaker, as well as the particular register employed for the specific setting [...] each individual will tend towards a particular phraseology, use of certain vocabulary and even, in some cases, distinctive sentence construction. Then, naturalistic dialogue has to conform to the general messiness of spoken language—the unfinished or ungrammatical sentences, hesitations, repetitions, interruptions, simultaneous speeches and verbal shorthands, much of it resulting from interaction between individuals [...] dialogue is fundamentally affected by the agendas—conscious, semiconscious and unconscious—of each character. (2008: 44–45)

Davis understands that screen dialogue is not and cannot be faithfully mimetic, though some will strive harder than others for that goal. Selective naturalism, as exemplified in his account, in different flavors, by Arnold Wesker, Mike Leigh, and U.K. television series *The Bill* (ITV 1984–present) *edits* real speech:

> Selective naturalism is the style of writing which attempts to faithfully imitate dialogue as we normally speak it, but, unnoticed, manages to omit all those passages—not only beginnings and endings but also all sorts of other uninteresting sections—which would add nothing to the production. For it is not enough merely to imitate life: scripts are not straight, one-for-one imitations of slabs of life. In selective naturalism they are crafted, moulded to appear as if they were. (Davis 2008: 48)

In thus pinning down selective naturalism, Davis is able to identify one possible alternative mode—*extreme* naturalism, as exemplified by *The Royle Family* (BBC 1998–2006; Davis 2008: 46–47; see also chapter 3 in this book). Writers who focus more exclusively on television in their accounts offer characterizations that are congruent with Davis's description of selective naturalism, while seeming to understand it as even more selective than in his account:

> The TV writers who rise to the top are those who know what real people sound like when they talk, but also know how to edit that reality so their characters are more intense, more clever and more expressive than real people usually are. Everyone's

been through the real life situation where, after an emotional verbal confrontation, you wake up the following morning and thing, "Damn! I should've said *this* last night instead of *that*." In your teleplay, all your characters, especially your hero or heroes, should say what you would if you had the time to second-guess yourself. Because, as the writer, you do have the time to second-guess and third-guess and fourth-guess the words that come out of your characters' mouths, and every reader expects that's exactly what you'll do. (Brody 2003: 213–214)

Screen dialogue is not real-life talk. It is sharper, more directed, highly constructed to fit story, layered with subtext and conflict, and though it may sound like a real conversation it is more like polished speech. (Batty and Waldeback 2008: 62–76)

Eavesdrop on any coffee shop conversation and you'll realize in a heartbeat you'd never put that slush onscreen. Real conversation is full of awkward pauses, poor word choices and phrasing, non sequiturs, pointless repetitions; it seldom makes a point or achieves closure. But that's okay because conversation isn't about making points or achieving closure. It's what psychologists call "keeping the channel open." Talk is how we develop and change relationships. (McKee 1999: 388)

Heightened naturalism for Davis is a separate affair. He starts with certain playwrights in mind (including, e.g., Bernard Shaw and Caryl Churchill). Such writers, he claims, "have not always been content to leave dialogue as being closely imitative of speech in 'real life'—they have taken it beyond naturalism [but] they do not positively draw attention to their artifice" (2008: 100). Some TV writers are included in Davis's conception of heightened naturalism, notably Alan Bleasdale (author of *GBH*—Channel 4, 1991—and *Boys from the Black-stuff*—BBC 1982). Davis contends that this mode is acceptable to audiences when it is consistent, whereas an internal consistency also creates opportunity for intratextual deviation. A passage of poetic or rhetorical eloquence may be effective against a background of more naturalistic speech, as in Trevor Griffiths's *Comedians* (1975) or Arthur Miller's *Death of a Salesman* (1949).

The third kind of dialogue in Davis's model is nonnaturalistic: "... the line into non-naturalism is crossed when the dialogue appears to acknowledge the hand of the author" (2008: 130). One subtype of nonnaturalistic dialogue for Davis is a political kind, inspired by Brecht, and another is an absurdist kind deriving from Beckett. The former kind, for instance, Davis illustrates with reference to Edward Bond's play *Restoration* (1981), which includes "many asides, poetic speech direct to the audience and also songs [...] the dialogue is about the *idea* of the character (Lord Are) [...] it is not pretending to *be* the character. ..." (Davis 2008: 133).

Davis is clear that we should not expect to find much reflexive speech in the popular media of film and television, as opposed to the more literary market-places of the theater (radio, at least in the United Kingdom, has space for a wider spectrum of possibilities). One reason for this is that the industry itself is prescriptive about what constitutes acceptable writing, and treats selective naturalism as the norm. Novice writers with no produced work cannot afford to go off-piste if they want freelance commissions, and journeyman writers have to respect the conventions of the shows they work for. Epstein even suggests that the latter do well to regard themselves as ghost writers: "Your job is to write the show the way the showrunner would if he had had time to do it himself. One of the greatest talents a story editor can have is not only to write well, but to write well with the showrunner's style, in the showrunner's voice" (2006: 228). The *showrunner*, in the parlance of the American television industry, is the executive producer of the show who outranks all other personnel and who is that show's creative source, even when he or she delegates writing and directing responsibilities down the line. Joss Whedon (*Buffy the Vampire Slayer*, WB 1997–2001; UPN 2001–2003) is a notable showrunner in the United States, and although that terminology may be less common in the United Kingdom, Russell T. Davies has certainly been so described in relation to the relaunched *Dr. Who* (BBC 2005–present).

If, in Davis's terms, selective naturalism is the default choice for television drama (with some scope for stylistic variations among genres and for distinctiveness in particular series), then, both in the United Kingdom and in the United States, this does not entirely eliminate work that rejects that default option. Some of this may fall outside the standard *series* format and take the form of a made-for-television movie/feature/miniseries. An example of this in the United Kingdom is *God on Trial* (BBC 2008), a drama written by Frank Cottrell Boyce, based on the premise of holocaust victims spending their last day on earth formally debating whether their God had broken his covenant with the Jews. This drama exploited the "trial" idea to allow its characters to make long and rhetorical speeches—not generally acceptable for mainstream drama on television and thus arguably an instance of heightened realism. In the United States, the mannered dialogue of *Mad Men* (AMC 2007–present) could be considered to push the boundaries of selective naturalism, not by lengthening of lines to turn them into speeches, but by an even greater move in the direction of indirectness and ellipsis.

STORY IS KING

The telling of stories may be an aspect of life that is universally present in human cultures. The demand for stories in Western popular culture has led some writers to see it as a kind of addiction: "The world now consumes films, novels, theatre and television in such quantities and with such ravenous hunger that the story arts have become humanity's prime source of inspiration, as it seeks to order chaos and gain insight into life" (McKee 1999: 12). It is certainly true that television's own rate of consumption for stories is a phenomenal one:

Television is more story-driven than any other medium. TV shows eat stories up and spit them out again in a never-ending binge-purge that usually ends up leaving writers and producers emotionally and creatively exhausted. What's the protagonist's need? What's the protagonist's problem? What's a new way to show the need? A new way to express the problem? What's a new way to satisfy the need? To solve the problem? (Brody 2003: 59)

The centrality of storytelling in popular culture generally and television in particular is the reason that story is king in the creation of television shows. It is king in the sense that other aspects of a drama production are understood to be of lesser importance to overall productions. It can also be seen as the default level of textual organization. At a superordinate level there will be some idea of what a show, or an episode, is *really* about—its thematic content[5]—whereas dialogue takes its place at a subordinate level, when the story comes to be materially realized.

If this structural view of storytelling corresponded to the processes of TV drama production, then one person or group might be responsible for thematics, another could take care of story, and yet another could attend to dialogue as one of the many *modules* of story realization. In fact, all three are aspects of *writing*, understood holistically. A screenwriter is meant to be able to create story form as well as its action and talk realization, while doing so in a way that carries some kind of thematic content prosodically distributed throughout the text. She would be free to decide which, if any, took priority in the planning process. Sometimes, especially in the United States, a separation is made between the creation of story structure and its expression in dialogue and action, so that a team of writers takes care of the story and an individual author takes this forward to the next written stage, providing the core text upon which other professional groups can base their own contributions.

Theme and Dialogue

Thematics has a Cinderella part to play in the process of TV drama creation, perhaps out of the fear of being didactic or propagandistic by making themes too obvious, or too crudely propositional.[6] Nevertheless, screenwriting advice, even when it does not use the words *theme* or *thematic*, certainly thinks that this is something that good stories will have:

Plot is hard. So when you find a series of events that actually string together to make a story—a beginning, middle, end—it's tempting to consider the job done. In fact, it's tempting to throw your arms in the air and caper in circles singing "We Are as Gods." But unless the story is *about* something, all you've done is come up with a pile of stuff that happens. And that can leave readers and viewers with a sense of arbitrary action, a sense that a different pile of stuff could've happened without it making a lot of difference.

When writing a spec (or even an episode of a show for which you're being paid), the mistake is in starting with the story. Instead, think first about what you want the

episode to be about—is it about the triumph of love? The destructive quality of
envy? About how expecting the worst in others brings out the worst in oneself?
About how emotional resiliency is better than virtue? About kindness trumping
truth? About how love isn't blind, but wishes it were? About how emotional infidelity is worse than physical? About how an anticipation of betrayal can cause that
betrayal? About how denial can sometimes be a choice? About how living a happy
life is also a choice and not an event?

Find something like that—something you believe in. Now, you're ready to find a
story. (*Jane in Progress*, http://www.janeespenson.com/, blog entry for September
22, 2006; see also the thread "Theme in Screenwriting and TV Too," http://www.
TVwriter.com, posted September 17, 2007)

Writers understand as a matter of practical accomplishment, that thematic concerns such as these have an impact on the plot. Analytically speaking, actions
(including verbal ones) mediate the plot, which in turn mediates the theme.
Propositional expressions of thematic content can take the form of actual speeches
by particular characters—the atypical *God on Trial* has many such expressions. The
beliefs and opinions of the screenwriter him/herself are generally thus hidden,
displaced on to the characters so as to downplay authorial didactic intent. Although
it is possible to find writers like Jane Espenson (writer on *Buffy the Vampire Slayer,
Battlestar Galactica*, Sky One/The Sci-Fi Channel 2004–present, and others) who are
committed to thematic meaning, it is also possible to find others who seem much
more nervous in this area: "A show's job is to entertain. It's plot-driven, and the
writer should commit, tell the story and let nothing get in the way—not educating
the audience or political correctness or 'arias.' The hero must have desire. He must
be thwarted. There must be complications" (Ann Donahue, showrunner for *CSI
Miami*, quoted in Littwin 2004: 126).

Plot and Dialogue

Story production, in the sense of working out a particular narrative form from
beginning, to middle and end, with all parts in between, is nowhere more
organized than it is in American television production. Another significant
term of art from the discourse of screenwriting is the verb-noun *break*. In
journalism, to *break* a story is to announce a news event to an ignorant world.
In screenwriting, breaking a story refers to the articulation of the plot. In
productions that make use of a writers' room, story breaking is likely to be a
collective activity:

In an assignment situation, once you've worked out the beginning, middle and end
and gotten someone to hire you based on that, you're going to come in for a meeting
with the staff of the show (or the rest of the staff if you're already on the weekly
payroll), or the development team if it's a TV movie or pilot. Together, everyone
involved is going to dig in and "break" that story. They—you—are going to figure

out every single scene you will write in the teleplay, with each scene defined as an "event" (sometimes a long one, sometimes just a moment) in the development of the situation you created in your leavebehind, moving it from the beginning to the end. (Brody 2003: 75–75)

The result of the breaking process is, as Brody indicates, an outline composed of 25–30 scenes (in a 1-hour episode). The most significant breaks, however, are the breaks between acts. This is where art meets commerce. On the level of the art form, stories need acts as markers of significant transitions or *turns* in the narrative. On the level of commerce, American TV dramas need acts, because they need to create spaces during the course of a broadcast into which commercials, trailers, and sponsor announcements can be inserted. Some television drama (e.g., on the BBC in the United Kingdom and HBO in the United States) has no need for commercial breaks. For artistic reasons it may still be appropriate to structure such drama in terms of discrete acts. Those who believe in the universality of a certain kind of narrative form would undoubtedly agree with this:

> I view the need to include essential scenes in drama the same way I view the need for every story to have a beginning, a middle and an end. It's not a formula, it's a way of satisfying an audience that has proven itself over time. Just as a story without an ending feels incomplete, so does a fantasy show without a quest. Certain events move an audience. That's why they're there. Certain events work and make the entire story work as well. Take those events away and the audience is confused, dissatisfied—and ultimately scarce. This isn't a matter of giving viewers what they've had before because they want it, it's a matter of giving them what they need. (Brody 2003: 132)

One of the recurrent injunctions to screenwriters is that dialogue is a potential *danger* to good storytelling on TV and in the movies, for three reasons. First, TV and the movies are both audiovisual media (and increasingly produced in film-like ways), so that the storytelling needs to depend more upon the visualized action than the verbalized action. Second, dialogue as such is the "icing on the cake," mere decoration in relation to story as the more fundamental basis of the entertainment. And third, the multifunctional properties of dialogue in drama can be abused: exegetical, story*telling* requirements can damage the realism of exchanges among characters as authentic expressions of what *they* understand and believe within the diegetic world:

> Many developing screenwriters begin with scripts that sound more like radio or theatre plays, heavy in dialogue with little attention to how the screen can be used to tell the story. (Batty and Waldeback, 2008: 3)

> Dialogue is the Christmas lights on a story . . . The story is the backbone of your script. If everyone is so flavorful that you begin to show off in the writing, rather than sticking to the spine of the story, that stays fun for the audience for about four minutes. (Anthony Zuiker [*CSI*], quoted in Epstein 2006: 103)

Writers often try to rid themselves of exposition quickly and early, so that they may concentrate on moving the story forward visually. This is a noble intention but you get lumpy exposition if you try and impart it all at once, rather than gradually over the course of a story. It is also poor choice to try and reveal too much information or information that is not crucial. Here's one view of "taking your lumps."

MORTIMER

Don't you understand? The reason I can't marry Edna is not because I don't love her. When we met seven years ago at the hot dog stand at the greyhound races, I was deliriously happy. Of course, that was before I was involved in the freak anvil accident which not only crippled my left kidney but my confidence as a soy bean futures salesman...and as a lover.

(Brad Schreiber, *Student Filmmakers*, May 2006, also on http://www.TVwriters.com, forum "13 Things Bad Screenwriters Commonly Do")

Whereas story making is recognized to be so hard that it may be better to assign this work to a team of writers rather than to any individual, the production of dialogue is not thought to offer the same degree of challenge for a career writer: "You can't overestimate the importance of good dialogue. One of the paradoxes of television writing is that, although the story is king, writers are judged by their dialogue. That's because stories can always be constructed by the entire staff, with everyone pitching in, but your dialogue reflects you, the writer." (Brody 2003: 213). Dialogue also threatens good storytelling when its use for expositional purposes (explaining the story-world to the viewer) originates outside the consciousness of the characters chosen to deliver it:

Feel the need to have your characters tell each other something they would already know so you can make sure the reader or viewer knows it too? Resist it! People discussing a "plan" at a point where they would already have planned it or when they're already putting it into effect immediately sticks out as unrealistic. The surgeon who tells his assistant, "First we do this, then this, then this," when the two doctors have worked together on similar surgeries 600 times is guaranteed to make a showrunner shudder. Find another way to give the information. Or, better yet, re-examine the need for giving it at all. Most of the time you'll find that the reader or viewer can live without it quite easily, thank you. (Brody 2003: 218)

DIALOGUE

"Good dialogue has a generally accepted definition. It's dialogue that is concise, witty, believable, and revealing of human character and emotion" (Brody 2003: 213). If Brody is to be believed, the industry agrees on the characteristics of strong dialogue. Particular productions are vulnerable to criticism whenever the dialogue is found unsatisfactory on any of these counts.

DIVISIONS OF LABOR

Screenwriting as part of an industrial process is conditioned to know its place within that process. Writers accept constraints on what can go into their screen-plays, and on how these texts are to be presented to their readers. Specifically, these constraints carry prohibitions on writers trying to control the behavior of either directors or actors. The industry wants something left on the table for other professionals to sink their creative teeth into.

The trend in Hollywood is toward the reduction of directorial indications in scripts for television. Brody (2003: 155–165) talks about a shift from the *classic* format to the *contemporary* format for screenplays. The latter approach calls for fewer indications as to how the viewer sees the scene:

<pre>
                    P.A. SYSTEM (OFF SCREEN)
All non-military personnel, clear the
airfield-

No one listens, <u>as we ANGLE WITH the descending jet, TO:</u>

INTERIOR. MILITARY TRANSPORT JET—DAY—
MASTER SGT. EZRA JACKSON
Haggard in his dress uniform, gazing down at the base eagerly.
Jackson is about 40 years old, Black, a career non-com who
looks like he's returning from hell

                    BRANDON<u>'S VOICE (OFF SCREEN)</u>
...Remember, Ezra, short and sweet. 'Yes,'
you're glad to be back. 'No,' you've got no
comment on the negotiations.

<u>WIDENING, we see that</u> seated next to Jackson is MARTIN
BRANDON, 35, dark-suited, immaculate, the perfect State
Department undersecretary.
                    JACKSON
Don't worry, Mr. Brandon. I'm not saying
anything that might hurt those poor bastards
still in Baghdad. (Brody 2003: 157)
</pre>

This is a small part of a scene representing the return of a newly released hostage, presented in the older, classic format.[7] (I have spelled out Brody's abbreviations for the convenience of the general reader.) The underlined words above are the ones that Brody omits when he re-presents this material in the contemporary format. There is some reordering as well, so that in the contemporary version it is left to the director to decide whether to include or exclude Brandon from the shot that initially shows Jackson to us: the stage direction between Brandon's first line and Jackson's is incorporated into the previous one, making the two lines of dialogue contiguous.

There is a belief that the absence of directorial indications in actual scripts makes for a draft that reads more easily (Brody 2003: 164–165). The convenience of the reader, who may have to scan hundreds of such texts, thus outweighs considerations about the appearance of the final product. But the prohibition does also relate to professional demarcation. Epstein (2006: 104) argues that TV writers are more likely to break the rule against directing the camera than movie writers are. Given that it is directors rather than writers who take the principal creative credit for a movie, the greater protection of their privileges in the motion picture world makes sense. If television screenplays are becoming more like those for feature films, then perhaps this is indicative of a shift in which drama production for TV and for movies is converging.

The avoidance of instructions to actors regarding their performances is also a matter of professional distinction:

> It would be a waste of time, an exercise in futility, and an insult to your co-workers to say too much in your script [about direction, set design, and props], just as it would be an insult to write in such a way that the actors are forced to say their lines as you, the writer, believe they should be said, and not as they, the actors, feel would be appropriate. It would be more than a waste of time because the wonderful thing about working with good actors is that they can come up with readings, and facial expressions ("character shadings," we call them) that no writer—or director or anyone else—would ever think of. (Brody 2003: 48)

> Don't coach an actor on how to say his lines. You'll be wasting precious words. Once a good actor has learned his lines, they are part of his character, not your screenplay. [...] Throwing in acting directions does not do anything but add extraneous words to your screenplay that you do not need, cannot use, and they slow the reader down. Let the dialogue represent the character, and let the actors bring out the character. (Flinn 1999: 66)

This injunction covers the use of adjectives and other descriptive glosses—"melancholy," "with sudden passion," and so forth—as directions in the script, as well as delivery indications such as underlining, which are overlaid on the lines themselves. In the latter case, the prohibition follows the lines of the culturally familiar argument that in well-written expression, it will be obvious from the words and their context where the emphasis should fall:

Don't tell the actors which words to punch:

```
                    JENNY
The minute I don't shine for you, you can fire
me. But I'll be damned if you're gonna pass on
me because of my watch! That's not me.
    (thumps her chest)
This is me. Guts!
    (pats her temples)
And brains. You can't do any better.
```

[. . .] Too many stage directions drive actors crazy, and nobody ever follows them. They're just in the way. If your dialogue needs that much thumping up, maybe it really needs polishing instead. (Flinn 1999)

At the start of this chapter I discussed how particular *word* forms and the meanings they represent—specifically the "um," "er," "uh" forms that stand for filled pauses—are also viewed by script readers as undesirable instructions to actors regarding their performances. If there is good dramatic reason to include such forms, the actors will introduce them in accordance with the selective naturalism of their mode and genre of production. If there is no such story-led dramatic reason to make speech hesitant, then fluent lines in a screenplay will become fluent lines in a performance. "Normal nonfluency" (Abercrombie 1963) might be more naturalistic, but would tend toward "extreme" naturalism, in Davis's (2008) terms and would occlude the meaning of particular disfluent utterances as signs of hesitancy, embarrassment, uncertainty, disbelief, and so forth.

PROHIBITIONS AND RECOMMENDATIONS

Beyond these considerations of the proper responsibilities for writers, directors, and actors in the production of screen dialogue, the profession has developed some more specific ideas about both its form and content. With respect to form, one major concern is that dialogue should strive to be concise, and this leads to specific recommendations on what television's selective naturalism can afford to leave out. But recommendations do not cover only the exclusions of scripted talk. Writers are also encouraged to *include* a particular kind of meaning, referred to in their discourse as *subtext*. With respect to content, it is the revelation/expression of character that is most important.

Questions of Form

With respect to the form of screen dialogue, two sorts of generalizations occur repeatedly. One of these prescribes that dialogue be *concise*; another prescribes that it should possess *subtext*—both aspects of selective naturalism as described at the start of this chapter. Though the meaning of these two terms is not self-evident to an outsider, there are more specific recommendations, as well as illustrations, in the advice that writers give one another.

If the elimination of filled pauses is one way that selective naturalism chooses to make dialogue more concise, then two other ways are the reduction of what sociolinguistics refers to as *hedges* and *discourse markers*:

The third most common dialogue mistake made by new writers is to put what I call "qualifying words" into speeches. Phrases like "I think," "it seems," and "kind of," and words like "pretty" (as in "pretty good") and "fairly" (as in "fairly certain") are common in real conversations, but you should avoid them like the proverbial plague when you're writing for TV. They take up space, they take up time, and when you hear them they always sound unnecessary and redundant. (Brody 2003: 215)

"Handle" is one of my favorite writing terms, and one of the most common. It refers to those words at the beginning of a line of dialogue. Handles include, but aren't limited to:

Well, Look, Listen, Hey, Oh, Say, Um, Actually, So, Now, I mean, C'mon, Anyway, Yeah, You know, and the name of any character used when speaking to that character.

I hear that some show runners object to handles in general, and will cut all of them out. I heard today about an editor who did the same thing when cutting episodes. But usually, handles are freely employed, with certain limits. (http://www.janee-spenson.com, "Actually Not," September 8, 2006)

The elimination of hedges, as per Brody's edict, as well as achieving the goal of more concise speech, should also have the effect of realizing *characters* as altogether more emphatic in their views than their counterparts in *real life*—corresponding also to his suggestion that characters in drama are "more intense" (2003: 213). The professional equivocation around the use of discourse markers is also interesting. As Espenson, one of the most analytically minded writers about TV drama dialogue, appreciates, there may be particular uses of certain handles that will be dramatically significant. Her entry on this subject includes some discussion of what sociolinguists have learned to call the "dispreferred response." Espenson does not use this terminology, but the usage she describes is certainly in the same area:

CHARACTER ONE
I think I've lost weight, don't you?
CHARACTER TWO
Actually, I think you might've found it again.
  (Remember, this is demonstration comedy, not actual comedy.)
  Certain handles, like "actually" and, sometimes, "well" are used to contradict the previous line. That means that when Character Two starts the line with "actually," the reader/audience already knows they're about to hear a contradiction. In the example I've given, they know, in fact, that they're about to hear a slam.

(http://www.janeespenson.com, "Actually Not," September 8, 2006)

For the sake of the comedy, Espenson argues against using "actually" in this and similar cases. The word signals to the reader to expect the slam, the reversal, the dispreferred response. The humor is better, she says, if it comes as a surprise.

Keeping It Real: The Uses of *Subtext*

If the writers' term *handle* approximates to, but does not quite equate with the sociolinguistic term *discourse marker*, so, too, the professional term *subtext* does not quite equate with any of the specific categories of indirect meaning elaborated within pragmatic theory—conventional implicature, conversational implicature, presupposition. The concept of subtext owes something to an appreciation of what indirectness can accomplish in unscripted talk, and thus to the requirements of naturalism, as well as an idea that subtext makes dialogue *more interesting* for audiences than direct expression of feelings and motives:

> Real people—and realistic television characters—don't blurt out what's on their minds. They don't ask directly for what they want, if they even know what they want, they manipulate and insinuate, either unconsciously or intentionally. (Epstein 2006: 101)

> In good dialogue writing, two characters can seem to talk about the weather, a neighbour or their favourite colour, when what is really going on underneath is that they are challenging each other, one trying to draw the other into a trap, or trying to tell each other how much they care and are sorry for what they did. A script which avoids dialogue which is "on-the-nose" (stating the obvious) and instead allows space for the audience to figure the subtext out by themselves makes them active participants in the drama and therefore more likely to stay engaged. (Batty and Waldeback 2008: 63; for an example, see also http://www.janeespenson.com, blog entry for May 4, 2007, "Also Good for Swimming Pools with Diving Boards")

Subtext as understood here might therefore refer to the illocutionary force of an utterance as opposed to its locutionary value, or it might refer to *off-record* meanings as understood in politeness theory—intentionality disguised and made deniable because of its face-threatening potential. The term can also be used when speakers are thinking things that they cannot convey to one another, but where the audience gets some indication of these unspoken thoughts, or infers unspoken thoughts based on knowledge of what the character has done or said previously. Consider the case of scenes that require body language and facial expression to express something about the character's state of mind that is at odds with the verbal meaning that her words express. That state of mind could be considered to be the *subtext* of the dialogue. Yet this subtext is heard only by the audience, and is withheld from other character(s) in the scene. Because this use of language in screen dialogue implicates the relationship between writer and audience independently of the relationship between the characters, it has more in common with dramatic irony than with instances of subtext in which (for example) implicature is involved.

Observation of actual broadcast drama demonstrates that scriptwriters are adaptable in their use of subtext. They do not use it just for the sake of it.

Thrillers, which rely more on action than on dialogue, may find direct speech more serviceable, especially in scenes of confrontation. There is little subtext in this, transcribed from *24* (Fox 2001–present; also quoted in chapter 3):

1 DEREK: Don't shoot me!
2 JACK: What the hell are you doing here?
3 DEREK: I'm sorry I followed you, I'm just—I'm just worried about my mother.
4 JACK: Get up. Get up. Get up. Dammit! Come here. You're going with me.
5 DEREK: This is none of my business. This is none of my business. I won't tell anyone. Just let me go, okay?
6 JACK: I really wish I could, kid, but I can't. You're going with me. Now, get in the helicopter.

(Season 5, episode 1, "7:00–8:00 A.M.," written by Howard Gordon)

If a particular relationship is characterized by indirect strategies, the emotional temperature will rise should they, at any point, allow themselves to be direct. But this, too, is conditioned by genre and viewers' expectations. The viewers of *Pride and Prejudice* (BBC 1995) were treated to a visual, embodied "moment of truth" between Elizabeth and Darcy: their one and only kiss at the end of the series, *after* their wedding. But there is a verbalized moment of truth in an earlier scene. Darcy renews his declaration of love and marriage proposal. Elizabeth finally expresses her own reciprocal feelings. Jane Austen never wrote the words that Elizabeth spoke on this momentous occasion, but screenwriter Andrew Davies supplied the lack. Did he allow them to be direct with one another? Almost. They are embarrassed, and their embarrassment makes them oblique. Darcy tells Elizabeth that his feelings are the same as when he originally (ardently— and very directly) declared his love for her. She tells him that her feelings are "quite the opposite" from what they were when she rejected him on that previous occasion. For a brief moment they look into one another's eyes. Verbally and visually it is enough for them, and it is appropriate, for their characters and their world.

Questions of Content: Delivering Character

When they reflect on these matters, professionals agree that story and character are interdependent (Brody 2003: 33, McKee 1999: 100, Epstein 2006: 14, Batty and Waldeback 2008: 18–20). Ensemble drama distributes heroic behavior across a number of characters, and all TV drama individuates characters above and beyond their basic plot functions. TV drama differs from drama in films and the theater by offering characters that viewers can invest in over a period of time. (Radio can also do this, though long-running drama on radio is much more low profile than on television, with the possible exception in the United Kingdom of *The Archers*, BBC4 1950–present.) This is relevant in different ways to continuing series (*Days of Our Lives*, NBC 1965–present), series with story arcs (*Life on Mars*,

BBC 2006–2007), and episodic series (*Diagnosis Murder*, CBS 1993–2001). A long-running soap such as the United Kingdom's *Coronation Street* (ITV 1960–present) has characters like "Ken Barlow" and "Sally Webster" that its viewers have grown up with—who have aged as they have aged, and gone through narratives appropriate to their age and stage of life.

Characters in drama are distinguished by their roles in the plot (protagonists, antagonists, helpers) and by their distinctiveness from one another, realized through the content and style of what they do and say, as well as what is done and said to them. They are also embodied and costumed, though as with direction and action, these are matters that writers are steered away from specifying in their scripts. Screenwriters say that in television no dialogue should be included that does not advance the plot. Characterization through dialogue is allowed only to the extent that it respects this principle.

What does that allow in practice? At a minimum it allows characters to perform speech acts appropriate to their function in the story. In romantic comedy we can expect declarations of love between the lead characters; in action thrillers, both heroes and villains will use threats (I do not mean to deny the possibility of nonlinguistic threats and expressions of love). Hero-doctors in medical dramas will need to use orders while their patients will make cries of pain. In TV writing, a *beat* is a single event in a story: the smallest unit of storytelling (Epstein 2006: 77). Beats do not have to include any dialogue but if they do there will, in sociolinguistic terms, be at least one key speech act in its realization:

> Blues comes home to find Charlie there waiting for her. He apologizes for standing her up the other day—but he can't explain. There were 'things he needed to do.' Blues blows up at him. She's sick of him being so mysterious. She tells him to get the hell out of her house. (Epstein 2006: 77)

There are several speech acts here—an apology, an excuse, a rejection of the apology, a complaint, and an order. The meaning of the beat for the story is a hazarded reconciliation that does not come off. Although "Blues" and "Charlie" are characters in a science fiction drama (*Charlie Jade*, CHUM Television 2004), and his mysteriousness is linked to the existence of parallel universes, the character roles, as played out here, are simply those of lovers at a difficult moment in their relationship.

Dialogue can go beyond this in delivering character. Television displays to audiences what characters say and do. It does this in such a way as to indicate that they also think and feel. Their inner lives, their subjectivities, are understood to direct their outward behavior. Stories require characters that make decisions and act on them. These decisions help determine the course of story events. Davis talks about people possessing "agendas" when they engage in talk:

This is some sort of idea of what we want from the conversation.[. . .] for example, a man meeting his partner after a long separation might have an agenda consisting of the following, not necessarily in this order:

(a) Making it clear to her how much he has missed her, (b) telling her how well he has used the time while she has been away, (c) the need to sort out major financial problems. (Davis 2008: 26)

Writers give agendas to characters to make the stories work, and also so that they will seem like real people. But agendas are not umbrellas and handbags to be waved in front of the camera. If appropriate agendas can be inferred from characters' behavior, then to that extent the writer has been successful. More accurately, we should say that the writer *and the actors* have been successful. The earlier discussion of professional demarcation lines makes it clear that there is plenty for an actor to do to ensure the inferrability of agendas that are fit for purpose—no more and no less than the narrative circumstances require.

DISCUSSION

It is not my intention in this chapter to suggest that the concepts and accounts used to discuss dialogue by screenwriters are theoretically unsatisfactory in comparison to the concepts and accounts used within sociolinguistics. The comparisons I have been drawing are not for the sake of evaluation in that sense. The purpose of the chapter, is, rather, to explore the professional metalanguage and its underlying principles, to discover where those principles focused on the similarity of dialogue and unscripted speech, where they focused on the differences of the two modes, and how the industrial subcultures influence the nature of the product.

Screenwriters do, consciously, know about such things as hesitation phenomena, discourse markers, and hedges, and about some of the functions these can serve in spoken interaction. The use they make of them depends on the following:

- The particular stylistic effects they are producing
- The importance of naturalism among those effects
- Their relationship with the actors who have to speak the lines

Writers' own role as top-down designers of spoken interaction in a story context allows them to use dialogue for purposes that have nothing to do with characters' imaginary mental lives and relationships. They know how to use dialogue as a way of advancing the narrative, and they also appreciate that such usage creates a source of problems for the naturalism that they are also obliged to sustain.

This is important because it underlines the point that when it comes to understanding dialogue in TV drama, sociolinguistics has something to learn from the professional discourses, as well as something to contribute. The strategic naiveté of sociolinguistics, as described at the outset of this chapter, needs this kind of corrective in a full account of what we can expect from talk when it appears in television's dramatized genres.

The professional angle also makes it harder to ignore, even for strategic reasons, the industrial circumstances that condition the kinds of things that characters on television can be allowed to say to one another. Despite these circumstances, *creativity*, in the sense of something out of the ordinary, something more ambitious than usual, is possible in TV drama dialogue, as I showed in my discussion of *The Royle Family* in chapter 3. But *The Royle Family* was not an easy show to get made, because of its unconventional approach. It did get made, and in the way its writer had wanted. It was a comedy, so humor could be a justification for that approach, and it was unconventional in an accessible way, taking account of, rather than resisting, popular modes of expression. Similar arguments will be made in chapter 9, which focuses on the American medical mystery drama *House*. Questions about what writers can "get away with," given the nature of the medium they have chosen to work in, often focus on the issue of swearing (though this is not restricted to drama), and there are some well-known parameters here—British mainstream broadcasting has become more accepting of "bad" language than equivalent channels in the United States, where the main divide is between the networks and cable TV; a temporal *watershed* ensures more permissiveness after 9 P.M., the tolerance of swearing by regulators is much greater overall than in the earlier years of television, and so forth. But in truth this is just one rather prominent aspect of a much more general question, where it is likely we will need a combination of scholarly and professional frames of reference in further exploration of the issues.

5

What Audiences Know about Dialogue

This chapter complements the previous one. Both offer reflections on dialogue from beyond the text itself. Both try to sidestep the limitations of formal textual analysis alone by focusing on the production and consumption (interpretation) of dialogue as situated cultural practices, open to ethnographic exploration. In the case of writers and dialogue, this exploration is easy to justify: writers are part of an industry that has a compositional view of texts as product and draws on different professional craft skills for different parts of the whole. It is instructive to learn about how and where the lines are drawn between writing, acting, and directing, and the effects of these demarcation lines on the product.

In the present chapter, focusing on television audiences, the rationale for the inquiry is less obvious. It involves extracting dialogue from the compositional mix that has been so carefully constructed for viewers' benefit. What is the point? Surely audiences respond to the drama as a whole, and to its meanings, not to its forms? Is this chapter an artificial exercise undertaken simply for the sake of the complementarity with the previous chapter? This is a serious point, and I will address it in this chapter by demonstrating that (a) some audiences, at some times, *do* single out the dialogue in their responses, (b) attention to dialogue varies according to which audience we are talking about, (c) when audiences respond to meaning (in their interpretations of particular characters for instance), dialogue—in other words, form—helps create those interpretations, as it is intended to do, (d) the creation of *new* dialogue for characters invented by dramatists for television has become a significant activity for one segment of the audience, and (e), some bits of dialogue are appropriated by the audience, taking on a second life in the form of catchphrases.

The approach is also justified for me by its value in trying to extend ethnographic perspectives so as to encompass cognitive concerns. Cognitively speaking, the question is this: how are texts interpreted, and what does dialogue contribute to interpretation? The ethnographic issues are as follows: Who and what is "the audience"? How does it use its interpretations? How are interpretations expressed by viewers and negotiated in their social relationships, including relationships conducted through public forums? From this point of view, audiences' relations with dialogue are just one aspect of a more complex inquiry into their relations with media texts more generally.

Writers and audiences bring their real-world identities and interests into their media literacy practices, as producers and consumers of texts. The practices of audiences as textual consumers include their ways of hearing dialogue. Potentially, there are many ways in which these practices might be turned into *data* for research purposes, including experiments, interviews, focus groups, and participant observation. The approach adopted here is to focus on some of the secondary texts that audiences themselves write and publish as a result of their encounters with the primary texts, and to treat those as research data. Such data exist in a variety of generically distinct forms—critical reviews and previews, blog entries, online discussion threads, Twitter streams, and fan fiction. All but the last of these are straightforwardly about the primary texts. The last involves attempts to create something new, but in the spirit and style of the primary text and under its influence.

There is an inevitable bias here toward the *articulate* audience—viewers with the desire and ability to verbalize their reactions and opinions, and to do so in writing. It is a common viewing experience to watch a program without ever finding occasion to speak about it, and it is likely that a significant proportion of the viewing public rarely say much about what they have seen. On the other hand, for those who do like to verbalize their response, the contexts of text messaging, Twittering and blogging, which have emerged in recent years, may have weakened reluctance to put this verbalization into written form, because these genres impose much less prescriptive conditions on writing than more traditional ones. The Internet, as a multimodal textual environment, also permits a certain rather limited kind of *nonverbal commentary* on media texts by their viewers via YouTube, in which contributors draw attention to scenes and images they find significant by cutting and pasting short audiovisual extracts from shows they have enjoyed, to share the pleasure. To the extent that this constitutes infringement of copyright, it seems that copyright holders are not energetic in enforcing their rights, under YouTube's own conditions, to have such material removed from the site.

As well as making a number of general observations about audiences and dialogue, I will focus on some audience activity provoked by and responsive to dialogue in one particular episode of one particular series. The chosen series is *Doctor Who* (BBC 1963–present), and the episode is "Partners in Crime," first airing April 5, 2008, in the United Kingdom as the launch episode for the season as a whole.

THE INFLUENCE OF DIALOGUE

As chapter 4 showed, screenwriters appreciate dialogue as an element that can contribute to textual meaning in naturalistic as well as other kinds of drama. In respect of naturalistic drama, there is a default reading position that is "innocent," nonanalytic. Drama productions of this kind situate audiences as flies on the fourth diegetic wall, colluding with the constructed, fictional reality. From this position, dialogue is meant to help bring off interpretations of character, story, and theme, while passing unnoticed in its own right. See how this viewer talks about a character from *Doctor Who*:

> Donna's her own woman. She's lived a bit. She's confident; as likely to enter a new situation with a healthy skepticism as with wide-eyed excitement. And she'll fight her corner—she's not afraid to tackle the Doctor, to challenge his actions or beliefs. You could argue he learns as much from her as she does from him. (Laura Pledger, "Why I Love...Catherine Tate as Donna Noble," *Radio Times*, "Why I Love...," blog, http://www.radiotimes.com/blogs/339-why-i-lovecatherine-tate/, June 16, 2008)

This overview of Donna's personality is not limited to a single information source: it extrapolates character information from dialogue, from performance, and from storylines. It is unnecessary for the writer in offering this sketch to refer to any specific act of Donna's, much less to refer to or quote the words through which that act was performed.

Not all *noticing* is off-limits when the audience colludes with the naturalistic illusion, only the kind that *recognizes its artifice*. Viewers can attend to what characters say, can notice their sayings, just as they can attend to any other kind of speech, mediated or otherwise. They can then quote or refer to these utterances subsequently in their own talk or writing. Thus, in relation to a hypothetical apology scene, for a viewer to notice the dialogue and write, "They both said they were sorry," in which "they" are characters in that scene, is different from "He had them apologize to one another," in which "he" is the writer of the scene. The former colludes with the fiction, the latter does not. Yet, because it can be tedious for someone who is perfectly well aware of textual artifice always to write such things as, "They had her say *x*," rather than "She said *x*," it will not always be apparent from single statements like this just how much recognition of constructional work is involved on the part of particular viewers.

There are certainly circumstances under which the default, "naive," reading position is not observed. Its limitations can be overcome or bypassed. Particular sectors of the audience, such as professional reviewers, may have interests that predispose them to take a more analytic view. The text itself can invite a more conscious attention to dialogue (e.g., verbal humor). Or it can attract such attention despite itself (e.g., when the writing, or the performance, or the story-line, is perceived as "bad" in some way). Each of these circumstances will be explored in the sections to follow, starting with some preliminary work on the concept of the audience and its genres of writing about television drama.

WHO IS THE AUDIENCE?

It is important not to oversimplify the concept of *audience* here, or to treat it purely as a construct of the text. Market research can be used to categorize the audience in terms of demographic variables: children/young adults/older adults/the elderly; unemployed/manual workers/white-collar workers/professionals/entrepreneurs; males/females. Academic research, also focused on audience demography, can be used to take this further to investigate more specific fault lines in the viewing and listening public, such as political partisanship. Such differences within the audience may variously lead to differences of comprehension, differences of interpretation, and/or different evaluations.[1] All of these questions about the variability of audience uptake are concerned with *overall* interpretation/response, and not, as in this chapter, with specific *aspects* of texts. The relevant fault lines in this case are rather different, and the most important subgroups from this point of view would include wannabe writers, journalistic reviewers, scholarly critics, fans, and casual viewers. These groups are *ideal types*: in practice their interests overlap and merge.

Wannabe writers are themselves learning the craft skills of dialogue production, and this gives them a reason to pay attention to how specific effects are achieved, including effects that depend upon dialogue. Reviewers are under an obligation to entertain as well as inform through their criticism, the balance between entertainment and information varying with the context. Judicious quotation of the dialogue can give flavor to the commentary. Scholarly critics are less interested in the value of the production on its own terms than on what it signifies symptomatically in respect of the culture that produced it. Dialogue for them can have important social subtext. Fans have become particularly significant with the growth of the Internet, as they became more accessible to one another and much more able to self-constitute as *communities* (Baym 2000; see also Gray et al. 2007). Fans have an interest in fostering textual features they appreciate, and are alert to uses of dialogue that disappoint them, for instance, when characters are given lines that seem inappropriate for their personalities.

As for viewers who are not recruited into any of the previous categories—the phrase "everyone's a critic" captures the rueful mindset of the cultural producer whose disappointment is that this audience, too, has engaged in some deconstruction unfavorable to his or her work. The disappointment is also tinged with the frustrated awareness that members of the general public are *merely* critics:

freely, happily, licentiously able to comment on the deficiencies of the product and to that extent possessing power over its producer, despite the inability among themselves to produce equivalent texts and submit them for reciprocal judgment. Criticism demands no qualifications. The situation is the same for athletes. We spectators and audiences often think we know what has gone wrong, even though we do not and cannot ourselves perform. It is true that everyone is a critic, in the sense that everyone has some kind of response to what they see and hear, including the responses that involve turning a show off or not watching any more episodes. But not all criticism is shared, let alone publicized, or even articulated. It takes more effort to discuss a text than merely to watch it, think about it, and move on. That effort is still more or less private when the discussion takes the form of oral communication in a domestic setting. The Internet, in providing a channel and a range of genres for sharing opinions, has lowered the barriers to the publication of those opinions, and expanded the range of commentators to include more "ordinary" viewers alongside fans and critics.

AUDIENCE GENRES

Whatever audiences know about dialogue, these understandings remain their own until they talk about them with others. In television studies there are various approaches to the production of data on audience responses generally: quasi-experimental approaches in which respondents are systematically recruited from the general audience and participate in protocols designed to examine the effectiveness of television discourse; interview approaches with similarly recruited participants who watch material under research conditions and talk to researchers afterward, individually or in (focus) groups; and quantitative approaches with multiple-choice questions about aspects of viewing and large-scale sampling. There have even been observational approaches, in which cameras are installed to watch and record processes of watching.

In the era of the Internet it has also become possible to investigate audiences on the basis of texts that they themselves produce, not under research conditions. Undoubtedly the kind of viewers who actually take up this opportunity is self-selecting and unrepresentative of the full range of actual viewers. However, a significant selection of two important viewer categories do use the public sphere for commentary on television productions: professional critics (reviewers) and fans. The genres they use for these purposes are, in no particular order, the fan forum thread, the blog entry, the published review column, the customer review (e.g., for DVD box sets on Amazon), and fan fiction. Whereas the first four all call for commentary about television shows, the fifth demands an ability, using words alone, to *reproduce* significant aspects of its discourse. For obvious reasons, dialogue design is prominent in this genre. Fans are likely to use fan fiction, fan threads, customer reviews, and blogs for their discourse; professional critics use reviews and blogs. Amateur criticism can also turn up in threads, blogs, Twitter streams, and customer reviews. Threads, blogs, and Twitters are native to online communication; fan fiction and reviews both existed independently before the arrival of the Internet, and continue to do so. Newspaper reviews are produced both electronically and in print, though the electronic versions are easier to access once the publication date has passed.

Threads

Threads are the online equivalent of face-to-face conversation but with significant differences. Online interaction comes in two main forms: synchronous, in which messages follow one another in real time, and asynchronous, in which any amount of time may pass between contributions. Forum threads are of the latter kind. On most threads there are more than two active contributors (and unknown numbers of passive auditors, both *lurkers*, who attend to the development of a thread as it happens, and others who access contributions retrospectively, as I did in the research for this chapter). Threads may be manifestations of communities with shared interests and goals, or the mutual links of participants may be minimal and thin. Messages orient to previous messages, producing the equivalent of adjacency pairs such as question-and-answer. But the ordering of these messages in linear sequence is not controlled by adjacency sequencing. Messages take their place according to when they are received on the server, so the linear organization of the textual product is to that extent arbitrarily imposed by technology. Contributors could have been typing and sending at the exact same moment but without mutually displaying this until after the full message is received on the server. Cohesion devices within the authored text indicate how contributions relate to one another. There may also be technological (rather than authorial) displays of textual relationships, as when degrees of indentation from the margin place contributions at a certain depth in relation to the originating contribution, this indentation being automatically generated by the software depending on which contributions are replying to which.

Blogs

Blogging is sometimes compared with diary keeping because, in the standard blogging template, entries are date-stamped and accumulate chronologically, the most recent displaying at the top of the screen. But offline diary keeping is essentially a private activity until such time as the diarist, retrospectively, chooses to publish (this option being mainly for celebrities—such diaries have to be marketable). Online, blogging incurs minimal publishing costs after initial investment in the technology, so does not require a market, and publication occurs on the day of writing, not retrospectively. Blogging is monologic, though bloggers can choose to enable the receipt and publication of comments on their entries. Compared with forum threads, the result is more hierarchical: the original entry has a necessary superiority in the discourse over comments. Blogging has overtaken the less structured personal web page as the most popular way for individuals (as opposed to institutions) to contribute to the World Wide Web. In addition, it seems now that many blogs are themselves produced under the auspices of an institution, and these have more in common with authored newspaper columns than they do with personal web pages. Nevertheless, anyone who can access the Internet can find a way to blog if they want to. Blogs may be freestanding, or they may be part of more general websites offering other resources such as images for downloading, video clips, and message boards. Entries related to television shows may be their main fare or just one possible area of that writer's blog. Blogs may be the work of individuals, or they may be offered within an institutional context. Television-themed blog-gery thus exists in three main contexts: as part of general TV/film-related websites (TVheaven.com; televisionwithoutpity.com), as part of websites focused on specific shows (whovianet.co.uk; drgreghouse.com), and as occasional topics on miscellaneous blogs.

Review Columns

Daily and weekly periodicals, in print and online, are the principal source of TV reviews and previews. Reviews are addressed to audiences either to help them decide what to watch ahead of broadcasting or to reflect on what has been broadcast in an entertaining way. Reviewers are professional writers and are expected to write *well* about TV shows, not just to emit statements of like or dislike. They are surrogates for the audience in general, but highly articulate surrogates. Reviews are the least interactive and most monologic of the audience genres here discussed. Traditional print reviews may result in no interaction at all in the public domain (private correspondence between reviewers and their readers does not count). Online reviews may, like blogs, enable comments to be reviewed and displayed.

Fan Fiction

Fan fiction involves contributions of varying lengths, from short scene fragments to book-length stories written about characters created in various kinds of fiction, including television drama. Authors may be wannabe writers *for real*, or fan fiction may be enough to satisfy their creative and publishing desires. These writers imagine additional encounters, within or very close to the parameters of the original text, and supply dialogue and action to bring these encounters to life, though without any expectation of performance by actors or any kind of production. Fan fiction writers do not necessarily see themselves as writing scripts or even fragments of scripts. They are mostly writing prose fiction. They do not write stage directions, as scriptwriters do, and they elaborate the thoughts of the characters, which scriptwriters do not. But prose fiction can incorporate dialogue, and fan fiction certainly does.

THE WRITING PERSONA

As indicated above, audience members who write about their viewing experiences in any of these forms may be individual viewer-critics (whether fans or more detached viewers), they may be professional critics, they may themselves be writers of TV drama, and yet it is not always possible to determine an *offline* identity, distinct from the persona the writer adopts within the text itself.

It is in its online *voices* that the writing audience identifies itself—that members of the viewing public constitute themselves as ordinary viewers, fans, or critics. Stances are variously offered by writers to their readers. At one end of the spectrum viewers provide unarguable expressions of personal taste at the level of "I never liked *ER* as much after George Clooney left," whereas at the other end there are lengthy and highly articulate accounts of strengths and weaknesses in particular productions. In genres that enable discussion, disagreements may break out. Commentators do not want to deny one another the right to an opinion, and they appreciate that preferences as such (e.g., the inclusion of a comic dimension in "serious" drama) are essentially beyond argument. But they do want to test and examine the perceptions on which preferences are based. Any statements about shows that go beyond "I like *x*," however tentatively phrased, are likely to be propositional and invite some kind of intersubjective validation. Not all viewers were equally irritated by Catherine Tate's "loud" performance in her first episode as companion Donna Noble in *Doctor Who*, but in this case there was little dispute that it *was* a loud performance. Other propositions are more contestable.

In the rest of this section I will illustrate and explore the different ways that the writing audience responds to TV drama shows. This general picture will provide a background for examining the presence of *dialogue* in such responses. The British science fiction series *Doctor Who* is a good choice of series for this purpose because of the extensive amount of attention it attracts as a flagship BBC production with strong overseas sales as well as a large cross-generational audience in the United Kingdom. The popularity and longevity of the series has given rise to such enormous quantities of commentary as well as secondary and tertiary intertexts available via the Internet (and beyond) that a full overview is not possible within the scope of a single chapter. I focus on a single episode,

"Partners in Crime" (series 4, episode 1, written by Russell T. Davies). This episode is recent enough to be regarded as contemporary television but old enough to be available in DVD format at the time of writing (either as part of the full-series box set, or with three other episodes on a single DVD). There is a related downloadable episode of *Doctor Who Confidential* (via BBC i-player) with behind-the-scenes commentary, and a copy of the shooting script (via http://www.thewriterstale.co.uk). When it was first broadcast in the United Kingdom it attracted the second largest audience of the day (8.4 million viewers—almost 40%; of the viewing audience that night), beaten only by a major sporting event, the Grand National Steeplechase, a daytime broadcast.[2] Even with the focus on a single episode, my approach is selective rather than synoptic. The selections have been made to encompass the varieties of voice/identity as discussed above and to incorporate in each case commentary that at some level showed attention to the dialogue. A more traditional approach might have been to analyze the episode's dialogue first, identify some significant scenes/lines on the basis of that analysis, and then discuss whether and how audience commentary responded to those same scenes and lines. Instead, I have constructed this as, essentially, an analysis of the secondary texts themselves, with the original episode as a background intertext. I will provide information regarding this intertext as appropriate to the discussion—starting here with a brief plot summary.

In this episode the Doctor (David Tennant) is reunited with Donna Noble (Catherine Tate), who will be his companion for the rest of the series (Tate's character was previously introduced in a one-off Christmas special). Before their reunion they have each independently decided to investigate what lies behind a mysterious new dietary product and the company marketing it. The plot hinges on the role of the company's CEO as an intermediary between an alien civilization and Planet Earth, using the fat tissue of human bodies to produce, illegally, the next generation of the alien species. Human hosts do not necessarily die as a result of this process, though death is a possible outcome in certain circumstances. The Doctor and Donna discover the plot and defeat the villain who perishes, while the "monster-children" escape to their home planet on a space machine. Before Donna and the Doctor depart together for new adventures, a previous companion makes a surprise reappearance, though only to Donna, who, in a moment of dramatic irony for the viewers, does not react, not knowing her to be the much-missed Rose Tyler (Billie Piper). The return of Rose is constructed to serve as an important highlight of the episode for the audience, albeit one that is dependent on familiarity with the story so far.

A Google search for "Doctor Who: Partners in Crime" leads to thousands of sources, some of them rather predictable: Wikipedia, YouTube, BBC, Amazon, the Internet Movie Database, and various newspapers. Along with critical judgment, the material at these locations included episode summaries and production information. In such cases, the authorial voice tends to be either impersonal and descriptive, or promotional, or a mixture of both.

"The Professional Reviewer"

The first episode of the latest *Doctor Who* season was bound to attract the attention of the mass media, especially in the national Sunday press (*Doctor Who* is a Saturday evening program), including the *Sunday Times* and the *Sunday Mirror*, and then beyond, in more restricted and specialist publications (*Metro, Digital Spy*). The following is an extract from a professional review (note that I have made some cuts to save space):

> Nerds rejoice . . . *Doctor Who* is back! And oh look, he's brought his mum.
> [. . .]
> Anyway, it's a racing cert that the Doc's vast army of devoted fans will not have been disappointed by last night's silly curtain-raiser. They never are.
> But it didn't exactly ooze tension.
> All we got in the way of terrifying space enemies was Sarah Lancashire hamming it up as an intergalactic super nanny, a couple of security guards with guns and lots of cute little fat babies. Err, that's it.
> Meanwhile, Ms Tate unwisely entered the BBC's weekly *Doctor Who* overacting contest.
> A word of advice Catherine—try as you might, you'll never beat David Tennant on that score.
> Crazy-eyed Dave is the king of the OTT performance [. . .] (Kevin O'Sullivan, "Not Bovvered by the Doctor," *Sunday Mirror*, April 6, 2007)

This review exists as a monologue: no reactions to it were solicited by the paper. Reviewers like O'Sullivan will almost always be writing to a specific word length. O'Sullivan distances himself from the fans in the second quoted paragraph, makes only negative comments about the episode, and does so with mocking humor: "Crazy-eyed Dave is the king of the OTT performance," to entertain his readers while evaluating the show. He disapproves of Tate on account of her age, which he humorously exaggerates ("his mum") and her acting style ("overacting"). The dramatic qualities of the plot dissatisfy him ("it didn't exactly ooze tension"), and he implies that "lots of cute little fat babies" are a perverse way for an ostensibly shocking series to represent monstrosity. It is fairly typical in not making *any* explicit reference to dialogue, only to performance.

Other critics reacted positively: some approved of the very same things that O'Sullivan disapproved of, notably the relative "lightness" of this particular episode in "shock, horror" terms. This is a difference of judgment, but it is founded on a substantive agreement. Other critics disagreed substantively— Andrew Billen in the *Times* regarded Tate's performance as "toned down," not overacted. Not all the journalists ignored dialogue, though they do not converge on any single line, scene, or dialogue function.

"The Fan"

It is more difficult to illustrate the voice of the fan with a single quotation than to illustrate the voice of the critic, because of the huge amount of material and the different flavors of fandom. This is complicated further in relation to *Doctor Who* because of the longevity of the series and the various changes it has undergone since the 1960s. The most important change is the 15-year break between the original series, 1963–1989, and the 2005 relaunch. This creates space for fans to diverge in respect to whether or not there is some *essence* that new episodes should honor. Generally speaking, however, what distinguishes fans from reviewers is a level of *detail* in the critical engagement—a more acute, often reasoned, perception of how and why things could have been done differently. Unlike reviewers, they are not restricted by the number of words they can use. What interests me about this is how it relates to the "us" and "them" relationship between viewers and producers. Whether sympathetic or unsympathetic, in this discourse, we-the-(serious)-viewers identify with the project of textual production. Fans are not just sitting on the sofa, throwing casual brickbats, nor writing entertainingly on behalf of the ordinary viewer. They are attempting, through their discourse, to make the producers *accountable*. The standards they ask the series to uphold are often precisely those it would wish to be judged on: production values, quality of acting, convincingly dramatic shock values, balance of humor and seriousness, and character consistency. An important exception to this relates to the internal logic of the diegetic world and the plot. Fans tend to set a higher standard regarding the internal coherence of the fictional universe than producers do, and there is potential here for considerable tension between the producers and this section of the audience.

On the *Doctor Who Ratings Guide* (a website for fans), the "Partners in Crime" episode featured five reviews on January 11, 2009 (4,000 words total), two of them favorable and three unfavorable, all of them monologic:

> Aside from the new companion, the plot is somewhat blah. The Adipose company has its new miracle diet pills out on the market in London and about to go nationwide, but, as we all immediately suspect, there's something unpleasant going on behind the scenes. The actual effects of the pills are actually quite inventive. It's such a shame that Davies had to ruin the potential surprise and shock by dropping a painfully obvious hint early in the episode (made all the worse by the line delivery from the otherwise solid Sarah Lancashire which just screams "this is a big hint!"). It was interesting to see a villain who could match the Doctor in terms of technology, though this idea was used in fairly obvious ways. Tennant has slipped back into the role of the Doctor without missing a beat and he maintains

that wonderful almost manic energy that makes him so engaging and he also forges
a very interesting connection with Catherine Tate that I'll be very interested in
watching develop. And the scene when they first see each other after a half
an episode of near misses is just delightful. (http://www.pagefillers.com/dwrg/
partnerscrime.htm)

This viewer-writer identifies as a fan in the way he shows his familiarity with
Tennant as the Doctor, as well as with previous *Who* villains, and in his plans to
watch future episodes of this season. The paragraph is full of positive language,
such as "inventive," "interesting," "without missing a beat," "wonderful, almost
manic energy," "engaging," "delightful," as well as more negative terms, such
as "somewhat blah," "painfully obvious," "screams," all of which focus on plot
management. The viewer-writer is conscious of not just the characters, but also
the actors (cf. his reference to Sara Lancashire's performance) and the writer,
Russell T. Davies, objecting to the undercutting of shock effects by early hints as
to what might be involved.

As for dialogue, the "painfully obvious" hint that this viewer refers to is the
early, dramatically underlined revelation (in both written and spoken forms) of
the company's advertising slogan for its new diet aid: "The fat just walks away!"
The writer does not find it necessary to remind readers of the hint's actual
wording, though some other commentators did quote the line. Because it is
textually foregrounded (the Doctor later repeats it in a private context), and has
the function (at one level) of a slogan, it seems *designed* to be remembered and
quoted. The slogan meaning is, of course, subsumed in the text by the play across
figurative and literal meanings of the same word sequence. (The version performed by Sarah Lancashire as evil Miss Foster has been audiovisually extracted
from its context by someone and made available online as a free downloadable
mobile phone ringtone.)

As well as commentary on *Doctor Who*, audiences—fans, specifically—have
produced huge amounts of fan fiction. The writers of successful fan fiction are
also in the business of understanding dialogue—dependent on their intuitions
and sensitivity to patterns of interaction, without reliance on the ability to make
their understanding explicit. There is an element of imitation in this approach,
along with an ability to develop tacit models for how these characters should
behave, sociolinguistically, in the scenarios they create for them. The largest
online collection of fan fiction is hosted at fanfiction.net, and this is where
I looked to see what such writers were doing with dialogue. On this website,
January 21, 2009, a search revealed 13,170 samples of *Doctor Who* fan fiction (for
comparison purposes, the less well-established science fiction series *Heroes* had
3,336, and a non–science fiction but long-running series, *ER*, had 4,628 samples). The earliest published (i.e., uploaded) samples on *Doctor Who* dated from
1999, and much of the material is therefore related to the "old" *Doctor Who*, not
the series as reinvented in 2005. None of the samples attract the MA (Mature

Adults only) grading (explicit language and adult themes), but around 850 were deemed to be unsuitable for under 16s because of possible strong but nonexplicit adult themes, reference to violence, and strong coarse language. By contrast, about 4,500 samples had the lowest grading, deemed suitable for anyone over the age of 5 (content free of coarse language, violence, and adult themes). I report these observations to convey the point that this is not, as some might suspect, an enclave restricted to the "dirty-minded," exercising lurid fantasies about the sex lives of fictional characters. At the same time, about 1,000 samples are generically coded as romance, mainly when the Doctor is imagined in a romantic/sexual relationship with the companion-of-the-moment. One of the functions of fan fiction is as an outlet for imaginative directions that the official version of the *Doctor Who* story (and the same applies to fan fiction in general) does not want to take, but (some) fans do.

There are just 25 samples that take their point of departure from the "Partners in Crime" episode. The majority are inspired by the reappearance of Rose Tyler. Not all of them offer the reader any dialogue. Several purport to present the thoughts of one or more of the characters, either the Doctor or more commonly Rose or Donna. For example, one contributor (whom I will refer to as Contributor 1, and assume him to be male) describes the thoughts of Rose as she appears and then (nonrealistically) vanishes at the end of the episode. Contributor 1 reproduces in his account the utterances that Donna spoke to Rose, but does not invent any new dialogue.

Another fan fiction writer in this collection does invent new dialogue. I will refer to this person as Contributor 2 and assign female gender for the sake of differentiation from Contributor 1. Contributor 2 rewrites the Donna/Rose encounter so that (a) the two characters become known to one another in their relations to the Doctor, and (b) their exchange has consequences for the plot. In this "improved" ending, the Doctor and Rose are romantically reunited and the Tardis departs with not one, but two, companions. A key line in this rewrite is the following:

> Tell him "Rose Tyler." If he doesn't come, I'll know he's moved on.

Contributor 2 is setting up a "good" reunion, welcome to both characters and not unwelcome to Donna, either. She is attempting to do this while sustaining Rose as a tough character who is robustly prepared for possible disappointment, and likewise sustaining a frame of melodrama around the romance, true to the spirit of the broadcast series.

The "Ordinary" Viewer

As suggested earlier in this chapter, there are more opportunities than ever before for viewers to publish their opinions via the Internet. Although on the one hand, the act of "going public" separates this group of viewers from those who feel no need to respond publicly to what they have watched, there is no doubt that *feedback* from the consumer has become more culturally significant than ever before, along with *interactivity*—both viewed as positive trends to be encouraged. Viewers who do respond may not, therefore, be truly "ordinary," but they are perhaps exemplary. If there is a "best practice" for television consumers, this is it.

Although the review column is the best genre for critics, and fans can adapt to most genres as well as create their own in the form of fan fiction, the best genre for our exemplary viewers is an interactive forum of some sort. So far, I have examined only monologues and not looked at any of the more interactive spaces where commentators exchange views about shows. One such space is the "comment" section following certain blogs and online columns by reviewers. Published replies to critical evaluations can demonstrate the existence of different views on the same show, though the engagement among contributors with reference to one another's arguments may be very thin. This is partly because such commentaries are often not generated in the same "conversational" way as forum threads (of which, more below): each comment is a response to the original column, though contributors may also mention one another.

A favorable review by Stephen Brook in the *Guardian*'s Organgrinder blog[4] provided a feedback facility that generated 52 comments (under 40 different nicknames) before the entry was closed to new contributions. Contributors (other than the original columnist) are writing as interested ordinary viewers, not as fans or reviewers; however, there is variation in the commentary suggestive of different degrees and kinds of engagement with the series. The ironic, "displaced" reading (cf. Richardson and Corner 1986), in which writers talk about why *other* people (probably, here, of poor taste and discernment) might or might not like the episode, is one possibility:

> Another episode about aliens hiding out on Earth exploiting humans and yet again the sonic screwdriver solves everything. If the public moans, throw in the Daleks. Everyone likes them and it gets you column inches in *The Sun.*
> Four series in, the formula still works.

Comments were both general ("I thought it was a great laugh and very clever") and specific, with Catherine Tate's performance being the most commonly cited feature attracting attention. The original columnist approved of Tate's performance: it was "spirited" and had a "lighter touch" (than her comedy sketch caricatures and her previous performance as Noble in a Christmas special). The character itself is found by at least one viewer to be interestingly headstrong compared with other companions and not romantically interested in the Doctor:

> Finally a companion that is in fact an adult and doesn't have a stupid school girl crush on The Doctor (Although he is quite sexy). I think she brings a whole new

side to the doctor's companions in the fact that she will challenge him and stand up to him as an equal, not become all awe struck every time he looks at her.

There is no explicit reference to dialogue in this description. But as discussed above, viewers' interpretations of character and plot derive information from dialogue while forgetting the specific input(s) that made their inferences possible. This viewer-writer (I will assume him to be male) gets that Donna is "headstrong" but does not feel any need to explain how he gets this meaning. As for character, so also for plot. Another viewer-writer (I will assume her to be female) in a different thread, discussing this episode, observes: ". . . there was never a real sense of danger. It was hinted that a million people might die, but it did not feel possible."[5] This viewer understands how she is meant to use dialogue information in her interpretation of the plot, but finds herself unable to *trust* the dialogue without sufficient support from elsewhere in the production.

As this example shows, when viewers do attend to the artfulness of the work that has gone into producing specific effects of plot and character management, the attention is often negative: faith in the fourth wall artifice has broken down. In this example, the dialogue hint itself is not the problem. The hint is significant, and necessary—it is just not enough.

There is disagreement in this thread, though not about dialogue—it is about Catherine Tate's performance. Those who did not like her simply assert disagreement without argument: "By the way, Catherine Tate can't act. She was useless." Asserted disagreement develops into debate only over the general point of what Tate's ability to produce good sketch comedy caricatures implies for her general acting ability, not about her performance in this episode.

Although it is common for dialogue to get attention when something has gone wrong in the production from the viewer's perspective, offenses against credibility are not the only "trigger" that draws viewers' attention to dialogue, even in a naturalistic production. As I observed previously, it is not inconsistent with the logic of naturalism for viewers to remember (and repeat, not necessarily verbatim) lines of dialogue from a drama episode, just as they might remember and repeat utterances from any other context. They might, for instance, remember a line of dialogue because of its importance to the plot. Or other kinds of artifice will become significant: wit/humor, rhetorical or poetic styling, or thematic resonance. "Partners in Crime" offers two candidates for "memorable line": the advertising slogan "The fat just walks away" (see above) and later, from Donna, "I'm waving at fat"—a comment revealing the character's own sense of the ridiculous, as one of the Adipose "monster children" at the end of the episode waves goodbye to her and the Doctor on Planet Earth. The humor of this moment is not lost on the audience, and the line was indeed memorable for many. It has been quoted many times since, in blogs (e.g., forapples.vox.com); on social networking sites (e.g., Facebook) and on the websites of media-related organizations (bbc.co.uk, imdb.com, digitalspy.co.uk). The scene as a whole was reproduced as a brief YouTube clip, uploaded by a fan in August 2008. The line then starts to take on a new life, at some remove from its origins. One viewer uses it as a heading for a blog entry about her latest homemade stuffed toy, in the shape of an Adipose baby, whereas another uses it as a witty way of talking about her own weight loss, while acknowledging Donna's contribution to her phraseology.

A specific line, uttered once in a show, may be memorable for a moment, but usually a certain amount of repetition is required before lines of dialogue turn into *catchphrases*—lines whose memorability/reproducibility has become part of their meaning and social function.

MEMORABLE DIALOGUE: THE TELEVISION CATCHPHRASE

One particular kind of collaboration between TV screenwriter and audience that celebrates dialogue is worthy of note, though hard to do justice to in the present context. The creation of catchphrases—mainly, of course, from comedy rather than serious drama—depends on screenwriters, who must ensure that the phrase in question is repeated sufficiently often to get itself noticed as something distinct from the less fixed language elsewhere in the production (while avoiding excessive use that would diminish the impact of the expression). But it also depends on a disposition in audiences to appreciate the familiarity of the phrase and to make it into something that they themselves can (re)produce in their own conversational behavior.

"I don't believe it" is a banal expression of incredulity that anyone might use in the appropriate circumstances. But there is also a catchphrase variant of this expression, which comes from the British situation comedy *One Foot in the Grave* (BBC 1990–2000), and is (or was) associated with the character Victor Meldrew in that series. The catchphrase is characteristically delivered in Victor's regional accent (Edinburgh Scottish) and with a particular pitch contour, with strong emphasis on "believe" and a prolongation of the stressed vowel. Victor and his wife Margaret are a just-retired couple living in England. When Victor says, "I don't believe it," his incredulity is often a response cry (in the sense of Goffman 1978). He says it when there is no other character to hear what he says. Its focus is some real or perceived outrage perpetrated against his desire for a comfortable, untroubled suburban life. Of course, he himself often bears some responsibility for the outrage.

For a TV viewer to deploy the phrase, with Victor's delivery, is to evoke, though not necessarily to identify with, Victor's sensibility and circumstances. Not everyone who says "I don't believe it" is consciously manipulating an intertextual reference to *One Foot in the Grave*. The ordinariness of the wording itself resists such comprehensive appropriation. "I don't believe it" may or may not be formulaic in everyday use, but it was meaningful before David Renwick (the writer of *One Foot*) put it into the mouth of his character, and continues to be meaningful without reference to Meldrew. But the Meldrew connection made available, to certain parts of British society, another layer of meaning above and beyond its core significance. To understand that meaning was to belong to the cultural community. *One Foot* ceased broadcasting in 2000 and, despite repeats on secondary TV channels (UK TV Gold), has now passed into cultural history. The community that can unite over a shared "Meldrew" interpretation of "I don't believe it" is shrinking and will continue to shrink. The catchphrases of the future are less likely to achieve the distribution that those of the past were able to do, as the proliferation of TV channels and, arguably, the drift away from television as the domestic entertainment medium of first choice continues to fracture national audiences.

A recent dictionary of TV catchphrases and related expressions (Brookes 2005) covers a substantial range of material with a British flavor, though with many American examples ("To boldly go"; "Good thinking, Batman"; "How you doin'?") and several of Australian origin ("I wouldn't give a Castlemaine XXXX."). Situation comedy and sketch comedy provide the bulk of the instances, advertising contributes a sizeable subset, and the rest variously come from straight drama, sports coverage, and light entertainment, including quiz shows and reality television. The ordinariness of "I don't believe it" is not untypical. Others, like Joey's chat-up line, "How you doin'?" (*Friends*, NBC 1994–2004), are just as unremarkable, linguistically. The unity of words and specific broadcast context constitutes the *catchphrase* in many cases. "And finally" is a case in point: this is a catchphrase from news discourse introducing a lighthearted item at the very end of a bulletin. A catchphrase does not have to be witty or linguistically playful or poetic, though it sometimes is: "Can we fix it? Yes, we can" (*Bob the Builder*, BBC 1999) was the catchphrase of the eponymous Bob in a British children's animated series. It has a poetic rhythm based on simple monosyllables, and a call-and-response structure, and became the lyric of a spin-off record. There is no direct evidence of any relationship between this upbeat assertion of a builder's confidence and the equally optimistic "Yes, we can!" of successful presidential candidate Barack Obama, though there has been online discussion of the similarity.[6] Tilove's article illustrates the important point that when utterances involve simple words, simple constructions, and basic ideas, they cannot convincingly be claimed as any single originator's personal property. Catchphrase variants can be constructed through strong contextual associations (Obama) and/or with witty or poetic qualities (*Bob the Builder*). "And it's goodbye from him," as the sign-off line in a sketch routine spoofing the news (*The Two Ronnies*, BBC 1971–1987), was witty because the other presenter had previously said, "So it's goodbye from me." It could be argued that the wit evaporated with repetition, leaving only the comfort of familiarity that it shares with other catchphrases. In the Unites States, the expression "more cowbell" is a comparable example of a phrase that has passed into general usage with some attenuation of the humor that gave rise to it. It references a famous *Saturday Night Live* sketch from 2000, where Christopher Walken, playing a fictionalized celebrity music producer, farcically demands to hear "more cowbell" from the band cutting a track in his studio, circa 1976. It is a joke at the expense of a real song by Blue Öyster Cult (*Don't Fear the Reaper*), which does indeed feature a cowbell, though not as prominently as in the spoof. As with the British examples, the familiarity of this phrase may now be more important to its continuing usage than the original joke.

The role of the audience in creating and sustaining catchphrases is enhanced when the catchphrase comes in the form of a template: partially structured and fixed, but with a "slot" into which new elements can be inserted as appropriate. A classic example from the British comedy tradition is the catchphrase associated with the character "CJ" from the sitcom *The Fall and Rise of Reginald Perrin*. CJ was Perrin's boss, an overbearing, opinionated, self-centered individual. His catchphrase began, "I didn't get where I am today . . ." (the dots represent the rest of the utterance). These have been collated online by a fan at http://homepages. nildram.co.uk/~culttv/cj.htm. Here are a few:

> I didn't get where I am today . . .
> . . . without knowing a favorable report when I see one.
> . . . without recognizing a real winner when I see one.
> . . . by selling ice cream tasting of book-ends, pumice stone and West Germany.
> . . . by waffling.
> . . . without learning how to handle people.

The context would often be where CJ had been warning an underling to follow or not to follow some course of action, and holding himself up as an example of the right course. Some of the above considered in isolation come across as sensible attitudes, but the third one illustrates the kind of absurdity to which the formula could be turned. The point here is that the template leaves audience members using this expression to finish it off in ways appropriate for their own circumstances. Not that this kind of incompleteness is necessary to encourage audience creativity. Even the more fixed catchphrases can be played around with. There was a blog (no longer actively maintained) at http://thepime.blogspot. com/ titled "This Blog Will Self Destruct in Five Seconds." This is a variant on a catchphrase that goes back to the American drama series *Mission: Impossible* (CBS 1966–1973). Because I did not watch this series, I will quote from Brookes:

> In each episode of the series, the team would receive its mission from the mysterious "Secretary" in the form of a tape. The tape would always exhort the team to action with the words "Your mission, should you choose to accept it, is . . ." and then

conclude with "This tape will self-destruct in five seconds," after which time smoke
would start to emerge from the tape recorder, providing a cue for the opening titles
to begin. (2005: 128)

The original series may have ceased production in 1973, but a new version
was broadcast from 1988 to 1990, and repeats kept this alive until the first
Mission Impossible movie came out in 1996. The sequels, which date from 2000
and 2006, have kept the franchise—and, seemingly, the catchphrase—alive till
the present day.

One final thought regarding the role of the audience in the creation of
catchphrases. I have focused on viewers as private individuals in this discussion,
but there is also a commercial aspect to be considered. Some catchphrases
(cf. the Castlemaine XXXX example, above) originated in the world of marketing,
but commercial organizations can also, in their own discourse, exploit the
resonances of catchphrases originating elsewhere, for instance, in product
names and other branding strategies. The idea of messages "self-destructing"
after a set period of time has been developed recently for SMS (text) messages on
mobile phones (messages disappear from the recipient's phone 30 seconds after
delivery). The company responsible used the *Mission: Impossible* link in their
promotions.[7]

DISCUSSION

This chapter has focused on drama dialogue from the perspective of the audience. It has shown that dialogue can be used as a point of entry from which to
explore complex configurations of comprehension, appreciation, critique, and
appropriation in viewers' relations with a particular set of semiotic cultural
objects, while recognizing that the textual genres that viewers use in displaying
those relations are themselves mediations of social identities and social relationships within the viewing public.

When viewers write about TV shows, they sometimes mention the dialogue
and/or display what it is that bits of dialogue have meant for them. This meaning
may be appropriated "naively" by writer-viewers, within the parameters of naturalistic conventions, or the interactional context and genre—blog, review, thread,
and so forth—with its attendant social relations, may help to elicit something
more attentive to underlying authorial and production strategies. Both of these
dispositions are respectful, even when they involve criticism of the production, in
the sense that they relate to the dramatic discourse on its own terms. By contrast,
when viewers remember and use lines such as "I'm waving at fat" for purposes
other than recounting or evaluating the original program, this respect has
begun to dissipate. By the time that lines of drama dialogue have joined other
cultural catchphrases, the narrative context(s) of the original use are of very little

significance, although the indexical link of such expressions back to the program may be meaningful as the expression of a cultural bond.

The object of this chapter was to explore and map the modes of engagement that viewers have with dialogue in TV drama: the attention they give to character speech and what they think it means in context. Viewers of all kinds—critics, fans, ordinary viewers, wannabe writers—can all be said to *use* dialogue in two different but related senses. First, they allow dialogue to influence their compre-hension/interpretation of the text itself. Such uses do not have to be verbalized—they are essentially cognitive. But viewers who do discuss TV shows produce texts of their own that offer clues about their own cognitive processes, as when they metacommunicatively refer to shows "dropping hints" that they have (dutifully) noted.

Second, audiences use dialogue in relation to their own social relationships and social interaction. Talk about TV faces two ways: it faces "back" to the show, and records aspects of what happened in the text/viewer encounter; and it faces forward, into the relationships that viewers have with one another, in which the TV shows are their common ground. These are different kinds of relationships. The relations between professional reviewers and their readers take place within a commercial communication matrix—the review is another kind of product for the consumption of a paying audience (even when advertising mitigates the sense of direct monetary transaction). In online discussions there is greater scope for relations to be negotiated, as fans come together to share their appreci-ation and possibly exercise influence over the shows they enjoy, whereas less committed viewers at least find others who have seen what they have seen and heard what they have heard. In all of these cases, dialogue is a resource. Lines can be cited in evidence of a particular interpretation, they can be criticized as unsatisfactory in a range of different ways, quoted as tribute to the pleasure they has provided, and remembered, as catchphrases, in sustaining a sense of com-munity with others who remember them too.

6

Dialogue as Social Interaction

LANGUAGE IN SOCIAL INTERACTION

One of the functions of language in everyday life is the management of social relationships in face-to-face interaction. People talk to one another, and as they do so they adjust their expressions to display their understanding of previous contributions, to fit in or stand out, to convey deference or dominance, to form bonds of solidarity or resist and challenge such bonds, within the scope of contextual constraints, their own repertoires of performance, and their interactional goals in terms of sharing information and cocoordinating action. Sociolinguistics has long been interested in language use from this perspective, and has developed a variety of concepts, theories, and approaches for exploring this territory. Not all social relationships are constituted through directly interpersonal face-to-face conduct, so these approaches have their limitations. A perspective grounded in the ethnography of communication (cf. Hymes 1972) is wide enough to encompass not only this kind of interaction but also more attenuated relationships conducted over time and/or at a distance. The relationships between TV dramatists and their audiences are of this more attenuated kind, without the opportunities that interpersonal face-to-face encounters provide for ongoing immediate mutual influence. This chapter does address the dramatist-audience relationship, but it focuses primarily on how dramatists display the relations of characters in their imagined direct interactions, drawing on interactional sociolinguistic approaches for this purpose.

Sociolinguistic perspectives on interaction direct attention toward speakers' calculation of what the relationship needs, what it will bear, and what they themselves are credibly capable of producing. Calculations regarding the interactional dynamics of a company board meeting will be very different from those regarding the dynamics of pillow talk. Not all speakers will have the cultural capital, not to mention the sociolinguistic performance skills, to carry off a "chairperson" identity in the former. Speaker strategy (for want of a better word) is only part of the picture. The other part is hearer response, because whatever that strategy may be, and however consciously adopted, speakers

cannot ultimately dictate what aspects of their utterances hearers may be sensitive to, and orient to, in their responses. The most politely formulated request
for help, if expressed in an obviously foreign accent, is not proof against
racist or xenophobic prejudice on the part of a hearer. Wordings, too, can
have interpersonal significance beyond anything that a speaker can plan for.
A degree of mutual goodwill is therefore necessary for interlocutors who want
to manage these interpretative hazards cooperatively, though such cooperation is
not part of all talk. Some relationships can be obstinately uncooperative, with
speakers using their turns to obstruct and frustrate each other's communicative
efforts. This should not be taken as a denial of the more fundamental cooperative
basis of talk as such, in the Gricean sense, in which cooperation is a condition of
intelligibility of both helpful and difficult talk.

Represented talk—in other words, dialogue—whether in novels, plays,
films, or TV dramas, is, like its real-world analogue, more or less coded
and calculated for interpersonal effect. Social encounters are not just events
in the realization of story structures, but also moments in the characters'
relationships with one another. Characters can be shown to adjust their
modes of expression depending on whom they are talking to, to be more or
less articulate, more or less equipped to cope with particular interactional
circumstances, and more or less in control of how the interaction unfolds
and of the outcomes that result from it. These displays are crafted, whether by
instinct or by more conscious awareness of what sorts of things are possible
(cf. chapter 4), from the same resources that are generally available to language
users.

In relationship-based productions (such as soap opera) this interpersonal
significance is in the foreground, whereas in action-led work (e.g., thrillers)
it is in the background. Screenwriters have to understand, subconsciously
or otherwise, the kind of interactional work that can be performed
through talk in order to produce dialogue that displays comparable properties.
Actors and directors too must appreciate what can, interpersonally speaking,
be *meant* when dialogue is realized in performance, and not just what is to
be said.

The primary function of general communicative resources, like the cooperative principle, or turn-taking rules, or metalanguage, is to underwrite the intelligibility of dialogue in drama, and ensure that it is credible, within generic
constraints, as a surrogate for speech in real life. But such resources can also
be exploited to produce dialogue that is creative or playful (function 8 in Sarah
Kozloff's typology: see chapter 3). They can also contribute to the creation of a
drama's thematics (function 9 in the same typology). When appropriate, I will
draw attention to examples of this kind too—if only to avoid the assumption that
the rules and conventions of language use are important to drama on TV only
insofar as they relate to its pursuit of realism.

SOCIOLINGUISTIC NAIVETY

When we, as researchers, write about dialogue as social interaction, we tend to treat the characters as if they were actual people, with communicative intentions as part of their mental lives, variously expressing "their" thoughts and emotions, and negotiating "their" social relationships. Other functions of dialogue, such as anchorage and exposition (see chapter 3), tied more to the real communicative intentions of the dramatist than to the virtual ones of the characters, fade into the analytic background.[1]

There is nothing wrong with this mode of analysis, as long as it is treated as offering only a partial perspective on the language of drama. When realist and naturalist writers and directors have nurtured the transparency and easy listening effects (see chapter 1), the naive stance is congruent with the dramatic intentions. It can have the unfortunate effect of suggesting that the analyst has simply accepted the transparency effect at face value, however sophisticated the sociolinguistic apparatus in its deployment of Gricean pragmatics, conversation analysis, or politeness theory.

Table 6.1 presents a short and fairly unremarkable extract from Britain's long-running soap opera *Coronation Street* (BBC 1960–present), to illustrate the strengths and weaknesses of this orientation. I have tabulated the dialogue to provide parallel indication of shot sequences.

Narrative Context

Jason (Ryan Thomas) and Sarah (Tina O'Brien) are young newlyweds, recovering from a ceremony that went awry because Sarah's younger half-brother David (Jack P. Shepherd) apparently attempted suicide and then her wedding dress was destroyed. Brother and sister are on bad terms; husband and wife are on awkward terms. Gail (Helen Worth) is the mother of Sarah and David; Audrey (Sue Nicholls) is Gail's mother and thus Sarah's grandmother. Audrey runs a hair salon where both Sarah and David work. The five of them are in Gail's house at the start of the day. This studio scene is configured to represent an open-plan living area in the small house.

In narrative terms, the point of the scene is David's negotiation of his return to work in the salon, along with some display of the current configuration of relations between characters: Sarah's annoyance with Jason and his somewhat irritated supplication for the return of her goodwill, Audrey and Gail's concern for David, and David's low-key tolerance of this, along with his determination to be independent. The scene moves through 15 discrete shots, varying in length from 1 second (some of the close-ups) to 18 seconds (the initial establishing shot), for a total scene length of around 1½ minutes. The longer takes tend not to be static, but allow for some camera movement, tracking along with character

Table 6.1 Domestic Life Dialogue in *Coronation Street*

	Lines	Shots
1	J: Well how many times can I say I'm sorry? [pause] All right, yes, I was an idiot for leaving the dress in Roy's. But someone else took it, not me.	SHOT 1 (Establishing), 18 seconds, turns 1–7. JASON, SARAH, AUDREY, GAIL
2	S: Yes, so you keep saying.	
3	J: Please, babe.	
4	S: See you later.	
5	G: See you love.	
6	A: I'll be over now sweetheart.	
7	J: Well, wait up.	
	SILENCE	JASON AND SARAH LEAVE
8	A: When are you going back in?	SHOT 2, 9 seconds, turns 8–11. GAIL AND AUDREY ONLY
9	G: Oh I don't want to leave him on his own. Not yet anyway.	
10	A: How is he?	
11	G: Well he's not his usual self.	
12	A: Hah, huh, well you say that like it's a bad thing, that.	SHOT 3, 4 seconds, turn 12
		D enters off-camera ready for shot 4.
13	G: Hello sweetheart. Want some breakfast?	SHOT 4, 4 seconds, turns 13–14. GAIL, AUDREY, DAVID
14	D: No. Not really hungry to be honest.	
15	A: Oh, you should have something David.	SHOT 5, 1 second, turn 15
16	G: I'll put some toast on. You hardly ate yesterday.	SHOT 6, 7 seconds, turns 16–18
17	A: How are you feeling?	
18	D: Well I'm not ill, gran=	

19	A: =No, I know=	SHOT 7, 2 seconds, turns 19–20
20	G: =Stop badgering him mam.	SHOT 8, 5 seconds, turns 20–22
21	A: No, I just asked how he was.	
22	D: Well I'm fine, OK? I'm not going to stick my head in a microwave.	SHOT 9, 1 second, turn 22
	PAUSE	
23	Uh, I were wondering if, maybe I could come back to work or something?	SHOT 10, 2 seconds, turn 22
24	G: Oh I'm not sure that's a good idea.	SHOT 11, 3 seconds, turn 22
25	D: But I'm all right. There's nothing wrong with me.	SHOT 12, 9 seconds, turns 23–25
26	A: Actually Gail, you know that might not be such a bad idea to help get back to normal. I mean, maybe just part-time to begin with, eh? To see how we go, right?	SHOT 13, 5 seconds, turns 25–26.
27	D: Yes, that's fine. Right I'll go jump in the shower then.	
		D LEAVES
	PAUSE	
28	A: Ah.	SHOT 14, 4 seconds, turns 26–29
29	G: Hope it's not too much for him.	
30	A: It's a hair salon G, not a fire station. Hhh. Mind you, I don't relish having to tell S. See you later.	SHOT 15, 8 seconds, turn 29.
	SILENCE	

Source: Broadcast November 7, 2007. Episode writing credit not available.

movement. (The preceding and following scenes are shot in different locations and with different character groupings.) The scene is designed to give the effect that the audience is being introduced to an interaction that has begun before the cameras arrived. Various aspects of language use could be examined here, including accent and dialect, disfluency, number and footing of participants, turn transition, turn selection, turn sequencing, cooperation, and indirectness. The following comments relate specifically to politeness and its management in the extract.

Politeness is often considered to be a part of pragmatics (see Leech 1983, Verschueren 1999), particularly when pragmatics is related to the study of social interaction, as well as, or in addition to, its value to the study of linguistic form and meaning. Both the expression of ideas (Gricean pragmatics) and the management of social relationships (politeness theory) have to contend with questions of directness and indirectness in talk.

The most well-known approach to politeness (Brown and Levinson 1978) proposes viewing conversation as a dangerous activity, in which the faces of both speaker and hearer are constantly at risk. These risks can be strategically mitigated, either by positive politeness behavior—compliments and the like— which enhances the face of the addressee, or by negative politeness, which is designed to avoid intruding on the addressee's personal space. Not all talk events value politeness as a good thing. Sometimes, in emergencies, for instance, interpersonal niceties take a backseat to the immediate, urgent need to coordinate action. On other occasions, one or more of the speakers is seeking the satisfaction of confrontation, purposefully seeking to offend, humiliate, and insult an interlocutor (perhaps in reciprocation for perceived insults from *them*). Brown and Levinson have been criticized for building a model of interaction wrongly designed around a normative principle of commitment to harmony in social relationships (see, e.g., Eelen 2001, Mills 2003)—with the consequence that too little attention is paid to the analysis of *im*politeness—though the literature on conflict talk and argument is certainly useful here (Grimshaw 1990a; see also chapter 7 in this volume). TV drama dialogue, arguably, goes too far in the other direction, making conflict, argument, threat, and other kinds of interpersonal discord more prominent, more overt, and more common than we experience it as being in corresponding real-life situations.

The world of the soap opera gets more than its fair share of confrontation, including confrontational talk, and there is some of that here between Jason and Sarah, albeit mild by soap standards. "Apologizing" can be remedial facework, recognizing an offense in the form of a prior face-threatening act, taking responsibility for that act, trying to restore the interlocutor's goodwill and restore the relationship to the preferred condition of mutual respect. Alternatively, it can itself be face-threatening, putting pressure on an addressee to accept the apology. Here, Jason offers a grudging formulation:

> Well how many times can I say I'm sorry? [pause] All right, yes, I was an idiot for
> leaving the dress in Roy's. But someone else took it, not me.

Jason gives redress with one hand and takes away with the other. Although he
admits that he was in the wrong, he also implies that *Sarah* is in the wrong, too,
for not accepting an apology so many times proffered.

Another participant seemingly concerned to get the facework right is David.
Later in the exchange, David has cause to make a request of his elders—he wants
to resume his job in the salon. Regular viewers of the series would readily agree
that the power differential between David and his mother and grandmother is
not usually enough to make this character deferential—but the extensive amount
of hedging in his formulation seems to be a sign of deference here. As Gail says
in turn 11, David "is not his usual self": but as Audrey suggests in turn 12, this
"other" self may be a nicer one. The conversation with David that follows these
exchanges confirms this commentary, displaying the new David as a "politer,"
more tractable youth than viewers have become accustomed to, by making him
hesitate and hedge his request—"I were wondering . . . ." David's request to come
back to work is, if not an imposition in the usual sense, at least a request that he
is willing to treat as more than a formality. His attempted suicide is an important
piece of mutual knowledge for the purposes of this encounter and the terms on
which it is managed, because he knows, and the women know, that it gives them
a possible reason for rejecting the request. The politeness helps him to achieve
his goal, and may lead viewers to conclude that the "usual" David, who rarely
shows anything but disrespect for these matriarchs, is strategically standing
behind the "polite" David and animating him, thus manipulating the women
into cooperation. If David here is a doubled being, the polite, deferential persona
being the creation of a less well-intentioned one, this does not rule out the
possibility that the latter, too, can be taken as a persona, that of the adolescent
(from a broken home, and with a chaotic family history) who, powerless in other
ways, "acts out"—in spite of his "real," better self—so as to impress himself upon
the world. Tension between soap's melodramatic and its realist impulses are
strongly indicated here, though we are probably at the limit of what can be
claimed about the meanings of dialogue without reference to audience uptake.

Throughout this analysis it has been convenient to adopt a sociolinguistically
naive stance, and refer to what "Jason" does, and what "David" does—what they
say, what they mean, what they think. This stance is possible because of what the
scriptwriters have given us, and what Ryan Thomas and Jack P. Shepherd, the
actors, have themselves made of those lines. The naive idiom is a useful analytic
protocol, one that allows us to make use of theoretical ideas from pragmatics, in
collusion with the fiction. The protocol does not stand in the way of more critical
approaches. It is possible to move from the naiveté of transparency readings, as
above, through to more speculative reflections on the possible interpretative

consequences of particular communication displays, or types of display. TV drama in general has always had a particular interest in domestic space and personal relationships. Soap operas like *Coronation Street* are the epitome of this domestic focus. The dramatists who write scripts for such productions are specialists in constructing, from general resources, a certain kind of interactional behavior that is appropriate to such space. Within its generic frame, the dialogue required for such encounters can be emotionally intense or comic, confrontational or solidary, sentimental or matter-of-fact. David's negotiation with his mother and grandmother is overtly matter-of-fact, though emotionally colored because of the storyline to which it belongs, including the apparent attempted suicide, with a "subtext," for want of a better word, that hinges on his self-presentation here as contrasted with his usual conduct. The underhand scheming speaks of melodrama, but the framing conventions are those of realism, as is (arguably) the social psychology. The relative weight of these two dynamics will depend on the audience.

DIALOGUE AS COMMUNICATION DISPLAY

The various branches of the sociolinguistic literature, from the ethnography of communication, through pragmatics and politeness theory, to conversation analysis and interactional sociolinguistics, are helpful in any attempt to understand and demonstrate the strategies by which particular communication displays have been dramaturgically managed—misunderstanding episodes, re-presentations of verbal offensiveness, constructions of characters as ineffective speakers—not to mention "normal," untroubled talk exchanges built to fit the settings established for them and (in the case of TV drama) partially realized visually. The next sections of this chapter will deal, in turn, with three different, sociolinguistically grounded ways of approaching this particular kind of talk—communication ethnography, pragmatics. and conversation analysis.

Communication Ethnography and the Dramatization
of Communicative Events

Drama dialogue, as suggested above, involves putting communication on display. This provides opportunities to explore imaginatively different kinds of communicative events and scenes. Dramas may be more or less ambitious in how they exploit these opportunities. The pull toward realism, and toward the generically familiar, on television are both factors liable to limit the extent of the ambition, though there will always be a range of possibilities even in quite safe productions.

Ethnographic perspectives on the uses of speech are sometimes referred to under the rubric *ethnography of speaking*. But this label is unsatisfactory in a wider perspective: speech is not a necessary component in all communicative events, nor is it always the central component when it is present. Communication using written language can also be approached ethnographically (Basso 1974). *Ethnography of communication* (Hymes 1972) has thus become the favored term. The ethnographic perspective is relevant to drama on the outer plane of the production as well as on the inner, diegetic plane in relation to depicted events and situations. On the outer plane, when we approach dramatic performances on stage, screen, or radio as culturally conditioned communication events, issues such as taboos of representation become salient, including questions of "bad language" and other taboos related to dialogue. In relation to television, nothing has been more risky in recent times than the mainstream broadcasting (in Britain) of a theatrical performance of *Jerry Springer: The Opera* (BBC 2005). *Swearwords* were a noticeable part of the show's discourse, calculatedly excessive in tribute to the American TV talk show that it parodied (in which they are generally *bleeped out*). The swearing drew attention to the production both before and after the screening, and the fact that many of the obscenities were sung, not spoken, did not seem to lessen the offense:

> The BBC has been flooded with a record number of protests after deciding to screen a show with more than 8,000 swear words.
> *Jerry Springer The Opera* includes 3,168 "F" words and 297 "C" words.
> The Beeb has had 15,000 complaints about the show, to be screened by BBC2 on Saturday at 10 P.M. And TV watchdog Ofcom has had a record 4,500 protests—also the most it has ever received. (Stewart Whittingham, *The Sun*, January 6, 2005)

On the inner plane, many different types of communicative events can in principle be dramatized and displayed, both public and private. Audiences have learned to expect that particular kinds of drama will feature particular kinds of communicative events. In police dramas, audiences will expect to see several interviews of witnesses and suspects, with police officers asking questions and interviewees answering them, or refusing to do so. Optional additional participants include the witnesses' lawyers and other police officers.

The staging of an interview or interrogation in a dramatic context is liable to be very much abbreviated compared with equivalent events in real life, though audiences may assume some ellipsis in the former. Length is not the only difference. Accounts of real-world practice include, on the one hand, an instructional literature for police officers (e.g., Inbau et al 2004; Zulawski and Wicklander 2002: very goal-oriented, while fully mindful of legal constraints on coercion, etc.), and, on the other hand, more critical academic accounts including the forensic linguistic research of Roger Shuy (1998). The emphasis in the latter readily demonstrates important differences between what dramatists need in their staged interviews and what the criminal justice system needs—for example, valid confessions, properly obtained. Some of Shuy's analyses are about delicacies of phrasing and paralinguistic features that cast doubt on interpretations of defendant speech offered in the context of a criminal prosecution. Others are about inconsistent police reports (in the absence of taped evidence) of what defendants may actually have said. Matters like this are somewhat resistant to dramatic staging, except when they carry narrative significance in their own right. But this is more likely to be the case in a courtroom drama focused on the outcome of a case, than in a police drama focused on crime and detection. In constructing a police interview as an event worthy of dramatization, the dialogue and its performance are required to display the significance of the scene for the drama either in terms of narrative development, as when an interview produces a surprise confession, or in terms of interpersonal relations, as when two officers play out a *good cop/bad cop* routine (see also chapter 6).

In hospital dramas audiences will expect to see sudden emergencies. Patients who go into cardiac arrest have to be kept alive. This calls for short, functional utterances, briskly delivered, co-coordinating the actions of the medical team. The emphasis is on speed and efficiency, with tones of panic present or absent, depending on the need to make the scene emotional or relatively cool.

Although both the police interview and the hospital emergency are both very familiar communicative events in their respective genres, they do allow for variations, according to dramatic requirements. Their length may be expanded or contracted, measured in turns; they may involve a minimum number of speaking persons (two in each case) or a larger number; they may have different outcomes in terms of information revealed or concealed, and bodies saved. Nonlinguistic choices include the length of the scene (as opposed to the length or number of speaking turns), its completeness, and its mise-en-scène.

Pragmatics and the Management of Subjectivity

Pragmatics has roots in the philosophy of language, and its point of departure is the inadequacy of *literal* meaning as a guide to the meanings of words in context. Thomas (1995: 22) defines *pragmatics* as the study of "meaning in interaction." As Cameron puts it, "Pragmatics concerns itself with the principles language users employ to determine the meaning behind words—how we get from what is said to what is meant" (2001: 48). Something equivalent to these principles will also be required to get from what is signified *non*linguistically to what such nonverbal semiotic behavior means in context. That is to say, if there is a gap between literal meaning and intended or taken meaning in respect of language use, there is also a gap between what any other semiotic *code* tells us that a nonverbal sign (e.g., a wink) means, and the meaning we attribute to any particular wink as used by a real person in an interactive situation. There is no one-to-one relationship between any given signifier and a single unambiguous meaning.

The landmark studies in the development of pragmatics include early work on the concept of *speech acts* (Austin 1962, Searle 1969), followed by important research on the universal principles of utterance interpretation by H. P. Grice (1975). Austin's concept of the speech act is the starting point because of its crucial role in undermining the distinction between *saying* and *doing*, speech and action. This distinction is obviously valid when a contrast is being drawn between saying "I'm painting a chair" and actually painting a chair. But this kind of comparison is only part of the overall picture. It overlooks the ways in which speech is, itself, a kind of behavior (and not just a mode of representation). Considered as behavior, "I'm painting the chair" is not the action of painting a chair, but it is still an action of some sort, and whatever it is will depend on who is saying it, to whom, in what circumstances, and for what effect. It may, for instance, be said by a speaker as a way of accounting for why he did not answer the phone when it rang.

Grice proposed that all interaction takes place on the basis of an assumed cooperative principle. "Make your contribution such as is required, at the stage at which it occurs, by the accepted purpose of direction of the talk exchange in which you are engaged" (Grice 1975: 45). Cooperation in this sense is not the same as cooperation in respect of the topic or the substantive business of the talk exchange. That is to say, the cooperative principle is understood here as the fundamental basis of all talk, which includes arguments and disagreements just as much as forms of talk in which speakers collaborate harmoniously. Cooperation for the Griceans is the foundation of *intelligibility* in talk. Grice went on to formulate a prescriptively worded set of maxims that spelled out what full cooperation would normatively look like. These are the well-known maxims of quantity, quality, relation, and manner. The quantity maxim specifies that speakers should produce as much information as the occasion calls for, no more, no less. The quality maxim specifies that the information should be true to the best of the speaker's knowledge. The relation maxim requires the information to be relevant, and the manner maxim requires it to be clear. In practice, as Grice knew, much talk fails to live up to these standards. But that is not the point. The point is that the maxims constituted a point of reference for a kind of calculus of communicative intention/interpretation. All coherent communicative behavior takes the cooperative principle as a given. This is an act of faith on the part of speakers and hearers in any exchange. Speakers may *appear* to have parted company with one or more of the maxims, but that very departure is motivated. When speakers are blatantly providing less information than they and the hearers both consider the occasion requires, they draw attention to their departure from the maxim of quantity, and provoke the hearer into providing some kind of rationale for this "offense." The rationale that the hearer comes up with is the indirect meaning (or "conversational implicature," in Grice's terms) of the utterance. If speaker A asks speaker B, "Is C honest and hardworking?" and speaker B replies, "C is hardworking," then, by this logic, A is entitled to assume that B is not confident in C's honesty.

The calculus here works just as long as the speaker is obviously, blatantly, at odds with the maxims. The departure from what is normatively required has to be noticeable to the hearer or else the hearer will have no reason to generate an explanatory implicature. He or she will instead take the utterance at face value. This is particularly relevant in relation to breaches of the maxim of quality. This is the maxim that enjoins truthfulness: Do not say that which you believe to be false; do not say that for which you lack adequate evidence (cf. B's inability to say "C is honest" in the scenario above). To "break the rules" in this blatant way is called *flouting* the maxims, and is communicatively cooperative. Verbal irony, for example is communicatively cooperative, despite flouting the maxim of quality. The following example comes at the start of an episode of *Law and Order* (NBC 1990–present). The exchange takes place between two police officers, called to a crime scene while the murder victim is still lying there:

1   GREEN: Looks like somebody just knocked off a street dealer.
2   BRISCOE: Yeah, what a shame.

(Season 13, episode 12, "Under God," written by Marc Guggenheim and Noah Baylin; Green is played by Jesse L. Martin and Briscoe by Jerry Orbach)

"A shame" is a very mild expression of regret for a death, and the inappropriateness of this mildness may thus constitute a violation of the relation (relevance) maxim. Alternatively, between two characters who share the belief that drug dealers are a vicious element of humanity who do not deserve to live, "a shame" is not a mild expression of regret at all but an ironically untrue statement, manifestly breaching the quality maxim and generating the implicature that this wicked man deserved to die. Nevertheless, their subsequent pursuit of the criminal case carries for the viewer indications that the speaker is not *professionally* committed to the contrary proposition that the victim deserved to die. In subtle ways like this, *Law and Order*'s dialogue realizes a disjuncture in characterization between the personal and professional self.

Another way of breaking the rules is to *violate* them. This is communicatively uncooperative. To violate the maxim of quality is to lie: to produce discourse that will not generate a true implicature but that will, instead, get the hearer to believe an untruth or at least believe that the speaker believes the untruth. If speaker B believes that C is not honest, but responds to A's question by saying, "Yes, C is honest and hardworking," B is committed to C's honesty and A has no reason, in the absence of any other information sources, to think otherwise.

In relation to naturally occurring speech, one of the concerns about how the Gricean approach, and others of a similar character such as relevance theory

(Sperber and Wilson 1986), model communication has to do with the importance attached to *states of mind* on the part of the speaker or hearer or both. As Cameron puts it, "Because we cannot read our interlocutor's minds, but can only attribute intentions, thoughts, feelings and so on, to them on the basis of what they say and do, it is problematic to treat linguistic meaning as dependent on the accurate retrieval of a speaker's intentions by a hearer" (2001: 71). The study of *lying* ought therefore to fall outside the purview of linguistic pragmatics. Lying and truth telling are indistinguishable from the interpreter's perspective. However, the existence of these two possibilities in our culture is congruent with dominant ideas regarding subjectivity, in which an inner or *private* self may be quite different from the self that is projected to other people. The *Coronation Street* extract discussed in an earlier section of this chapter demonstrated one way of dramatizing this kind of construction. Lying is just one of the ways in which selves, or subjects, may use the resources of language to keep information to themselves, to the private realm, while still participating in social interaction.

The significance of this for the study of drama dialogue is this: because of the *double discourse* of drama, any production that subscribes to the dominant view of what constitutes subjectivity will itself, via the narrative and/or via the discourse of other characters, supply its virtual people with whatever private knowledge, motivations, intentions, and so forth that the story requires them to have, and will be able to manipulate audience's access to those private realms—though not quite as easily as a novelist can. Among other things, this means that whereas it is true that in "ordinary life" we cannot know whether speaker B is lying or telling the truth when he says "Yes, C is honest" (though our access to other information sources may influence our judgments), in the context of a (realist) drama we certainly can, should it be dramatically relevant for us to know this. This includes the possibility that there will be paralinguistic and kinesic signs preceding, following, or contiguous with the false utterance that are for the benefit of the audience and not for the benefit of the fictional interlocutor. Such signs may or may not be interpretable as "leakage" on the speaker's part—signs that are inadvertently given off, in the manner of poker "tells," by those speakers, in which the audience may judge that the interlocutor could have picked them up as signs of deception, but did not. A character who cannot meet an interlocutor's gaze while telling a lie may avoid the danger of doing so by occupying themselves in some mundane task—doing the washing up, watering the plants, tidying the room. These behaviors—*business*, in theatrical parlance—might not be written into the script but instead be matters for directorial discretion or an actor's own judgment on what kind of performance would be appropriate. But truth tellers, just as much as liars, might have reason to talk and wash the dishes at the same time. Audiences will need to rely on the designed combinations of narrative context and nonverbal signs to come to some decisions about who can be trusted and to what extent.

Turn Taking and Turn Sequencing

Sociologists in the 1970s, frustrated with the logics of mainstream sociological explanation, sought to develop methods that would take seriously and seek to account for the orderliness of lived experience, on the premise that this orderliness was not in the first instance imposed from above, but was a practical accomplishment of social actors in everyday life. The orderliness of conversation, of talk, was of particular interest because of its ubiquity. *Data* in the form of audio recordings was easy to obtain in the era of light, inexpensive tape-recording equipment, and the properties of interest to such scholars were to be found in even the smallest fragments of talk exchange (though for certain purposes, large quantities of similar talk fragments proved very useful). This research was able to draw attention to many significant (and hitherto unremarked) regularities in the construction of talk exchanges, making use of such concepts as transition relevance place (TRP), adjacency pair, and preference organization.[2]

Viewed in the light of this approach, the 100% hindsight possessed by writers, directors, and actors of screen dialogue, which is an advantage in terms of narrative production, is a denial of talk's very essence as emergent, coconstructed social order. Any dialogue scene that ends with a character "unexpectedly" bursting into tears was written, all along, to produce just that ending, and is directed and performed appropriately. The contrived talk, nevertheless, has to help foster the illusion of emergence and coconstruction. The crying has to come across to the audience like a spontaneous and unplanned but plausible, motivated, response to what precedes it. What precedes it will, of course, also have been written, directed, and performed to make crying plausibly "unexpected" as a response to what went before.

Audiences have been taught to accept dialogue scenes on these mimetic terms. The twists and turns of a talk exchange through self and other correction, insertion, and side sequences, preferred and dispreferred responses, skip connections, and so on may require them only to follow the utterance-by-utterance progression of the talk on the basis of the same constructional resources that they themselves use in spontaneous talk.

But these same constructional resources support more than just ability to comprehend the moves being made in a conversational exchange. They also help to support more playful and/or aesthetic communicative and interactive effects. For example, in comedies, one recurrent device involves extended sequences of skip connecting, in which each character in effect pursues his or her own monologue, without reference to the intercut speaking turns of the other character. This may have been formally creative once, but has become tired with repetition. It has, however, given rise to variations, such as the following short sequence from an episode of the successful American sitcom *Friends* (NBC 1994–2004).

Monica and Chandler (Courteney Cox Arquette and Matthew Perry), who are friends with one another in 4 of the show's 10 seasons, lovers for another 3, and a married couple in the rest, are in bed together. Monica is upset because Phoebe indicated that, were she lesbian, she would prefer Rachel as a girlfriend over Monica. Chandler is upset because he thinks he invented a joke that Ross has taken credit for and published in a magazine.

1 MONICA: She picked Rachel. I mean, she tried to back out of it, but it was obvious. She picked Rachel.
2 CHANDLER: He took my joke, he took it.
3 MONICA: It's wrong. You know what else is wrong? Phoebe picking Rachel.
4 CHANDLER: You know who else picked Rachel? Ross, and you know what else Ross did? He stole my joke. You know what? I'm going to get a joke journal. Y'know? And document the date and time of every single one of my jokes.
5 MONICA: That's a good idea.
6 CHANDLER: Yeah!
7 MONICA: Do you know what's a bad idea?
8 CHANDLER: Picking Rachel.
9 MONICA: That's right.

(Season 6, episode 12, "The One with the Joke," written by Andrew Reich and Ted Cohen)

The start of the conversation in turns 1 and 2 may suggest to the audience that it can expect a fairly standard (in sitcom) skip-connection routine. There is no thematic connection between what Monica says and what Chandler says, and they are not looking at one another as they take turns. But what actually occurs, from line 3 on, is more formally creative than that—and it also manages, as a bonus, to remain faithful to the dynamics of the relationship between the two characters. Each of the participants, in turns 3 and 4, uses that turn both to indicate (perfunctorily) an interest in the other's topic, and to shift topics. In turn 2, Chandler complains about Ross's plagiarism; in turn 3, Monica agrees that this is wrong. But having thus obtained the floor, she puts it to use in shifting the topic back to her issue. This pattern is repeated in turn 4, and, in more attenuated form, for the sake of variation, across turns 5–7. The topic is then rather than abruptly switched, by playing with semantic patterns to propose a connection between the two topics. The connection at turn 3 is one of similarity. The joke theft and Phoebe's preference are both "wrong" things. The connection at turn 4 has more stages. The first stage treats "picking Rachel" to be the connectable device introduced by Monica—the *given* information, in textual terms. "Ross" is the new information because he, too, "picked Rachel" as a girlfriend. The second stage draws from this the predicate "Ross did x" and treats that as given information. "Stole my joke" is then introduced as the new information—these are both "things done by Ross." In both transitions, there is a question-and-answer sequence, with the speaker answering his/her own question. In the third transition, in which the relationship is one of contrast rather than of similarity, between "good" and "bad" ideas, Monica does not have to answer her own question. She gets Chandler to answer it, and this time, although he manages to perform the collaborative, other-oriented part of the routine, he holds back on the more self-centered contribution: he does not attempt another topic shift. This can be seen as a characteristic deferral to Monica: their relationship, which becomes a romantic/sexual one at the end of series 4, is one in which it is more usual for Monica to "win" any contests they may have. This is made explicit later in the series as they prepare for their wedding:

1 MONICA: We're going to Las Vegas to see your dad. It's time you two talked, and I want to get to know my father-in-law.
2 CHANDLER: Y'know we already went over this and I won!
3 MONICA: No you didn't. Oh and honey just so you know, now that you're marrying me, you don't get to win anymore.

   [. . .]

1 CHANDLER: So I really never get to win anymore?
2 MONICA: Ah, how much did you ever really win before?

(Season 7, episode 22, "The One with Chandler's Dad," written by Brian Buckner and Sebastian Jones)

Hearings

This subheading relates back to a point made at the start of the chapter: whatever a speaker's strategy may be, and however consciously adopted, speakers cannot ultimately dictate what aspects of their utterances hearers may be sensitive to and orient to in their responses. The discrete subjectivities of speaker and hearer create at every juncture an *uptake gap*—and there are limits on how far participants can prepare themselves for the negotiation of this gap. Conversation analysis has shown how participants display, in their own contributions, their interpretations, or "hearings," of what has gone before. Among the meanings that participants can respond to in this way we must include errors, unintended humor, and unintended insults. Such meanings, for their producer, are tangential to the main through line of the talk. They can arguably be said not to exist *unless* they are explicitly attended to, and thus heard, in subsequent contributions.

Questions arise, however, about the influence of unacknowledged meaning on the conduct of talk. Accent convergence or divergence, for example, seemingly requires no explicit recognition, or even consciousness, of speaker identity, yet the phenomenon whereby speakers adjust their pronunciation to sound more like an interlocutor they feel solidarity with, or less like an interlocutor they are at odds with, is well established.[3] A speaker might refrain from drawing attention to a persistent malapropism in an interlocutor's speech, and even go so far as to use the malapropism herself, rather than substitute the correct word and risk insulting the speaker's linguistic knowledge. Alongside the influence or lack of influence of such meanings on the conduct of the talk, there may also be influence as regards impression formation. A speaker with a large repertoire of malapropisms is subjectively marked as lacking in education by a more educated interlocutor, though not by one who is at a similar or lower educational level.

In the context of multiparty and public talk, scripted or otherwise, unacknowl-edged meaning cannot be wholly dismissed as unreal. Audiences (I include here overhearers and eavesdroppers as well as nonspeaking but ratified participants) may notice and be affected by meanings that speaking participants (choose to) ignore.

In a multiparty conversation, when one speaker takes the floor from another in accordance with turn-taking rules, all other speakers are shut out. This includes any who had attempted or contemplated a contribution of their own at that point. Lost, in consequence, is the sequential relevance of whatever such shut-out contributions might have had on the progress of the talk.

The artificiality of scripted, performed dialogue has a lot to do with its lack of interest in either the shutting out of participants or in conversational roads not taken. All that is required is that the dialogue and/or its performance does not subvert the principles that, in real life, produce interactive speech in which things do go unsaid and unnoticed, and in which participants have routinely tried and failed to make their voices heard.

Imagine a scene set in a lingerie factory. British readers might like to think of "Underworld"—a factory in the fictional town of Weatherfield in which the soap opera *Coronation Street* is set. One of the factory workers is a cast regular— "Janice Battersby" (played by Vicky Entwhistle). But scenes in this location call for other bodies on screen beside hers to represent the workforce. The factory boss calls out for "someone" to lock up. The plot needs Janice to be that someone. It does not offend the principles of interaction if Janice now speaks, volunteering herself for this chore. Yet any member of the workforce could in principle have offered, and the rules of interaction at this point provide for any or all of the potential volunteers to indicate their offer through speech or otherwise. Dramat-ically speaking, of course, no one is interested in the other "possible" volunteers, not even them.

The proposition that dramatic dialogue should not overtly contravene the rules for naturally occurring talk-in-interaction is not an absolute one. In comedic contexts the subversion of these conventions may be the device on which the humor relies, as in a classic British comedy sketch, parodying the TV quiz show *Mastermind* (readers are invited to follow my example and locate this clip on YouTube using keywords "the two Ronnies" and "mastermind").

1 QUIZMASTER (RONNIE BARKER): And so to our first contender. Good evening. Your
   name please?
2 CONTESTANT SMITHERS (RONNIE CORBETT): Good evening.
3 Q: Last time, your chosen subject was answering questions before they were asked.
   This time you have chosen to answer the question before last each time, is that
   correct?
4 S: Charlie Smithers.
5 Q: And your time starts now. What is paleontology?
6 S: Yes, absolutely correct.
7 Q: What's the name of the directory which lists members of the peerage.
8 S: A study of old fossils.
9 Q: Correct. Who are Len Murray and Sir Geoffrey Howe?
10 S: Burke's.
11 Q: Correct. What is the difference between a donkey and an ass?
12 S: One's a trade union leader, the other is a member of the Cabinet.
13 Q: Correct. Complete the quotation "To be or not to be. . . . "
14 S: They're both the same.

(Episode from 1980, writing credit not available)

The question in turn 3, "What's the name of the directory which lists members of the peerage?" has as the correct answer "Burke's"—which Corbett/
Smithers duly delivers not in turn 4 but in turn 6, as required by the self-imposed
rule of this encounter. Meanwhile, in turn 4, he gives a correct answer to the
question asked in turn 1—"a study of old fossils." The humor comes from the
unwanted but inescapable relevance of turn 4 to turn 3, on the basis that the
British peers of the realm can indeed be metaphorically viewed as "old fossils."
Despite the introduction of a new rule of talk, just for this encounter, the
coexistence of the standard conventions is absolutely necessary for the humor
to work.

Meanwhile, within the bounds of normal talk conventions and for dramatic as
well as comedic purposes, characters may be required to do the following:

1. To hear meanings that other characters intend them to hear, directly
   or indirectly expressed
2. Not to hear meanings that other characters intend them to hear—to
   "miss the point"
3. To hear meanings that other characters do not intend them to
   hear—to "read between (or over, or under) the lines"

The third option here can be understood as a matter of unintended consequence—the malapropism that signifies "uneducated," the Freudian slip that
signifies a guilty thought, the foreign accent that signifies origins. In the following exchange, from the series 24 (Fox 2001–present), season 5, episode 1, Wayne
Palmer (D. B. Woodside) and ex-president David Palmer (Dennis Haysbert), who
are brothers, are discussing David's memoirs. Wayne hears silence from David

when it was his turn to speak (line 1). Not only does Wayne hear this silence as "distraction" (line 9), he also hears it as part of a pattern of distraction, the latest instance in a sequence. David's explanation (line 10) will later be shown to be a smokescreen. David, seconds before his assassination, was harboring an explosive political secret that he could not disclose to Wayne.

1 WAYNE: You didn't hear a word I just said, did you?
2 DAVID: Yeah, I was listening.
3 WAYNE: No you weren't.
4 DAVID: You're right, I'm sorry.
5 WAYNE: Are you OK?
6 DAVID: I could use a break.
7 WAYNE: What's going on?
8 DAVID: What do you mean?
9 WAYNE: I mean, you've been distracted ever since you got to Los Angeles. I don't know—it's like you're somewhere else.
10 DAVID: Writing my memoirs—maybe it's put me in a melancholy mood.

(Season 5, episode 1, "7.00–8.00 A.M.," written by Howard Gordon)

There is a difference between a scenario like this, in which a character is confronted with an aspect of meaning that he or she did not intend, and one in which only the audience is shown that a listening character has heard something unintended from a speaking character's talk.

In the following exchange from an episode of *CSI* (CBS 2000–present), our hero Gil Grissom (William Petersen) seems to "read" the other character, Dominic Kretzker (Stephen Lee), as simple-minded (he cares too much about the correct spelling of his name; he is too sycophantic), or guilty (his knowledge about bombs is quasi-professional), or both. But Grissom does not treat Kretzker as a suspect to his face. Instead, he panders to Dominic's "wannabe" display and offers him a role as an assistant on the case. Lest there be any doubt, his comment to Catherine (Marg Helgenberger) after the encounter colloquially says it all, for the audience's benefit as well as hers:

1 KRETZKER: Mr. Grissom. Oh, uh...hi, I've...I've, um, I've seen you on TV before. I admire your work.
2 GRISSOM: Well, thank you. And your name is?
3 KRETZKER: Uh, Dominic, with an "I-C" rather than with the "I-C-K"...uh, Kretzker. I'm the, uh, Hansen Building Security Detail.
4 GRISSOM: Did somebody from homicide talk to you yet?
5 KRETZKER: Yeah. As a matter of fact, they said that I was going to be talking to you, because, well, we are...you know, we're both in law enforcement, and...[...]
6 GRISSOM: Well, I mean, realistically, what could you have done?
7 KRETZKER: Well, I know a lot about bombs. You know, pipe, power, powder. The three "Ps" of mass destruction.
8 GRISSOM: Huh. Dominic...with an "I-C," not "I-C-K"...

9 KRETZKER: Yes sir?

10 GRISSOM: Would you be interested in helping me in my investigation?

11 KRETZKER: Are you serious? (*he chuckles.*) Yeah. Yes, sir. I'd be honored, sir. Oh. But we
   can't tell anybody on the day shift, though because they're going to get real jealous.

12 GRISSOM: That's good thinking [. . .] Would you excuse me a minute?

13 KRETZKER: Yes.

14 GRISSOM TO OFFICER: Keep an eye on that guy.

15 OFFICER: All right.

16 KRETZKER (TO HIMSELF): Oh, yeah!

17 GRISSOM (TO CATHERINE): Well, we got a live one out there. I got a cop
   baby-sitting him. How you doing?

(Season 1, episode 13, "Boom," written by Josh Berman, Ann Donahue, and Carol Mendelsohn)

Talk about Talk

As the *24* example above shows, it may be the case that when speakers produce
hearings of previous contributions that orient to unintended aspects of meaning,
they shift from *language* to *metalanguage*, from communication to metacommunication (Jaworski et al. 2004). In this case, Wayne Palmer metalinguistically refers to
the meaning of David Palmer's silence, for which there was no intended communicative effect on David's part. This kind of metalanguage is concerned with the
management and negotiation of meaning in talk and, as Cameron has said, is an
essential communicative resource, without which no kind of recognizably human
interaction would be possible: "Metalinguistic resources are necessary to allow
language to function as the extremely flexible means of communication we know
it to be. Without such resources we would be reduced to the level of Wittgenstein's
builders, able only to exchange a limited set of predetermined messages (and with
no recourse if the communication happened to fail)" (Cameron 2004: 312). To this
extent, therefore, we should not be surprised to find that human interaction as
displayed in dramatic works would also involve the staging of strategies that involve
metacommunication. The *24* example is a mundane instance of this, scarcely
noticeable as such because of its essentially realist grounding. Someone with
more important things on his mind finds it hard to pay attention to the business
at hand, and an interlocutor notices and comments on this.

But television drama is by no means restricted to the staging of metacommunication of this basic sort. Elsewhere in the repertoire of possibilities it is possible
to find rather more creative and expressive deployment of metalanguage in
dialogue. Notable in this respect is *The West Wing* (NBC 1999–2007). This series,
as I have argued elsewhere (Richardson 2006), makes use of metacommunication to a marked degree. Prospective and retrospective discussion of talk performances are a staple feature of the show. To an extent this would be expected in a
series with this particular subject matter: the behind-the-scenes world of White

House politics. In real life and in fiction, the publicness of politics is understood as itself necessarily "staged"—and much political action takes place in the public domain. But the staging of politics presupposes stagers—agents who take responsibility for performance, who prepare it before the event and explain it after the event. Preparation takes place "offstage," and in *The West Wing* it is the speech and behavior in the off-stage realm that is the primary object of dramatization.

The extent and character of the metacommunication (which is metasemiotic rather than narrowly metalinguistic) in *The West Wing*, however, goes beyond the basic requirement of keeping faith with the realities of political life. It seems to have an additional, expressive function within the dramatic project of the series. The expressive function, as I read it, has to do with recruiting audiences to a positive and sympathetic view of the characters in this world—the president and his immediate aides. Thanks to the humor, and the wit, which underlies much of this metacommunicative discourse, we come to appreciate that the characters are smart, but also self-mocking and self-critical as occasion demands. We know from their actions that they are nobly well-intentioned. The combined characteristics that they thus display operate to counteract a widespread prejudice that audiences might be expected to hold—that these people, who are essentially *spin doctors*, are thus necessarily engaged in corrupt, deceitful work. In addition, the metacommunicative commentaries of these characters provide added appeal for the educated audience that this show seeks to attract.

DISCUSSION

I have suggested in this chapter that sociolinguists start from a position of strategic naiveté when they use pragmatic and other theories to explain the interactive conduct of speakers as if they were real people and not simulacra. I have also tried to justify this approach on the grounds that it works with the grain of what dramatists and their collaborators are trying to achieve, making explicit some of the interpretative work that is entailed in understanding the drama on its own terms. A secondary aspect of this justification is that the naive approach understands well enough that it *is* naive, that it is a strategy of interpretation that can be recast in more sophisticated terms through periodic reminders that the meanings thus derived have actually been put there by the dramatists and not by the characters.

As chapter 5 showed, actual viewers (at least those who produce their own texts on the basis of their viewing experiences) do not limit themselves to naive interpretations of characters and their interactive behavior. They frequently and variously address themselves to the construction of the text as a cultural product, telling each other, for instance, not what "Donna Noble" and "The Doctor" said to one another, but what Russell T. Davies as a writer and Catherine Tate as an actress are trying to put across in this respect to the audience. Strategic, analytic naiveté, developed as a scholarly method, thus runs the risk of seeming to be *less* clued in to the nature of dramatic discourse than viewers in general are. Caveats about the "real" source of the interactional meaning may seem rather gestural in this context. More important, though, viewers and sociolinguistic scholars alike, to the extent that they do sidestep one kind of innocence, arguably fall prey to another: the innocence of attributing meaning to an auteur of some sort when an important dynamic of critical theory in the last half-century has been to resist this auteurist model of meaning production through texts.

Seen from this perspective, there is another possible defense of the "original sin" of reading characters as people and crediting them with the mental states appropriate to the lines they exchange with one another. Our own everyday interactional behavior regularly includes encounters in which the consequences may be serious and/or the utterances are hearably unclear, ambiguous, indeterminate, or otherwise *difficult*. These are circumstances that push us into more than usually self-conscious work on the interpretation of our exchanges with other people, including remedial metalanguage: "What are you getting at?" "What's that supposed to mean?" and so forth. In such cases there will often be an experience of never *really* knowing why someone else said what they said, what they might have meant by it, what degree of intentionality to attribute to it, and how far to examine it for indirect meanings, both intended and unintended. If it is important for analysts and critics to appreciate the inconclusiveness/indeterminacy of all textual meaning, then a reading strategy that starts out as naively character-based may be a more satisfactory route to that appreciation than the superficially more sophisticated auteurist strategy. To focus on a real person, whether Shakespeare, Dennis Potter, or Russell T. Davies, is, misguidedly, to keep alive the hope of conclusive answers. To focus on the simulacra is to have an easily accessible reminder that "they" could never have intended anything.

What this chapter has also shown is that the conventions by which TV dramatists produce dialogue that is acceptable on generically conditioned terms as simulated talk are also capable of producing effects that go beyond the requirements of credible simulation, or diverge from those requirements. Even the highly artificial sociolinguistic patterning of the Barker/Corbett *Mastermind* sketch is possible only as a conscious and explicit manipulation of the normal and well-founded principle that question-and-answer is a coconstructed *adjacency pair* whose unity can be disrupted only in certain well-governed ways. *The West Wing*'s efforts to ensure goodwill toward its spin doctors give thematic purpose to the extensive displays of metalanguage and metacommunication that its characters deploy in the course of "business-as-usual" behind the scenes of American political life.

7

Dialogue, Character, and Social Cognition

All drama is in the business of creating and sustaining characters. In the realistic and naturalistic dramatic modes favored by television, audiences expect to read characters as *people*, to impute meaning to their behavior and their speech as they do to the behavior and speech of their real-life acquaintances. Writers, actors, and directors exert effort toward feeding and satisfying those expectations, and audiences who collaborate with these efforts are willing to take the embodied utterances they hear from the screen as signs of underlying identities, along with attitudes, stances, values, beliefs that may vary with the relationships and situations that characters are confronted with in the course of the story. Audiences are able to perform these interpretative tasks thanks to the considerable amounts of social knowledge they possess, derived from their prior experiences of real people and other fictional characters. The creativity of this process is thus very much a question of what dramatists feel able to assume regarding that social knowledge, and how they choose to engage with this.

READING FOR CHARACTER

The interpretation of characters and the interpretation of *people* are not identical processes. Impressions formed when real people are being assessed are normatively treated as meanings *given off* (Goffman 1959), by-products of their actions, rather than impressions consciously *given* by those people. From this normative and innocent perspective, when we surmise that someone talking to us is, for instance, distressed, Italian, and suffering from a cold, it is not because he has told us these things in so many words, or even because he wants us to know them, but because we assume, in the absence of any evidence to the contrary, that he is not conscious of, or not concerned enough to control, the indexical signs (including aspects of speech) that permit these guesses to be made. From a narrowly communicative perspective, however, they are optional inferences on our part.

Goffman showed that all speakers engage in the routine *manipulation* of meanings supposedly "given off"—with some risk to face, should the manipulation be detected, and construed in moral terms as a kind of attempted deception. This possibility of moral judgment arises only if the manipulation is covertly managed, not if it is explicit, and certainly not if it is framed as *play*. In a nonserious framing, it can contribute to the texture of everyday discourse, with speakers *putting on* identities to entertain, amuse, and enlighten one another. Drama, in this perspective, is just the most official and formalized framing possibility. And the acquiescent viewers of a dramatic performance know that they *should*, in this context, pay attention to the *indexical* signs, that this is a requirement for successful engagement with the production.

If a stranger on a train asks me if the adjacent seat is free, an expectation is created, and my subsequent behavior, linguistic and nonlinguistic, will be interpreted in the light of that expectation. If I do *nothing*, it will be a meaningful *nothing* in this context. My orientation to the communicative purpose of the utterance is required, or some account for the absence of such an orientation. One possible account is that I did not hear the question. My not-hearing is a meaningful moment in this scenario, albeit one engendered through me, rather than by me as an agent.

If I do hear the request, I may inwardly react to the speaker as being rude, polite, or neither, as well as reflect on what his clothes, speech, body language, and so forth "say" about him. His performance of the question and my performance of a response are publicly accountable also in terms of social norms of politeness and respect. But *person perception* (the term used in social psychology for this kind of assessment), which is ubiquitous, and consequential for social relations as well as the conduct of particular interactions, may go well beyond the matters that are significant for our respective performances of *politeness*. Our assessments of each other as British or foreign, straight or gay, shy or outgoing do not have the same consequences in generating accountable public performance. They take place in the background of the social encounter, possibly below the threshold of consciousness, with the communicative purpose of the event in the foreground.

In drama, these assessments become more consequential. They are subsumed by the overarching communicative event. Audiences are supposed to form character impressions in this context. The writing/performance/production is designed to promote particular impressions/inferences, even while trying to configure them as matters of background meaning, in the relations between the characters themselves, to accommodate the lateral and projective dimensions/axes of the discourse context (Herman 1995) or the embedded discourse structure (Short 1996).

Consider the case of the character "Philippa Morecroft" in Victoria Wood's situation comedy of the late 1990s, *dinnerladies* (BBC 1998–2000). The first episode of the series engages the British viewers' understanding of social class differences in contemporary Britain. Philippa (played by Celia Imrie) is established early in that episode as southern English, lower middle class, and in a white-collar occupation. She is newly entering the working environment of a tight-knit group of northern working class women in blue-collar jobs (factory canteen workers), varying in age from young adult to near retirement, as their human resources manager—a superior status to theirs. Philippa wants to bond with these women. She has the advantage of status; they have the advantage of solidarity. Because the audience is meant to be reading for character when they watch the show, it ought to pick up on aspects of the talk that are *background* as far as the characters themselves are concerned. Philippa's posh southern accent is a contributory factor in this context, contrasting as it does with the Manchester accents of the dinnerladies themselves. Audiences witness how the latter respond to Philippa, and understand that her accent, along with her clothing, demeanor, social address, and the content/force of her utterances, have influenced them to behave as they do. The northern women are guarded, funny at her expense, and they react with scorn to some of her suggestions for fun things to do together after work or during the lunch break: "Why not Scottish country dancing?"

CHARACTERS, PERSONS, AND VOICES

Characters

Chatman (1978), among others, has put forward the view that characters in fiction are entities that come off as having a life of their own—a kind of credibility that goes beyond the functional requirements of the narrative. "Tony Soprano" does not exist as a real person. "He" does not do anything, does not say anything, and does not own anything—outside of the scenes that feature him in the show. Of course, because *The Sopranos* (HBO 1990–1997) operates within formally realist conventions, a huge amount of effort is invested in having him come off as someone who *could* exist, and this effort is rewarded whenever audiences discuss the thought processes that might have led "him" to a particular course of action, write additional scenes for their own satisfaction and that of other fans, or demand backstories.[1] It is not necessary to go so far as sending "him" birthday presents, or letters asking if "he" feels better after his illness, to be imaginatively caught up in the reality effect. All that is required is collusion with the artifice—a slightly more active mental state than mere *suspension of disbelief*. This accords with Chatman's advocacy of an "open theory of character" (1978: 119–126): "A viable theory of character should preserve openness and treat characters as autonomous beings, not as mere plot functions. It should argue that character is reconstructed by the audience from evidence announced or implicit in an original construction and communicated by the discourse, through whatever medium" (1978: 119). Chatman was arguing against the purely structural view of character in fiction (deriving from the work of such scholars as Propp, Greimas, and Northrop Frye). Chatman believed that we draw on the same resources to interpret *characters* as we do to interpret the people we meet in real life: "The same principle (of inferring character and personality) operates with new acquaintances; we read between their lines, so to speak; we form hypotheses on the basis of what we know and see; we try to figure them out, predict their actions, and so on" (1978: 118). Herman (1995: 45) talks about the fragmentary or "gapped" evidence that drama provides about the nature of the characters featured in it. Our evidence about the nature of "real people" is likewise fragmentary.

Narratives need characters, but there is no requirement that the characters should be human beings. They can be whatever imagination allows and the medium affords, though *human* nature is always the point of reference. Discussing film characters, Chatman writes the following:

> There are animated cartoons in which a completely contentless object is endowed with characterhood, that is, takes on the meaning "character" because it engages in a suitably anthropomorphic action (that is, a movement on the screen that is conceived as an instance of human movement). An example is the film by Chuck Jones called *The Dot and the Line*, whose plot runs roughly as follows: a line courts a dot, but the dot is going around with a squiggle, a sort of hip jokester. Whatever we think of the dot and the line as geometric familiars, the squiggle is surely without meaning until it moves. That is, as a drawn object projected on the screen, no one would identify it as anything but a random assemblage of swirling lines. In context, however, in its visible movement-relations with the dot and the line, it becomes a character. (1978: 25)

Television exhibits a full range of character realizations. TV characters can be full, normal human beings (*Coronation Street*, ITV 1960–present, *Desperate Housewives*, ABC 2004–present), human beings with superpowers (*Heroes*, NBC 2006–present), extraterrestrial entities (like the Daleks in *Doctor Who*, BBC 1963–present), flesh-and-blood animals (the eponymous *Mister Ed*, CBS 1961–1966, was a talking horse), cartoon animals (*Tom and Jerry*, CBS 1965–1972), cartoon humans (*The Simpsons*, Fox 1989–present), graphic shapes (BUPA commercials on British TV, in which triangles and circles conduct social lives, various channels, 2007–2008),[2] animal or human puppets ("Sooty" and "Sweep," respectively, a glove puppet panda bear and a dog from *The Sooty Show*, ITV 1968–1992, and string puppets in *Thunderbirds*, ITV 1965–1966), or material artifacts (rubber gloves in the sponsor identifications for *House*, Fox 2004–present, and on British TV as animated talking puppets).[3]

As in the Chuck Jones film, entities in a TV dramatization can come off as characters, in certain circumstances, just because they have functions in the narrative. A narrative action of some kind is performed, and the entity performing it is, by default, a character. The triangles and circles of the BUPA commercials are characters in this minimal sense. Thanks to the health insurance company, granny (a flat white circle, with a dark gray stylized "hairstyle" on top) can go to a care home while the rest of the family (a pink circle and a red triangle) take a much-needed vacation. These characters have no dialogue, but a voiceover guides our interpretation of their onscreen movements and those of the camera.

Chatman, following Barthes (1974) speaks of "the quintessence of selfhood," which in written fiction attaches to a proper name as something over and above the unification of specific character traits, and in screen fiction attaches to a visualized (but not necessarily human) form: "The proper name in this sense is precisely the identity or quintessence of selfhood property.... It may well be what Aristotle meant by *homois*. It is a kind of ultimate residence of personality, not a quality but a locus of qualities, the narrative-noun that is endowed with but never exhausted by the qualities, the narrative-adjectives" (Chatman 1978: 131).

Persons

The triangles and circles of the BUPA commercials are characters, but they are not *prototypical* characters on television.[4] Prototypical characters here have bodies as well as functions—they are dramatic persons. *Persons* may be characters or they may be extras, actors paid only to populate a scene on camera. The embodiment of character in performance is important because, other things being equal, the dominant metaphysics of Western cultures predisposes us to impute subjectivity to all people we encounter in real life, and all "persons" we encounter on stage, loudspeaker, and screen. Possession of subjectivity is a default assumption for any moving human body and any speaking human voice. Subjectivity equates here with possession of a mind, capable of thinking, knowing, believing, judging, and so forth. The converse applies to nonembodied characters. By default, these lack subjectivity, though as in the BUPA commercials, we may be brought to construe otherwise as we watch and listen.

A degree of embodiment is present in radio drama, which can present the body through its voice. Staged drama, as well as the audiovisual kind, can also present the body visually, whereas audiovisual drama (film and television) can make use of cinematic codes of shot length, depth of field, take duration, and so forth to control how its audiences encounter the physical body. Use of the voice is characteristic across all dramatic modes, though, as in mime and ballet, it is not essential in those that also have a visual dimension, and speech has been regarded rather negatively in the world of film: "Basically, the perfect movie doesn't have any dialogue. So you should always be striving to make a silent movie" (Mamet 1991: 72; see also Kozloff 2000: chapter 1).The significance of all this is the power of the audiovisual conspiracy: first, to endow onscreen characters with subjectivity, and second, to make that subjectivity feel substantive, particular, *real*. Only when persons-with-subjectivity start to be differentiated one from another can we really talk of character in the full sense.

Voices

Embodiment of character is all too easily conceived of as a visual matter, something about what we see on the screen or on the stage. There is a real danger of forgetting that embodiment is also *aural*. In radio drama, and on the soundtrack of audiovisual drama, bodies are realized as voices. There is considerable debate in the film literature on the aesthetic merits of *synchronization*—in other words, whether and when speakers should be seen and heard at the same time. This is part of a larger debate about the kind of work that audiences should be expected to do. Too much synchronization arguably makes life too easy for the audience— beguiling it into referential readings of the characters and their world, at the expense of more imaginative/challenging/aesthetically worthy/ideologically open possibilities (Kozloff 2000: 96–104).[5] In defense of synchronization, Kozloff argues that "watching talk" is rewarding because "it allows viewers to study and compare so many simultaneous signifiers: the actors' words, their voices, their intonations; their facial expressions, the look in their eyes, their body posture, their gestures, their costuming; the setting and its use of light and art direction" (2000: 99). Voices, of course, deliver dialogue, and dramatic narratives are designed to foster the default belief that the point of origin for this dialogue is the mind of the character speaking it. But the *character* exists only as a virtual mind, not a real one, and unless the actor is improvising, dialogue originates prior to production, usually as written text, and from someone other than the performer.

Thus there is at this point a mismatch between production protocols and protocols of interpretation. From a production perspective, writing comes first and vocality (prosodic and paralinguistic delivery) is added. From an interpretative perspective, vocality and writing (verbality) coexist. Vocal characteristics (rhythm, pitch, intonation, volume, and voice quality) are not meant to be experienced as *add-ons*—though they may be, if performances are poor. They are experienced as part of the embodiment of character. Actors are chosen to bring appropriate vocal qualities to the part. A certain *natural* unity of body and voice is expected as regards age and gender. Professional skills also equip performers to adapt: accents can be learned (think of Anna Friel's American accent in *Pushing Daisies*, David Anders's southern English accent in *Heroes*); pitch levels can be adjusted upward or downward; monotonous or excitable delivery can be deployed to suit the character, the situation, or both. The effects of voices on audiences can also be affected by the ways in which the set or the performers are miked for sound. So argues Lury (2007) in relation to the soundscape of *CSI* (CBS 2000–present):

> The sound of the human voice in the dialogue in *CSI* is absolutely privileged in relation to the other sounds in the programme. Thus the voices of the CSI team and associated detectives are nearly always dry and close-miked. "Realistic" sound perspective—which would reproduce the sound levels based on how far away the characters apparently are from the camera—is rarely adhered to. [. . .] the fact that actors' voices are recorded via the use of radio mikes taped to parts of their anatomy allows them (except when dramatically necessary) to effectively whisper their dialogue. This means that the majority of the conversations in CSI are performed in a low-pitched, breathy and intimate manner—the register of secrets and caresses. (2007: 113)

Vocal distinctiveness and vocal expressiveness are generically conditioned on television. A Marge Simpson voice (as played by Julie Kavner in *The Simpsons*), with its unusual combination of "feminine" high pitch and "masculine" roughness is acceptable for a comic/cartoon character, but would sound artificial in mainstream drama. Sketch comedy, such as that in *Little Britain*, is well named. It offers vignettes of social life rather than full narratives, and vocal distinctiveness is part of its kit for indicating character types, many of which are extreme, comic exaggerations. The exaggerated subjectivities on display allow for comic exaggeration of voicing, too. David Walliams as a "lady"—"Emily Howard"—is a case in point. This character is no ordinary transvestite, but one seeking to construct himself as an Edwardian lady, with the petticoats and bonnets to prove it. A high-pitched voice is strenuously projected, consistent with an image of extreme effort in bringing off this caricature in twenty-first century Britain.[6] Situation comedy voices are closer to the naturalistic norm, but tend to be louder and tenser, and to offer a wider range of expressive variation—especially those, like *dinnerladies* (BBC 1998–2000), which are performed before a live studio audience. The effect of such a production space is to make more *theatrical* speech possible.

Voices on television have work to do when there are verbal lines to be spoken. They may also be called upon to produce nonverbal vocalization—to cry, to shout and scream, to laugh, to choke and splutter. Only one kind of production makes really significant use of such vocal sound—the crime reconstruction series *Crimewatch UK* (BBC 1984–present).[7] It is not always possible to reconstruct the speech of real-life crime victims after the event, or that of the perpetrators. Fidelity to the original event is important in this show, and it does not like to create imaginary dialogue in the absence of records as to what was actually said. But in the case of violent crime, *realism* can be salvaged by the inclusion of some appropriate wordless, or indistinctly worded, screaming and yelling. It is situation, rather than character, that is best served by such expression: faced with such a situation, anyone might respond in this way. Not all character performance on television favors the naturalistic acting mode, but this has been a baseline against which other approaches have been assessed—stylized, mannered, melodramatic.

CHARACTER AND SCHEMATA

If characters can be like people, then it makes sense to ask whether the discipline of psychology has anything to offer the study of character in drama. *Person perception theories* developed within social psychology have explored how people form impressions of one another in real life (see Hamilton 2005 for a representative collection of readings in this area). Those same theories have also been extended to research on character in drama, notably in the early research of Sonia Livingstone (1987, 1989, 1990):

> Parallels between the representation of television characters and real-life people allow the extension of person perception theories. For people's everyday experience of others is to some extent mirrored in the way that regular soap opera viewers immerse themselves in a particular social *milieu* for many years and build up a complex web of background knowledge, emotional reactions and personal judgments. (Livingstone 1990: 113–114)

Livingstone here singles out soap opera characters especially as justifying the use of these theories, because of the particular nature of soap as a genre, and audience relations with that genre. Using multidimensional scaling techniques, she determined, for instance, that audiences perceived characters in *Coronation Street* by distinguishing among those who were more responsible and those who were more staid. Characters' gender, though not their social class, was perceptually salient.

Jonathan Culpeper (2001) has also used insights from psychology in the exploration of literary character. Coming from a stylistic rather than a media studies background, it is cognitive psychology just as much as social psychology that has influenced his approach, and whereas Livingstone is concerned with the empirical study of variability in audience uptake, Culpeper is more concerned with general principles of interpretation.

Culpeper (2001) argues that one of the ways we read characters (form impressions of characters in our minds) is by a *top-down* process involving the accessing of relevant social schemata.[8] The claim is that audiences already know, for example, what police officers are, how they look, how they sound, and what they do, so that, given appropriate signs in the text to activate the schema in question (on television, of course, a police uniform would be enough), audiences are well equipped to mentally create the character. Preexisting knowledge, not the text, fills out the details and creates specific expectations regarding the possible conduct of that character. Audiences will interpret actual conduct thenceforward in the light of this prior knowledge. One of Culpeper's examples was illustrated and discussed earlier, in chapter 2.

The interpretation of real-life people begins in exactly the same way. A passing body in a police uniform is a police officer—unless and until proven otherwise. Police officers behave in a certain way—unless and until proven otherwise. In fiction, characters that are never pushed beyond this initial assessment are *flat* characters, or in Culpeper's terms, "category based character impressions" (Culpeper 2001: chapter 2; see also chapter 2 in this volume). But characters need not remain flat, and for Culpeper that is where *textual cues*, rather than existing understandings, come into play. The text will show us that the particular police officer, whether "Jack Frost," "Morse," "Frank Furedi," "Ed Green," or any other is something more than a body instantiating a category. Our impressions of him will develop and change as we become more familiar with him, witnessing what he says and how he says it, what he does and how he does it.

Such enlarged characters may also provoke revision of the original schema, what Guy Cook (1994) calls "schema refreshment"—not just in allowing viewers to say that *x* is "not a stock policeman, after all" but "If *x* is a policeman, and x is like that, then *I was wrong about policemen*" (trainspotters, women, Swedes...). Dramas have been written with the express intention of moving beyond popular schemata. In everyday language, we might call this *challenging stereotypes*. Consider this critical reaction to the British drama *Queer as Folk* (Channel Four 1999), about gay lifestyle in Manchester:

> The point of the TV series, written by Russell T. Davies, was to depict the lives of a group of gay men in Manchester, and to demonstrate with tremendous energy and gritty wit that homosexuals are not strange, but are as needy, horny, funny, dumb, lovable, and anguished as any comparable group of heterosexuals. Except the gay guys' stomachs were much flatter. If all these seem obvious facts, jolly good for you, but they invariably come as news to many people, some of whom were outraged by "Folk"'s graphic displays of sex. (*Entertainment Weekly*, Dec. 1, 2000)[9]

It is instructive to assess this review through the lens of Cook's approach. Cook recognizes three different types of schema refreshment (1994: 191)—schema destruction, schema construction, and schema connection. *Queer as Folk*, if it has indeed gone beyond popular understanding and is denying the audience a simple satisfaction of "understanding" by reading the schema into the bodies, would fall into the first of these three categories. The audience is asked not to create a new schema, but to rethink the original one in terms of differences, or even to move beyond categorical interpretation. For this critic, the series does not offer audiences a new or revised schema of northern English gay men. Such men are "as needy, horny, funny, dumb, lovable, and anguished as any comparable group of heterosexuals." Something in popular understanding is disrupted, but what that something might be is extremely vague—"homosexuals are not strange." What is put in its place is too diverse and/or too similar to the control group—heterosexuals—to be considered a *revised* schema of gay men, except in a very trivial sense of what can be considered a *schema*. The critic uses the final sentence of his review to reconstruct his readership by construing them as unprejudiced, like himself—"If all these seem obvious facts, jolly good for you." Other people, elsewhere in the audience, needed to have their schemas challenged. But the review suggests those same people were offended by the sex, even though promiscuous sexuality might well have been part of the original schema. There is more social "baggage" in this critique than is apparent from an initial reading.

According to Culpeper there are four groupings of character schemata: four sets of character categories. Three of these sets are social, and one is textual. The social groupings are as follows: (1) personal categories—for example, those based on likes and dislikes; (2) social role categories—for example, kinship roles and occupations; (3) group membership categories—for example, those based on race, age, sex, class, and so forth (Culpeper 2001: 75–76). He suggests that these three sets are organized hierarchically: group membership categories are at the top of the hierarchy, social role categories are in the middle (corresponding to the basic level of categorization in prototype theory), and personal categories are at the bottom. The textual grouping comprises dramatic role categories (Culpeper 2001: 87)—heroes, villains, heroines, helpers, and the like—closely tied to genre.

To make this particular version of top-down character interpretation work for TV drama, some further observations can be made.

First, there is the question of the activation of a relevant schema. Culpeper is working from literary materials and tends to think in terms of written language: on cinema and in television, schemata can be activated visually (and would often be supported visually even if they are activated verbally). Although the usual location for a trigger that activates a schema will be intratextual, it is also worth remembering that TV drama production is embedded within supporting discourses of reviews, trailers, and press interviews, so that schemata may be anticipated even before a single second of some show has aired. Genre expectations will also play a role. This suggests the need for a more contextualized view than Culpeper's of schema activation for this kind of drama. In addition, much television drama operates on presumptions of continuity: there are many more second and subsequent episodes of drama than there are first episodes, because there is much more series drama than one-off production. In terms of schema activation, this points to a real, practical tension for writers and producers in steering between presumptions of familiarity and presumptions of new acquaintanceship, given that many viewers will not join in the viewing experience from the start of the pilot episode.

Some standard ways of dealing with this have been developed. One is the "previously on . . ." recap section, before the opening credits and title sequence, which brings the audience up to date and prepares them for what is to come, with brief replays of key moments from earlier episodes. Others are more customized. Thus the start of series 2 of *Brothers and Sisters* (ABC 2006–present) contrives to have Nora, the matriarch (played by Sally Ann Field), create a webcam message for the benefit of absent son Justin, and to tell the absentee what has happened to his family over the summer—not coincidentally, the gap between the first and the second series. These updates function primarily to keep viewers abreast of the storylines, but they can also be helpful in the (re) introduction of characters.

Second, it is appropriate to allow for other, nonschematic ways of reading for character in real life and in representation. Culpeper argues that just as our understandings of real-life acquaintances become fuller with each subsequent encounter, so, too, as readers of texts, we can use *bottom-up* interpretative strategies, and construct "rounder" characters, piecemeal, from multiple textual clues—whether or not our first impression of them was schematic. There is no reason to believe that characters in TV drama cannot, in principle, be found to be "round" in this sense (or "person-based character impressions" in Culpeper's idiom). Culpeper himself believes that characters in at least some TV dramas are *not* round:

> However, many soaps [such as *Neighbours*, 7 Network, 1985–present] make almost exclusive use of flat characters. Yet these soaps are phenomenally successful: viewers come back day after day for more. It may be the case that some viewers positively value the schema-reinforcing nature of flat characters. Furthermore [. . .] the focus for viewers may be on what characters do with their attributes. (Culpeper 2001: 96; see also chapter 2 in this volume)

Third, there are questions surrounding the origins of schemata in individual consciousness, and the relations between first- and secondhand experience in their establishment. In the absence of any relevant firsthand experience, people may acquire a "police officer" schema that originates in their secondhand experiences as viewers of TV drama and/or other mediations. Specific *dramatic role* schemata, such as the schema for "Western hero" (Culpeper 2001: 87), must obviously originate in textual materials. This is not to deny the discursive or semiotic nature of schemata, even those that are built exclusively from firsthand experience.

Finally, there is a question of balancing authority and variability. We must acknowledge the potential variability of schemata, cross-culturally as well as across "internal" cultural fault lines (e.g., fault lines of gender, ethnicity, class, sexuality). In their interpretations of particular texts, critics and analysts will tend to activate their own schemata, with the same presumptions of legitimacy as linguists drawing on "native speaker intuitions" of grammaticality. As an analytic procedure, this is commendable. In television the default address has been to large and therefore necessarily mixed audiences. This encourages TV to use schemata that are already rather generally shared—as well as to cultivate schemata on their own account, and distribute these widely through repetition, possibly producing second-order interpretations of the type "this is how I am supposed to think."

Nevertheless, it is problematic automatically to treat schemata as normative, especially in relation to the heterogeneous audiences of TV drama. Although it is true, for instance, that some sections of the audience will have an "oppositional" view of the police, as agents of harassment if not oppression, a construct of the institution as dutifully upholding law and order is in force for mainstream production. This does not preclude particularizing individual police officers as corrupt, inefficient, lazy, and ill-intentioned, as the history of police drama in the United Kingdom, from *Z Cars* (ITV 1962–1978) through *Life on Mars* (BBC 2006–2007), clearly shows. It does not even preclude oppositional representations of the police force as such. It does suggest that writers who seek these effects will have to work harder than those who do not: that only police representations in which the police are the "good guys" or are not relevant to the central narrative can get by on schematic representations.[10]

Dialogue has two possible functions for a "schema poetics" (Stockwell 2003) of character in television drama. When characters first appear, dialogue can be a source of triggers, activating relevant schemata. Then, as the characters become familiar, their dialogue (and dialogue about them) will help us to learn how far their *real* character diverges from our prior understanding.

An Example: Redeeming the Underclass in *Shameless*

Shameless (UK Channel 4, 2004–present) is a good series for the purposes of illustrating how dialogue can contribute to impression formation within a schema-based approach. This British series, set on a fictional northern England housing estate, depicts the lives of the Gallagher family and their neighbors. These characters could be said to represent the contemporary underclass, many of them unemployed, some unemployable, living on benefits, and comfortable with fraud and deceit as survival techniques. It plays into schematic understanding of workless lives as wretched, disreputable, or both. Its project has been understood as one of particularizing the lives of the "work-shy," redeeming them for mainstream audiences:

The title of the series is both ironic and apt: apt because the Gallaghers oscillate wildly between good intentions, indifference and hurtfulness towards loved ones, but there is little sign of the overweening feelings of self-worthlessness and self-disgust that characterize real shame; and ironic because accusations of shame-lessness, for example made by "respectable" neighbors, represent moral condem-nation that tends (and intends) to render its targets beyond the pale of acceptable humanity. It reveals far more about the accusers, hinting at their deeper hidden shame and insecurity concerning their own lowly social status, and furthermore legitimizes in their eyes the hostile actions and persecution by "the authorities" that ultimately disrupt or preempt any meaningful sense of their own community. [. . .]

Shameless thus invokes several conventional discourses relating to the nature and potential of working class people, only to then flout and undermine them—and in the process to question the social and political philosophies and programmes that, at root, depend on class-based ideologies of moral deficit and ethical inade-quacy for their normative and pragmatic utility. (Tom Jennings, review of Shameless, January 18, 2008, at http://libcom.org/library/shameless-paul-abbott-series-1-2-channel-4-20034-television-review-%E2%80%93-tom-jennings)[11]

Before engaging specifically with the dialogue, I will spell out what this means in relation to the patriarch of the family at the center of Shameless. It is possible for parts of the audience to find "Frank Gallagher" (David Threlfall) appealing, despite his offenses against middle-class and "respectable" working-class norms. He is shambolic, uncouth, exploitative, irresponsible—and drunk as often as sober and seemingly without conscience. This characterization would make him (and the show generally) an excellent subject for audience research, teasing out the limits of ethical and interpretative common ground and the relation between them. How widespread, really, is "Frank Gallagher's" ap-peal—and is it based on empathetic identification, or the humor of a perceived caricature? How do viewers who like, or claim to like, the character, reconcile themselves to his amorality? Do critical viewers perceive the series itself, or just the character, as culpably amoral? Does Shameless have the potential to be schema refreshing, and, if it does, is that because of or in spite of Frank? The reviewer at libcom interprets Shameless as a left-leaning radical series, politically valuable because it questions the attitudes that help to perpetuate this kind of social exclusion. But this interpretation is a vulnerable one in the absence of any evidence that audiences themselves question those attitudes, and do so as a result of their responses to the character and the program.

Shameless is a series that plays into Britain's social class divisions in complex ways. Nelson (2007) argues that it avoids a straightforward sympathy appeal for the plight of the disadvantaged through its hybridization of comedy with social realism. But as he also notes, a reading position based on humor at the expense of the underclass is an awkward one if, at the same time, the realism makes the characters something more than comedic caricatures in the tradition of Steptoe *and Son* (BBC 1962–1974). The antics of the Gallagher clan also push up against the limits of normative morality. In one episode discussed by Nelson, motherless Debbie Gallagher kidnaps a toddler. Rather than explore the sensibility that might make her do something so outrageous, the story line is played for laughs. Eventually the child is returned unharmed to its parents. But there is no narrative moral justice punishing Debbie for her wrongdoing or making her confront it as such. Nelson believes that the times are not right for didactic moral or political lessons in drama, and that this text has a worthy openness that can stimulate thought. But this openness interacts with the sensibilities of real viewers, and this is difficult in the case of those who might, on economic grounds, identify with the Gallaghers. The comedy does not necessarily redeem the offensiveness of suggesting that baby kidnapping is something they would be capable of.

Frank Gallagher is to some extent contrasted with other members of the community, or at least represented as being at the extreme end of a continuum of respectability. His children, ranging in age from toddler to young adult, and his neighbors are mainly presented not just as morally "better" than Frank, but are also personalized so as to request from a mainstream audience a refreshed schema of underclass identities. Dialogue is one of the elements that draws viewers into cognitive processes of schema refreshment. Audiences also get the help of some monologue as well as dialogue, in the form of the following voiceover accompanying an introductory shot sequence:

> Now, nobody's saying the Chatsworth Estate is the Garden of Eden. Least, I don't think they are. But it's been a good home to us, to me, Frank Gallagher. And me kids, who I'm proud of 'cos every single one of them reminds me a little of me. Now they can all think for themselves—which they've me to thank for. Fiona, who's a big help, massive help. Lip, who's a bit of a gobshite, which is why nobody calls him Philip any more. Ian, lot like his mam—which is handy for the others, 'cause she's disappeared into thin air—and good luck to her. Carl—we daren't let him grow his hair. One, it stands on end and makes him look like Toyah. Two—nits love him. Debbie. Sent by God. Total angel. You've to check your change, but she'll go miles out of her way to do you a favor. Plus Liam, little rock-and-roller. Gonna be a star—once we've got the fits under control. You know, there's three things are vital to a half decent community. Space. You need wide open spaces, where everyone goes mental. And neighborliness, fantastic neighbors. Kev and Veronica. Lend you anything—well, not anything. But all of them, to a man, know first and foremost, one of the most vital necessities in this life, is, they know how to throw a party. Whe-hey! Scatter! (Season 1, episode 1 and subsequent episodes, written by Paul Abbott)

The images that accompany this monologue depict the named characters as they go about their normal lives (hitting one another, demonstrating how to unwrap a condom, running away—but also doing household chores and taking care of one another). Walters (2006) points out that the monologue is written to convey the good opinion that Gallagher has of himself and the positive relationships he enjoys with his family—but the imagery presented undercuts this self-presentation, showing one child hitting Gallagher, and a number of them running away from him.

Gallagher's introduction primes viewers to recognize and pay attention to these key characters subsequently. One of them, Lip (played by Jody Latham) duly appears in the very first scene. This is the scene I particularly want to consider in schema theory terms. During the course of the action, Lip arrives at a house on the estate, is admitted by one woman, Sheila (played by Maggie O'Neill), sets down to help another, younger one, Karen (played by Rebecca Atkinson), with her homework, and is disconcerted when Karen crawls under the table to give him a blow job, but complies on learning that she is not able to pay him to do her homework.

(*Lip knocks on door*)

1 LIP: Hiyah. I said I'd help your Karen with her homework.

2 SHEILA: Okay. Take your shoes off.

3 LIP: Fair enough. (*Lip starts to remove shoes*)

4 SHEILA: I'll get you a carrier bag.

(*Sheila disappears and returns with a plastic bag into which Lip puts his shoes*)

A cut at this point elides Lip's entry into the house and the start of his exchanges with Karen. Sheila is now in another room, visible in certain shots from the living room table where Lip and Karen are. Occasionally, the point of view is reversed, and we look past Sheila to see Lip and Karen.

5 KAREN: She's got this thing about people bringing soil into the house.

6 LIP: Right.

7 KAREN: She's not as mad as she seems. Agoraphobia.

8 LIP: Oh, right.

9 KAREN: So how come you know all this?

10 LIP: It's just something I do.

11 KAREN: What, like a hobby?

12 LIP: No, the plans.

13 KAREN: What, physics?

14 LIP: All sorts. Look. (*Lip starts drawing, Karen slides under the table and crawls towards him whilst he is concentrating on his diagram.*) I've got a great one for Newton's First. Watch. Every body continues in a state of rest or uniform motion unless acted upon by an external force (*Karen's head approaches Lip's crotch*).

15 LIP: Karen! Karen!

(*Karen's advances continue*)

16 LIP: To be honest I could do with the money.

17 KAREN: What money?

18 LIP: I charge for homework. I thought you knew.

19 KAREN: (*Looks up at Lip from under the table*) I'm skint.
20 LIP: [pause] OK.
(*Blow job action recommences, now with the active participation of both parties*)

(Season 2, episode 1 and subsequent episodes, written by Paul Abbott)

The combination of dialogue (its content, rather than its form, in this instance) and action in this scene establishes by inference the following about the character of Lip:

- Lip has sufficient "book smarts" to be relied on to help classmates with homework (his knowledge of Newton's First Law of Motion, line 14).
- He is shrewd enough to turn his abilities to financial advantage (lines 16–18).
- He is innocent enough to be surprised by the sexual advances (line 15).
- He is appreciative of the sexual opportunity (line 20).
- The sex is second best to the financial gain he was expecting (line 16).

A category-based take on Lip based on setting, physical appearance, and accent would see an English, northern, underprivileged, working-class youth—a cluster of group membership categories. This reading has already been partly offset by Frank Gallagher's initial introduction, inviting us to consider a more person-based impression, even before we know what that person-based impression will contain. Viewers who accept this invitation are rewarded by this scene—Lip's character both affirms the category (this is a young man "on the make"—a "scally" in northern parlance) and challenges it (he is a clever student). This short example further supports the description of film and TV audiences as "overhearers" of dialogue (Bubel 2008). If the character inferences I have drawn here are sound, the "open theory of character" proposed by Chatman would say that they have been drawn just as they would have been if Lip and Karen were real people. But audiences would never have this opportunity relative to Lip and Karen's supposed real-life analogues. Behavior like this, knowingly performed in the physical and attentive presence of others, would be even more extraordinary than it is in the depicted scene. Throughout the scene there is in fact another person (Karen's mother Sheila) within audiovisual range. Sheila is a potential onlooker or eavesdropper within the diegetic world, but shown to be distracted by other activities. Part of the pleasure of the scene comes from its *riskiness*, with Lip appearing (in nonverbal performance) more disconcerted than Karen at the possibility that Sheila, whom he does not know, might catch them out. Of course, the scene has been written in this way precisely to push audiences into making inferences like these—to get to know Lip as this kind of character as quickly as possible, and the narrative action of the scene (a house call, homework assistance, a sexual encounter) is inseparable from the dialogue.

Within a *referential reading* (Liebes and Katz 1990), the inferences about Lip's character can be treated as meanings "given off" by Lip about himself, just as his accent gives off that he was born and raised somewhere in the vicinity of Manchester. It can also be heard as Paul Abbott, scriptwriter for this series, implying that Lip is a clever and entrepreneurial but sexually immature working class youth.

The proposition that schematic or flat character impressions can give way to textually determined, round character impressions positions the reader/viewer/listener as someone whose prior beliefs about particular person categories are not so fixed as to resist "evidence" that a new character may not conform to these beliefs. After all, the new character is only one individual, possibly atypical. The audience is also positioned as susceptible to textual cues on the author's terms.

This account of Lip Gallagher is offered as a character reading that is appropriate rather than *correct* (a term that is too strongly prescriptive), and explicit about the prior schematic knowledge required to derive it—in other words, that male youths from the urban underclass in Britain are antisocial and uneducated. It also clearly formulates the textual cues that allow us to move beyond the schema in this case. It follows that audiences that do not possess this particular initial schema will make sense of the scene in other ways. One possibility is the existence of an audience that does not subscribe to a belief in the antisocial character of the male urban underclass, but is nevertheless aware of its existence in the wider society, and of its relevance to the representations in this show. This is the position taken by Jennings, the reviewer, in the review of *Shameless* cited earlier, as it also was in the *Entertainment Weekly* review of *Queer as Folk*. Interpretative positions such as these have sometimes been referred to as *displaced readings* (Richardson and Corner 1986).

Characters from the Bottom Up

Just as there is a question mark over the universality of any particular schema that might have interpretative relevance, so, too, there is a question mark over the audience's access to the knowledge/reasoning powers/codes appropriate for noticing the textual cues that allow them to develop elaborated impressions of characters—as indicated in my earlier discussion of how and when a Liverpool accent can be a guide to regional origins. The range of possible cues is vast and possibly limitless. Culpeper (2001: chapter 4) provides a checklist that ranges over conversational structure, conversational implicature, lexis (Germanic versus Latinate vocabulary, lexical richness, surge features, social markers, keywords), syntactic features, accent and dialect, verse and prose, paralinguistic features (tempo, fluency, pitch range, pitch variation, voice quality), visual features, kinesic features, appearance features, contextual features—and with a whole chapter devoted to politeness strategies.

In contemplating this list, two questions come to mind. First, why, in a book about language and character, are many items on the list about paralinguistic or nonlinguistic elements, including kinesic and appearance features? Second, in a TV drama, in which multiple semiotic modes are simultaneously in play, some involving speech and some not, and in which many different aspects of speech can potentially act as cues, how do we decide which signs to focus on and treat as character cues?

In response to the first question, it should be noted that nonlinguistic character cues, for instance, the way a character is dressed, exist in their own right, but they may also exist in the dialogue. Characters themselves can draw attention to relevant features.

Consider the case of "Philippa," in *dinnerladies*, already referred to above. Philippa is less than fastidious about her clothes. She knows this about herself but is not much worried about it. Others know it about her, too. It is a *signature* feature of this character, to the extent that it can be used to identify her. In one episode, a decorator, Bert, is asked to identify the person who gave him permission to paint the canteen.[12] He can't remember the name, and admits to being no good with faces either. All seems lost. Brenda (Victoria Wood) suggests it may have been Philippa:

1 BRENDA: Was it Philippa? Quite posh, little glasses?
2 DOLLY: A big blob of soup here (*pointing to chest area*) probably.
3 BERT: That's her. Tomato soup, left bust. Soup, I can recognize.

(Season 2, episode 1, "Catering," written by Victoria Wood)

In a less well written drama, such trademark characteristics would be constantly in play as a comedic equivalent of the political *claptrap*[13]—a signal for laughter at Philippa's expense. In fact, throughout the 16 episodes, there are probably no more than three references to sartorial carelessness of this sort. This low-key use of character cues is an advantage for a comedy that seeks to create characters that are more than just single-trait constructions. Furthermore, we never actually see tomato soup stains, or anything like them. This comedy is very theatrical in its mise-en-scène, with a virtual "proscenium arch" perspective on the action for establishing/ensemble shots. The kind of close-up that would be required to show messy clothing is incompatible with this. The nearest we get, in one episode, is Philippa going through the motions of trying to remove the remains of a mayonnaise stain from her blouse. But even here we need the dialogue in order to understand the meaning of Philippa's physical actions.

As for the second question, the short answer could be that we focus on whatever is contextually relevant (as a pragmatic approach, particularly one influenced by Sperber and Wilson's relevance theory, would propose).[14] Or it may be that we focus on whatever is textually foregrounded (an answer influenced by formalist poetics in the tradition of Jakobson, Murakovsky, and others).[15] Or perhaps we focus on whatever we are most interested in (an answer influenced by multimodal semiotics, after Kress and van Leeuwen,[16] and which would not seek to limit character inferences to those intended by an author or objectively present in a text). Culpeper (2001: chapter 3), whose general approach I have adopted and adapted, is drawn toward an explanation in terms of foregrounding. He also points out (a) that "any textual cue can yield character information in a particular context" (2001: 163) and (b) that textual cues are a matter of function, to which form is an unreliable guide.

These points raise theoretical issues beyond the scope and focus of the present work, so, rather than pursue them directly, in table 7.1 I will briefly elaborate on a model for understanding the basic ways that dialogue can contribute to the impressions we form of characters such as the Gallaghers and Philippa Morecroft.

There are eight cells in this grid, but only six of them are significant for the construction of character impressions through dialogue. In the top half of

Table 7.1. Character inferences in *Shameless*

		Say	Hint, imply, suggest, indicate
Benefit of character	About self	1 a i "I charge for homework": Lip to Karen about himself.	2 a i "To be honest, I could do with the money" = "stop sucking me off" = "I prefer money to sex." Lip to/for Karen about himself.
	About other character	1 a ii "She's not as mad as she seems": Karen to Lip about Sheila.	2 a ii "She's not as mad as she seems" = You, Lip, think Sheila seems mad.
Benefit of audience	About self	1b i (Monologue) "[E]very single one [of my kids] reminds me a little of me...."	2 b i "Every body continues in a state of rest or uniform motion unless acted upon by an external force" = Lip is smart (author Abbott to/for audience). Mancunian accent = Lip is northern English. "She's not as mad as she seems." Karen thinks Lip thinks Sheila is mad.
	About other character	1b ii (Monologue) "Debbie. Sent by God. Total angel."	2 b ii "She's not as mad as she seems"= (Karen thinks) Lip thinks Sheila is mad.

the grid (all of the meanings labeled "a"), characterization takes place within the diegetic world and characters themselves learn, or are invited to learn, about one another. In the process, audiences also learn about them. What we learn may be as much about the speaker as about the spoken-about. It is no accident that in *dinnerladies*, it is the character Dolly (Thelma Barlow) who refers to Philippa's soup-stained blouses. By contrast with Philippa, Dolly is fastidious, with pretensions to refinement—she "used to work in the Café Bon-Bon"—a far superior establishment to the works' canteen. Messy clothing would stand out for Dolly as it might not do, or do much less, for others. In the bottom half of the grid (the "b" meanings), other characters seem not to benefit from the dialogic cues, though the audience does. Note that statements and hints about other characters would in principle include the interlocutor—the *second person* in the speech situation, as opposed to the first person or speaker, and the third person or spoken-about.

I have quoted again from the *Shameless* dialogue to illustrate these possibilities, and I have not sought to differentiate among various kinds of information about characters (habits, beliefs, traits, biographical facts, etc.). "I charge for homework" is a direct statement by Lip about his business practice for Karen's benefit. If she did not know this before, she does now. Karen's "She's not as mad as she seems" is a direct observation about Sheila's mental disposition to Lip, seeking to "dial down" the extent of her mother's craziness. These direct statements have meaningful face value, but they also have implications. "I charge for homework" constructs Lip as the kind of person who charges classmates for doing their homework—clever enough to do this reliably, smart enough to make money from it, and not troubled by any ethical misgivings. The derived meanings belong more in the "b" section of the grid. The fact that Lip is clever and knowledgeable enough to do her homework is not something Karen is just now learning. She already knew this when she hired him. It is the audience that is getting to know the character through these lines.

This suggests that the difference between meanings in the first column and those in the second column is rather superficial. Both types are of interest for characterization in ways that either have nothing to do with their propositional face value (any utterance, conveyed in a Manchester accent, indicates a northern English identity), or else go beyond propositional content ("I charge for homework" = "I am good at schoolwork and make money from this").

CHARACTER SINCERITY AND PERFORMANCE

In drawing this chapter to a conclusion, I want to offer some observations that relate to the issue of character *sincerity* in TV drama, rather than to their particularity as possessors of traits. Because, as Goffman showed, people in real life will routinely engage in "impression management," audiences have every reason to be disappointed at some level when such impression management is missing from the behavior of characters in dramatized narratives—when characters seem to have only one-dimensional, "sincere" selves to offer, and especially (as in many TV commercials) when their sincerity is recruited to superficial causes.

Of course, drama is inconceivable without certain kinds of *identity work*. Audiences expect to be shown characters who lie and pretend to one another. Sometimes it is important that audiences are unaware of the pretence, until the *reveal*, when the deceit is finally uncovered. They take characters at face value, only to discover during the course of the narrative that they are not as they have seemed to be. *Treachery* plots (think of the series *24*, Fox 2001–present) depend on credible but insincere and untruthful performances that lead audiences up the proverbial garden path. In other narratives, audiences are granted the privilege of awareness. The pleasure of watching a formulaic series like *Columbo* (NBC and others, 1968–2000), in which there is no "whodunnit" mystery, is very largely derived from observing murderers construct, for the detective's benefit, "innocent" personae, variously antagonistic or cooperative toward him, according to how they perceive their strategic interest. Columbo (Peter Falk) also manages a downbeat persona of his own, while encouraging villains in their persona constructions, as part of his distinctive approach to crime solving, in which villains eventually betray themselves.

Theorists who write about the language of drama, and refer especially to the double articulation of its discourse architecture (communication *among* characters embedded as part of communication between author and audience *via* characters), usually go on to observe that this architecture can increase in complexity whenever there is a "play within a play." The examples in the previous paragraph show that such complexity is not restricted to such formally contrived situations, but can occur whenever characters are called upon to manage their relationships in a more or less self-conscious way. In *Columbo* episodes, the "true" character is a villain who controls the "false," innocent persona, but the fake is ultimately abandoned and the true is publicly revealed, beyond doubt or ambiguity.

There is another approach to the layering of characterization in TV drama— one that concurs with Goffman in regarding identity work as entirely normal conduct in social life, just another aspect of social interaction. The trend toward irony and reflexivity in contemporary culture favors representations that incorporate such identity work. The pleasure of a series like *Friends* (NBC 1994–2004) has a lot to do with its willingness to pursue the humor inherent in this. For instance, one of the characters, Chandler Bing (Matthew Perry), is concerned that he comes across to strangers as gay, when he is not. Rachel Green (Jennifer Aniston) misreads body language in a job interview and inappropriately kisses the interviewer, worrying subsequently about what he must think of her and how she can make it right. Ross Geller (David Schwimmer) tries out different possible nicknames for himself, including "The Rossitron." Characters will "thoughtless-ly" say things that have double meanings or stupid ones, and then act out their awareness of what "just happened."

For a subtle but convincingly funny, in-character example of *identity play*, consider this exchange. Phoebe (Lisa Kudrow) has arranged to go out with Joey for a meal, but a long-lost lover, David, has returned from Russia and has only one night when he can be with her. Phoebe has recently harangued Joey when he stood her up in order to go out on a date, and realizes it would be hypocritical if she did the same to him. On principle, she is at the point of refusing David's invitation when Monica intervenes:

1 MONICA: Phoebe, what are you doing?
2 PHOEBE: Well, I have plans with Joey tonight.
3 MONICA: So? He'll understand.
4 PHOEBE: No he won't. And that's not even the point. Monica, I made a
       whole speech about how you do not cancel plans with friends. And now, you
       know, what, just because, potentially, the love of my life comes back from Russia for
       one night only, I should change my beliefs? I should change my beliefs!
5 (*Monica smiles*)
6 PHOEBE: No, no. If I don't have my principles I don't have anything.
7 MONICA: God, you are so strong!
8 PHOEBE: Or, I could rush through dinner with Joey and I could meet David at nine.

(*Friends*, season 7, episode 11, "The One with All the Cheesecakes," written by Shana Godberg-Meehan)

The key to this is Phoebe's repetition of "I should change my beliefs." The first time it is produced, sincerely, as a rhetorical question to which the answer is "No." (However, Phoebe is already formulating the question to prefigure a "Yes" answer—this is not any old "better offer" but a unique opportunity.) Beliefs are important, and it is unethical to abandon them for expediency's sake. But the second utterance of the same words, with different intonation and body language, is no longer a question, but an exclamation—the articulation of a sudden, significant insight into the solution to her problem. The rest of the exchange sees Phoebe move back to her original position, finally settling on the compromise that the narrative will subsequently dramatize.

Identity play is not restricted to comic productions on television, as the example of *Dexter* (Showtime, 2006–present) shows. Dexter works as a forensic scientist in the Miami police force—but for dramatic purposes he is categorized by his extracurricular activity (killing people), not by his day job. The challenge of making a drama with a serial killer as the central character puts pressure on consensual values, though these are preserved in part by limiting Dexter to the killing of other murderers. But the Dexter characterization experiment is not just a substantive one: it has a formal aspect, too, that connects with this issue of character sincerity and performance above. A kind of double life identity is obviously a necessity for this individual, living in what passes for the same world as ours rather than some fantastic alternate universe in which killing is morally acceptable.

Introducing himself in voiceover to the audience in the pilot episode, he says,

> My name is Dexter. Dexter Morgan. I don't know what made me the way I am, but whatever it was left a hollow place inside. People fake a lot of human interactions, but I feel like I fake them all, and I fake them very well, that's my burden, I guess.

(Season 1, episode 1, "Dexter," written by James Manos Jr., from a novel by Jeff Lindsay)

The drama is therefore not just about Dexter's moral principles and how they relate to those of the wider society. There is also a character issue, about the extent of his hollowness, and the unavailability of *sincerity* as a possible mode of discourse for him. At the level of textual pleasure, this creates space for opportunities to display all of the character's various modes of insincerity, in his work life and in his relations with others—friends, family, and colleagues.

DISCUSSION

Schema theory, as developed by Culpeper for fictional characters more generally, offers a valuable perspective on what makes possible the creation of characters through dialogue. Dialogue can certainly be used to help activate an existing schema. In the example from *One Foot in the Grave*, discussed in chapter 2, an incorrect "police officer" schema was activated, and then replaced to comic effect by a "doorstep evangelist" schema. Both schemas were appealed to through the combination of doorstep setting and use of language by the visitors. Dialogue is also employed in the elaboration of categorical characters into more rounded ones. This is very necessary, for instance, in hospital series featuring not only a set of well-known cast regulars, whose traits have some kind of continuity from episode to episode, but also an endless supply of guest characters depicting the patients-of-the-week, who for the sake of credibility and entertainment need to be *fleshed out* beyond their initial category assignment. Dialogue can also be used in the challenging of categorical assignments, as we saw with *Shameless*'s Lip Gallagher above.

As Chatman proposes, though, the essence of characters goes beyond the use of language, and not just because characters can be represented in nonlinguistic ways as well. Character schemata are cognitive constructs, and the interpretation of TV drama's characters lies at the intersection of dramatic worlds and the world as it already exists in the viewer's mind. One of the lessons to draw from the foregoing account has to do with the nature of the collaboration between dramatists and audiences. It is by no means original to observe that meaning is not something inherent in a *text* (even if the concept of text is properly expanded from its original literary sense to encompass performance and production), but can only be achieved on the basis of the resources that consumers of texts bring to the tasks of understanding and interpreting what they have heard and seen. Sociolinguistic approaches to this (see chapter 6 in this volume) tend to focus on procedural resources: cognitive approaches like schema theory emphasize that substantive knowledge also has a part to play. On one side of the communicative relationship, dramatists relying on schematic knowledge are making assumptions about the beings—police officers, drug dealers, canteen workers, working-class youths—who already populate the cognitive worlds of its target audiences. On the other side, cooperative consumers themselves strive to supply appropriate schemata and thereby to *be*, to turn themselves into, the dramatist's assumed audience.

Some qualifications are necessary here. Not all consumers are cooperative; there are no metacommunicative disciplines of interpretation for popular entertainment, and well-intentioned efforts on both sides can misfire—the scope for misreading, resistant reading, alternate reading and nonreading is extensive. In addition, the contribution of character schemata to interpretation is only a starting point.

Generic constraints and the sociocultural conditions of TV production set limits on what dramatists are able to create by way of *new* characters, always feeding off the older ones. The greatest opportunities now are in countries that are in a position to exploit channel abundance to create niche markets on subscription channels. It is this situation that has given rise to the character of Dexter as perhaps the most extreme case of creative characterization.

8

Dialogue and Dramatic Meaning

Life on Mars

This chapter and the next each present a case study of a single series. This chapter focuses on a British-made show first broadcast on the BBC (*Life on Mars*, BBC 2006–2008), and the next focuses on an American series (*House*, Fox 2004–present). The fact that one of these series is British and one American is useful for promoting this book on both sides of the Atlantic, but these series have been screened in both countries, and a single-season American version of *Life on Mars* was broadcast in 2008–2009, with Harvey Keitel as Gene Hunt. As a British viewer, I can hear many national resonances in the original series that will be less apparent to viewers in the United States, and I may miss (or misunderstand) some American references in *House*. This is nothing new in the transnational trade. Both series can be seen as examples of the same kind of drama product: quality drama, a label that will be further discussed below. In each of these two chapters I will argue that the series use dialogue in interesting, untypical ways. But the emphasis is different in each case. The present chapter focuses on the contribution that dialogue makes to the meaning of *Life on Mars* as a dramatic work, whereas the next chapter will make a case that the dialogue of *House* is micro–sociolinguistically interesting.

There is general agreement that *Life on Mars* series is *good* television drama, and that its merit is, in large part, due to the writing, by Mathew Graham, Tony Jordan, and Ashley Pharoah. Although the production of dialogue is not a screenwriter's only concern, it is necessarily a very major part of it, as discussed above in chapter 4. I am interested here in where considerations of technique encounter standards of critical and popular evaluation, so the chapter offers a brief account of the latter, before embarking upon some textual analysis accompanied by relevant citation from the various commentaries that the series provoked. Because this will involve an apparent movement away from sociolinguistics and toward media research (though cf. chapter 2 on previous research at the intersection of these two fields), the discussion at the end of the chapter will reestablish connections.

LIFE ON MARS

Generically speaking, *Life on Mars* is a crime series in the police procedural
subcategory. Police series are traditionally viewed as being closer to the *popular*
than the *quality* end of the drama spectrum. Viewers follow police officers' crime
discovery, crime solving, and crime management, and experience the world
mainly from the officers' point of view. But in this series, there is a twist. The
central character, Sam Tyler (played by John Simm) is a man of the twenty-first
century, a detective chief inspector in the Manchester police force. After a
car accident, he finds himself transported back to the Manchester of 1973 as an
adult: a world he would have known in reality only as a 4-year-old child. He is
assimilated (with a credible cover story, about a "transfer from Hyde," and with
a lesser rank) into the equivalent detective force of that period. There is a mystery
story arc about where he really is and how he got there: "Am I mad, in a coma,
or back in time?" he asks each week, a question that is resolved only at the end
of the second and final season. While he is in 1973 he is subordinate to Detective
Chief Inspector Gene Hunt (played by Philip Glenister), and their relationship
gives the series much of its energy. Other police characters are junior to Tyler,
and one of them, WPC Annie Cartwright (Liz White), is also a confidante and
possible love interest.

The history of police series in the United Kingdom has been well researched.
(For an overview, see Leishman and Mason 2003.) The story of televised police
work (as opposed to *sleuthing*) starts with *Dixon of Dock Green* (BBC 1955–1976),
challenged in terms of *realism* by the 1960s *Z Cars* (BBC 1962–1978), until that
was itself challenged in the 1970s by *The Sweeney* (ITV 1975–1978), under the
influence of the American *Starsky and Hutch* (ABC 1975–1979). Other key series
and miniseries in the United Kingdom (excluding the softer *maverick detective*
programs of the kind epitomized by *Inspector Morse*, ITV 1987–2000) would
include *Law and Order* (BBC 1978), *Juliet Bravo* (BBC 1980–1985), *The Bill*
(ITV 1984-present), *Prime Suspect* (ITV 1991–2003), *Between the Lines* (BBC
1992–1994), and *The Cops* (BBC 1998–2000). In the United States an equivalent
list would include *Dragnet* (NBC 1951–1959); *Kojak* (CBS 1973–1978), *Hill Street
Blues* (NBC 1981–1987), *Homicide: Life on the Street* (NBC 1993–1998), *NYPD
Blue* (ABC 1993–2005), and others that have been significant in the United States
but less so (or not at all) in the United Kingdom.

In terms of audience appeal considerations, new series in old genres have to
show some element of originality, some variation on the generic formula. New
series in the past have often been successful when they have offered fresh
insights into the nature of police work (which itself has changed over the
years), including insights that might form the basis for social critique. A documentary as well as an entertainment impulse has informed this trajectory,
although it is a trajectory that may now have run its course, with the rise of the

docusoap format, along with more *postmodern* tastes in the upscale audience. Genre refreshment increasingly takes the form of generic hybridization (see articles in McCabe and Akass 2007) and genre parataxis (see Nelson 2007). *Life on Mars* fits this era well as a police drama that introduces an element of fantasy into its (arguably) realist but "period" diegesis.

The series is able to play with ideas of social change between the 1970s and the 2000s. Attitudes to gender and sexuality, race, and policing itself are especially significant, and accompanied by more incidental reminders of the past that was ours, whether we lived through it or not.[1] The present time is presumed to be both better and worse than the past. The 1970s "Wild West" attitudes to law enforcement have their attraction in terms of success rates and emotional release—not to mention their embodiment in the entertaining, as well as outrageous, Gene Hunt (Philip Glenister). But they are also problematic, so that the protocols of 2000s policing, such as the use of audiotape recorders in the interview room, can be presented as a positive advance. In some respects, Tyler's knowledge exceeds that of the people who now surround him (for example, he knows what will happen to some of them in the future). In other respects, he is the "innocent," unfamiliar with the custom and practice of the time. He does not know the wording of the caution administered when suspects are taken into custody for questioning—though he knows it is significantly different from the equivalent caution administered in the 2000s.[2]

1 SAM: Kim Trent. I'm arresting you on suspicion of armed robbery. You do not
      have to say anything, but it may harm your de ... No, that's not it, is it.
      What is it? Er ... You have the right to remain silent ...
2 GENE: You're nicked!

(Season 2, episode 2, written by Mathew Graham)

The past is also a place Sam can explore for answers to personal questions he has brought from the future, and specifically, in season 1, the question of what became of the father that disappeared from his life during his early childhood. Like much successful TV drama, the series aims for a mixture of the comic and the dramatic (including the sentimental). The relative proportions of comedic and serious elements, and the terms of their relationship, vary by genre, but the idea of such a mixture is not restricted to quality drama. Soap operas such as *Coronation Street* (ITV 1960–present), as well as situation comedies such as *Friends* (NBC 1994–2004), have certainly recognized the value of such a combination.

Despite the 1973 setting, the creative team responsible for the series has explicitly disassociated it from what they call "nostalgia" television. In the United Kingdom nostalgia television is associated especially with programs like *Heartbeat* (ITV 1992–present) and *The Royal* (ITV 2003–present). Though set in the past, these are not costume dramas as normally understood (e.g., *Pride and*

Prejudice BBC 1995, *Bleak House* BBC 2005) because their diegetic setting is, by design, within living memory, and there is no literary connection. They make extensive and rather pronounced use of evocative dress and other paraphernalia from the past. They use hit records from the past for the nondiegetic musical sound track but are not too scrupulous about the specificity of dates, so that tracks are often selected for the narrative appropriateness of the lyrics as well as for period feel (Nelson 1997). *Heartbeat* and *The Royal* shy away from the realism of contemporary police and hospital series in favor of a family-viewing, Sunday-night ethos. Series such as these are experienced by viewers who bring their own twenty-first-century sensibilities to the viewing. This may include a desire for reassurance that the past was simpler and less troubled.

By contrast, period detail is also important to *Life on Mars*, but with a grainier, harder, more downbeat take on the period in question. This is expressed in qualities of cinematography, designed to represent the 1970s not as a gaudy continuation of the excessive 1960s, but as a rather drab era of some privation. Its music is a mixture of specially composed new material and hit songs from the period. Most important, some very different thematic and comedic possibilities can be explored when twenty-first-century sensibility is explicitly built into the narrative premises of the text itself, rather than contributing unofficially to its character and interpretation.

Quality Drama

The following summarizes the problems involved in the exploration of television *quality*, at the risk of oversimplifying these important debates. Researchers have concerns about the relativity of value perspectives and the power hierarchies capable of validating some at the expense of others, so that, for instance, *masculine* sports still prevail over *feminine* ones in mainstream television broadcasting. These difficulties are compounded by questions about the relative contribution of values brought *to* texts by audiences and values that are the properties *of* texts (*bad* shows can be redeemed by *good* audiences; or the *badness* of shows can disappear altogether except insofar as audiences themselves criticize or reject them). Even when specific genres and programs are addressed as texts, it can be difficult to adjudicate between the respective merits of *truth*, *beauty*, and *virtue*, or to allocate particular textual features to one or more of these three subcategories of worth. But some such adjudication is clearly appropriate, given the vast generic range of television output. Different, though possibly overlapping, standards must surely apply to journalism on the one hand, and drama on the other.

In relation to TV drama, these issues form part of the backdrop distinguishing the study of soap opera on the one hand and shows like *The Sopranos* (HBO 1999–2007) on the other. There has tended to be more audience research in the former and more textual analysis in the latter, and either approach can lead to a conclusion that the series under investigation is *good*. Some drama appears to reward textual analysis, and it has been argued, especially with reference to American broadcasting, that more drama of this sort was being made since the introduction of satellite and cable television and the move into the digital age. Thompson (1996) was one of the first to write about the distinctiveness of this kind of programming, but in referring to it as "American quality programming," an indeterminacy was perpetuated: was the identification a judgment on the value of the shows or just a matter of identifying distinct generic characteristics? (McCabe and Akass 2007).

The characteristics that Thompson proposed are still much cited. They include the following:

- A large ensemble cast
- A memory
- A new genre formed by mixing old ones
- A tendency to be literary and writer based
- Textual self-consciousness
- Subject matter tending toward the controversial
- Aspiration toward realism
- A quality pedigree
- Attracting an audience with blue-chip demographics

For the purposes of this chapter, I want to remove the criterion dealing with subject matter—not in order to ignore it or dispute it, but simply to address it separately from the others. Subject matter is liable to be controversial when it is of sociocultural relevance, as with issues of policing and society. This is an area in which the evaluation of drama and the evaluation of nonfictional shows such as news and current affairs have something in common. The other criteria in Thompson's list tend to privilege merits of a broadly aesthetic or formal kind, but as far as subject matter is concerned, the grounding shifts. Viewers might be expected to *learn* something, for good or ill, from a drama's subject matter, and this must raise issues of ethics and truth alongside those of its style, construction, and pedigree. (The demographic criterion seems to be potentially circular in this company.) I will reserve the term *quality* for the checklist as a whole, and use the term *value* to refer to drama's relation with its subject matter. Although it is a British rather than an American production, *Life on Mars* can be regarded as a *quality* series because it satisfied a number of Thompson's desiderata for such programming. It is also arguably a *valuable* series because of its engagement with social issues, especially those that relate to policing.

Quality and value, as defined here, are no guarantees of success. *Success* is a designation that looks at responses to the product and other consequences of broadcasting it. *Life on Mars* was an enormously *successful* show. It was a critical success with the TV reviewers, a popular success in terms of viewing figures, in which about a quarter of the British public watched the first-run releases; it garnered prestigious awards, including BAFTA and Emmy prizes, was broadcast internationally, gave rise to an American remake and a U.K. spin-off (*Ashes to Ashes*, BBC 2008–present), and generated dedicated online discussion and fan fiction, which this chapter will refer to in trying to understand what viewers and critics liked and disliked about the show.

Quality Dialogue

> Good dialogue has a generally accepted definition. It's dialogue that is concise, witty, believable, and revealing of human character and emotion. (Brody 2003: 213)

This quotation has appeared before, in chapter 4. Brody is writing for, and on behalf of, the professional writing community, and the basis of his characterization of quality dialogue is an appeal to professional consensus. In the present chapter I have pursued a different approach, and adopted a definition based on the functions of dialogue in TV drama. *Quality dialogue* is multifunctional, and/or it goes beyond the six basic functions in Kozloff's (2000) schema for dialogue in feature films (see also chapter 3 in this volume). In this section, extracts from the series that can be shown to provide some kind of added value are analyzed to establish that dialogue is one of the features that warrants the genre label *quality* for *Life on Mars*, along with its high-concept premise and strong production values. Neither my approach nor Brody's can claim *objectivity*: both require interpretation of the materials they examine. But the functional approach can certainly strive for some degree of intersubjective plausibility in its demonstrations that particular functions (e.g., the service of realism and of characterization) are performed by particular conversational exchanges in the production.

Kozloff put the storytelling role of movies at the heart of her account, recognizing that the six main functions of dialogue—anchoring of the diegesis and characters, character revelation, communication of narrative causality, adherence to the code of realism, enactment of narrative events, and control of viewer evaluation and emotions—were all, in their different ways, concerned with servicing the story. She argued that these six functions did not exhaust the possibilities, and three specific additional functions—opportunities for star turns, exploiting the resources of language, and thematic/allegorical messages—were also recognized. Audiences should perceive creativity first when dialogue has been able to combine functions in unusual or striking ways, and second when it is allowed to move into these three *value-added* areas.

Life on Mars has plenty of dialogue that respects its audience's basic need to understand where the action takes place, who the characters are, what they are like, and what activities they are engaged in. If the initial scenes are, by default, in the present day, then the first major challenge for this particular series is that of moving Sam back in time. This is not primarily a matter of speech: the production creates a sequence of narrative moments to manage the transition from a contemporary to a credible 1970s visual mise-en-scène. But some device is necessary to make the new context propositionally specific, and the writers choose to do this using dialogue. They get Gene to tell Sam that it is 1973. The audience, who shares Sam's reality for the duration of the series, including its mysteries, learns as Sam learns.

When Gene tells Sam that it is 1973, he does so in a way that combines the obvious *anchorage* function of dialogue with the other basic functions of respecting realism and advancing characterization. This is how the moment is set up, and how the dialogue progresses. Sam has arrived in the Manchester CID main office immediately following the car accident that has brought about his transition. He has found his way to "his" office, but it looks nothing like the office he recently left, and it is filled with men he does not know and who do not know him. He is confused and angered by this and becomes noisily confrontational, disturbing Gene in a private office. Gene then makes his first entrance as master of the domain.

Now Sam can ask his question:

1 SAM: OK. All right. Surprise me. What year is it supposed to be?

(Season 1, episode 1, written by Mathew Graham)

This is how Sam asks the time, with emphasis on "supposed." He asks it in the persona of a man who knows he has been elaborately set up, who is accepting, not fighting, his victimhood with as much bravado as he can muster, and who now wants the truth confirmed. The joke has gone on long enough. He knows the year is still really 2006. He knows there is a conspiracy to make him believe otherwise. He is wrong on both counts, but these beliefs currently make more sense than those he will later entertain.

And here is how he gets his answer:

1 GENE: Word in your shell-like, pal. [*Grabs Sam by the lapels of his leather jacket, pulls him into the office and shoves him against the wall.*]
2 SAM: Big mistake.
3 GENE: Yeah? What about this? [Punches Sam in the stomach, grabs the lapels again keeping Sam pinioned for the rest of the conversation.] They reckon you got concussion. Well I couldn't give a tart's furry cup if your brains are falling out, don't ever waltz into my kingdom acting king of the jungle.
4 SAM: Who the hell are you?
5 GENE: Gene Hunt, your DCI. And it's 1973. Almost dinnertime [shoves Sam against the wall again]. I'm having hoops.

(Season 1, episode 1)

Although it is not epistemologically unrealistic for Sam to ask this question, given his context, it might be considered unrealistic for Gene to take it seriously enough to answer it. Gene is not meant to know, or even suspect, that Sam is a time traveler. No problem: the dialogue shows the audience that Gene thinks Sam's mental powers have been compromised by his road traffic accident: "They reckon you got concussion." Period realism is evoked by the unashamed sexism, as well as the reference to spaghetti hoops (a familiar canned product of the era, eaten mainly by children, served on toast, like baked beans)—though for at least one reviewer, such details helped to create a parody of the 1970s, not the real thing: "It's as if there's a voice shouting from the telly: THIS ISN'T NOW, YOU KNOW, IT'S 1973!"[3]

Characterization is also well served by this short exchange. It constructs this first encounter between the drama's two main characters as a physically and verbally confrontational one and it displays the new character, Hunt, as the alpha male who immediately takes charge of the situation and who has the formal authority as DCI to back up his claim of power. It also gives Hunt an expressive style that is not just sexist and brutal but also funny.

The skill involved in bringing all of this together could be enough to ensure recognition of its quality, but we might also want to give some thought to what it offers that *exceeds* the requirements of anchorage, realism, and characterization. Verbal humor, in which dialogue exploits the resources of language, is important to the show's character, both in the form of *one-liners* by Gene Hunt and in the form of anachronistic jokes that take advantage of the knowledge that Sam shares with the audience but not with the other characters:

1 GENE: I think you've forgotten who you're talking to.
2 SAM: An overweight, over-the-hill, nicotine-stained, borderline-alcoholic homophobe with a superiority complex and an unhealthy obsession with male bonding?
3 GENE: You make that sound like a bad thing.

(Season 2, episode 8)

1 SAM: God's sake, gov. Let's not resort to this.
2 GENE: Gotta charge him today, Sam. Gotta keep that bloke off the streets
3 SAM: This place is like Guantanamo Bay.
4 GENE: Give over, it's nothing like Spain.

(Season 2, episode 2, written by Mathew Graham)

The comedic strand of meaning in the dialogue is also important in that first encounter between Sam and Gene. Bharat Nalluri, who directed this episode and set the visual style for the series as a whole, has said that it was the Gene's final line, "I'm 'avin' 'oops," that made him want to take the job (DVD commentary). He did not say why. Here are some observations. The line has an element of mockery directed at Tyler's silly question, licensing Hunt to be equally silly in his response, and to end on a note of bathos. It carries an intertextual reference to *The*

Sweeney, in which, in a much recycled clip, John Thaw as Jack Regan announces to a witness/suspect, "We're the Sweeney, son, and we haven't had any dinner," playing with the idea of suspects as a kind of prey. The intertextual reference is colored by an overlay of self-mockery—Hunt claims *The Sweeney's* "hard" legacy through the intertextual reference, but then repudiates or undermines it, with the childish reference to spaghetti hoops. *The Sweeney* reference is likely to be deliberate, because it was precisely this series that was the early inspiration for *Life on Mars*, writers Ashley Pharoah and Matthew Graham claiming that back in 1998 all they really wanted to do was remake the original series that they had enjoyed as children (*Take a Look at the Lawman, Part 1*, DVD box set extra). There were certainly *Sweeney* fans who picked up the allusion, though not always admiringly:

> Glennister's opening line—"It's nearly dinnertime, and I'm havin' 'oops!" said in threatening tone was just too similar to Regan's famous line (which I'm sure I don't need to remind you of here) for comfort. (*The Sweeney* forum, http://www.thetvlounge. co.uk, January 10, 2006, retrieved April 17, 2009)

The comic ingredient in this helps to sustain an ironic reading of the script's excesses in its depiction of 1970s social interaction. The humor is part of Gene's character, but it is also a way of colluding with an audience that knows that this is ultimately a playful rewriting of the past, not particularly concerned with whether it references the past of police work itself, or the past of its dramatic representation.

Life on Mars viewers include some who are capable of appreciating the challenges of scriptwriting from the writers' perspective—its expositional obligations, for instance (the following quotations, unless otherwise indicated, are from the Internet Movie Database, http://www.imdb.com/):

> There's a bit of rushing around to get all this explained in the first episode granted, but I suspect that's needed to set the thing up (unlike US shows like LOST that run to 24 episodes or so, this thing will probably have to fit itself inside 6).

> [T]he first episode was not perfect—in particular the opening 10 minutes was overly crammed with exposition masquerading as dialogue.

> I must admit to not being totally taken with White in terms of character or performance. I suppose she was OK but her character felt a bit too convenient and maybe just allowed Sam to speak out loud and thus inform the audience what was going on in his head.

The humor does not hit the spot for everyone:

> There's also rather too many time travel "jokes" ("I need my mobile," "Mobile what?" etc.), which grate a bit after a while.
> Some of the "haven't things changed in 33 years" dialogue is a bit forced: Walks into a pub and orders "Diet Coke," keeps mentioning his "mobile," all women are "crumpet" etc.

However, Gene Hunt's predilection for one-liners is noted and commented on with approval, with references to "Sweeney-esque 'You watch this car or I'll come round and stamp on your toys' dialogue."

A former senior officer in Manchester is among those who object to a lack of realism:

> It could not be more inaccurate in terms of procedure; the way they talk or the way they dress. In all the time I was in the CID in the 1970s I never saw a copper in a leather bomber jacket and I never heard an officer call anyone "guv." (John Stalker, former deputy chief constable of Greater Manchester, a junior officer in Manchester in the 1970s)[4]

The specific issue of realism in dialogue is here just one aspect of Stalker's general concern for period, subsuming characterization, plot, visualization, and attitudes. For Stalker it is a matter of criticism that the show is so unrealistic, and coming from him, there is undoubtedly a political sensitivity to that criticism, but other viewers were quite content to understand it as a show with its anchor points in the films and TV police series of the era, and not in the actualities:

> The period is well established but in fitting with the coma theme it is very much a seventies that is based on childhood memories. Hence we have cops that are basically right out of the *Sweeney* and a world more in tune with similar shows from the period rather than reality.

The possibility that Tyler's imagination has constructed this world is a helpful rationalization of its failures in respect of realism for some of the viewers—as the previous quotation shows, along with the following:

> We the audience don't yet know whether Hunt and the rest of the team are real or just all in Sam's imagination. If it turns out to be the latter, then perhaps Hunt's OTT-ness is simply what Sam thinks coppers were like in 1973. (*The Sweeney* forum, at http://www.thetvlounge.co.uk)

Valuable Dialogue

One of the three *value-added* functions recognized in Kozloff's scheme for the functional analysis of dialogue in films is the contribution to thematic concerns/ allegorical messages; one of Thompson's 12 characteristics of *quality* drama is controversial subject matter. It is impossible to ignore the question of *content* in the evaluation of screen drama, and dialogue plays a role in the delivery of that content. But, as with any communicative behavior, it is impossible to separate the *what* from the *how*.

It is part of the duty of public service broadcasting to offer programming that is beneficial for audiences in ways that go beyond "mere" entertainment. Mainstream public service broadcasters like the BBC have to manage the risk that such programming could be a turnoff for their viewers; they also want to sell on some of their wares to commercial channels. Television dramatists may either be looking to broadcasting as a platform for their ideas, in the manner of someone like Dennis Potter, or else they may see themselves as being primarily entertainers. The latter will be just as concerned as the publisher to keep viewers happy, whereas the former will often be drawn to drama as a mode of discourse that opens up issues for reflection and debate, and thus seek to avoid anything obviously didactic. There may also be niche rather than mass markets for thought-provoking material, as America has discovered with its HBO (Home Box Office) channel. When the BBC's version of *Life on Mars* was screened in the United States, it was on another niche cable channel (BBC America), albeit one that carries commercial advertising (unlike HBO, and unlike the BBC in the United Kingdom).

Whatever the original intentions of the *Life on Mars* writers, the character configurations they devised gave them scope to depict different philosophies of policing without finally or unambiguously endorsing either one as better. At the same time, these thematic concerns were never allowed to overrule the entertainment dimensions of characterization, plot, nostalgia, and humor. Nelson (2007) praises the series, in terms that indicate the importance of its thematics for him. Following a brief discussion of how the narrative handles one particular issue of police ethics, Nelson summarizes:

> *Life on Mars* is a "quality popular drama" in that it is police series with a twist, but an original twist which opens up potential for it to be much more than a mere reworking of the ingredients in a formula. It offers the pleasures of the genre in resolving cases within the episodes but throwing out a serial hook in Tyler's quest to "get home. [. . .]"
>
> The ensemble is strong, with particularly powerful performances from Simm and Glenister, and the reconstruction of the 1970s is convincing. But *Life on Mars* is more than nostalgic "heritage" drama. In providing undoubted generic pleasures it has the potential also to be thought provoking and to invite complex seeing. (2007: 179)

Nelson approves of the show's originality in respect of the generic formula; he approves of the performances, and the realism; he approves that it has a story arc as well as episode-specific story lines—but the real key to his commendation is in the last line. A good show is thought provoking: *Life on Mars* has the potential to be so. It cannot force viewers to think, but the configuration of its ingredients ought to encourage this.

How does dialogue contribute here? There are three main ways: through personalization of issues with (arguably) merit and sympathy on both sides, through identification with one character's critical view of another, and through speeches in which a *writer-to-audience* address seems to coexist with a *character-to-character* address. I will discuss each of these and also, when possible, refer to relevant commentaries by viewers of the series indicating the possibilities of *uptake* in respect of these devices.

"I Know Only One Way to Police": Issues Personalized

Many critics and commentators have observed that the series allows for the display of two very different views of policing. Gene Hunt gets to articulate one of those views and Sam Tyler the other. Gene is the sheriff, doing whatever it takes to protect good citizens from lawlessness; Sam appreciates that the police force is part of society and the officers' own behavior is rightly a matter of public concern. When they argue, viewers have an opportunity to take sides. For example, in one episode, Gene wants to plant evidence on someone he knows to be a criminal, whereas Sam wants to avoid such unethical behavior. He also doubts its efficacy:

1 SAM: In "Hyde," we don't traditionally keep acid and knocked-off bling in our
        offices just so we can get home early.
2 GENE: So you wouldn't have pulled him in?
3 SAM: Not without evidence!
4 GENE: What, even if you knew people out there were in danger?
5 SAM: People are always in danger, guv.

(Season 1, episode 2, written by Matthew Graham)

Narrative outcomes can then suggest that one was right and the other wrong. In this case, Sam gets the suspect released for lack of evidence, and someone does indeed get hurt. Gene was right. But eventually they get their man, with sound evidence. Sam was right. Over a long(ish) series, the rights and wrongs can be balanced out, compromises can be engineered, and Gene can learn from Sam and vice versa:

1 GENE: See, I told you. I'll do you a deal. I'll listen to your little tape machine now
        and again, OK? So long as you, just sometimes, listen to this [*indicating
        his own head, to symbolize the value of instinct as well as technique*]. OK?
2 [*Sam, shaken, nods assent*].

(Season 1, episode 3, written by Mathew Graham)

1 SAM: Look, you know when I said I wasn't wrong? Well, I was. But, I was right about
        this not being the IRA. I was right to follow my instincts. Just like you always
        say, "Go with your gut feeling." Just taking your lead.
2 GENE: So I'm right?
3 SAM: We both are.
4 GENE: Right.
5 SAM: Right.
6 GENE: Just as long as I'm more right than you.

(Season 2, episode 3, written by Mathew Graham)

Nelson and others are disposed to recognize "complex seeing" in these arrangements. It could also be seen as fence sitting, as a way of dialing down the social critique and allowing entertainment values to prevail. Television can also be criticized for being *insufficiently* opinionated in its own right. *Balance* can be a cop-out. My own research in cyberspace suggests that entertainment-driven responses (i.e., those oriented to the characters and plot) greatly outnumber those that were informed by critical engagement with issues of policing.

Internal Criticism

Gene and his 1973 colleagues are shown to be unashamedly sexist and racist. But the story lines (and its depictions of black and female characters) do not collude with the unreconstructed attitudes. Dialogue, which supplies the non-PC characterizations, also displays Sam's reactions to their outrageous comments—and Sam is one of us:

1 GENE: Now. Yesterday's shooting. The dealers are all so scared we're more likely to get Helen Keller to talk. The Paki in a coma's about as lively as Liberace's dick when he's looking at a naked woman, all in all this investigation's going at the speed of a spastic in a magnet factory.
   [*Sam drops the radio he is holding*].
2 GENE: What?
3 SAM: Think you might have missed out the Jews.

(Season 2, episode 6, written by Mathew Graham and Ashley Pharaoh)

The writer Matthew Graham commented as follows:

We just had a feeling it wouldn't turn out to be a vile piece of offensive drama but might end up being quite cool and fun, and probably the only way to do that it is to take someone with our sensibilities and plonk them right in the middle of it, so that any time Gene Hunt says, "All right luv, go and make us a cup of tea and [bring] a Garibaldi biscuit," someone can roll their eyes. Somehow that lets us off the hook.[5]

The internal criticism can come from the performance as well as the words (as when Sam drops the radio), and, once the premises of the show and its characters are established, it may be enough that twenty-first-century Sam exists as part of the diegesis to activate a critical response from the audience, without *any* action or any speech on his part. His mere presence keeps the 1970s value framework safely distanced. On the other hand, it is a familiar problem in such cases that audiences who are sufficiently drawn to a *bad* character may affiliate with his or her attitudes *despite* the internal criticism. In 2009, as Gene appeared once more on British TV screens in the second season of *Ashes to Ashes*, there was some commentary along those lines:

In *Ashes to Ashes*, which is set in the early 1980s, Gene enjoys some equally sparky clashes with another right-on modern-day colleague, DI Alex Drake (Keeley Hawes). She has been sent back to 1982 from today and is constantly horrified by Gene's casual sexism. This is, after all, a bloke who, in 1973, declared in his characteristic, I'm-never-wrong tone: "As long as I've got a hole in my arse, there'll never be a female prime minister." He's the man political correctness forgot.

And yet, in spite of attitudes that would barely pass muster in the Stone Age, Gene is a hugely loved character. So why has this Neanderthal proved so ridiculously popular? "Gene is so well loved because he's gruff and difficult to please," says Hawes, 33. "He's the opposite of a New Man. People really like that. It's such a breath of fresh air. Someone who exhibits those old-fashioned ways in this PC era is very attractive. What more could you want?"[6]

The reception issues here would hinge not only on trying to establish just how widespread the favorable response to Gene really is, but also whether that popularity is *in spite of* or *because of* the attitudes. Hawes speaks on behalf of heterosexual female viewers when she points toward Hunt's charms; he also has subversive role model/folk hero charms for males. These subjective attractions may be so strong that they exceed the power of the diegesis (including dialogue cues) safely to contain them. Alternatively, the attitudes Hunt is allowed to articulate and possess as his own can also be read as separable, in principle, from that character, to the extent that they provide support for an existing critique of the *politically correct* present day.

Writer to Audience

Once upon a time in TV police drama there were shows that told their audiences, in direct address, what the thematic concerns of their stories were, and what views to adopt. George Dixon (*Dixon of Dock Green*) stood facing the camera at the start and end of every episode and said something along the lines of the following:

> Well . . . that was the only bad copper I ever met. They say you get a bad apple in every barrel, the police have to build on trust and the papers will print a page about one bad policeman and never mention the thousands who do their job properly . . . . When we find a bad one we're down on him like a ton of bricks. Well, I'd better be on my way. (Cited in Sydney-Smith 2002: 114)

The paternalist content of Dixon's discourse, his complacent attitude, his confidence in the absolute dividing line between "good" and "bad" policemen, and the authoritative speaking position the character is given belong to yet another world—not the Britain of 1973 and certainly not the first decade of the twenty-first century. As early as 1962 (in *Z Cars*), the main police characters included a wife beater and a gambler, though it took rather longer before institution-level issues attracted the attention of dramatists.

Because the audiences of 2006 no longer trusted the police as they might have (or could be treated as doing) in the 1950s and 1960s, police characters cannot be allowed to address the audience in this straightforward fashion. But perhaps they can still make credible points about the state of society in their conversations with other characters? In one episode of *Life on Mars* there is a murder to solve: the victim is a supporter of the football team Manchester United, and suspicion falls on fans of the local rivals, Manchester City. Sociologically speaking, the issue in this episode is "football hooliganism in Britain: its origins and consequences." It turns out that the killer is another Manchester United football fan. He has killed a fellow supporter, not in anger but to turn rivalry into war, by inciting the United fans to blame the City fans for the death. The police pursuit of the real villain eventually leads to a "confession" scene between the Sam and the killer, Pete.

1 PETE: A good punch-up's all part of the game. It's about pride. Pride in your team, being the best.
2 SAM: No it isn't. [*pause*] This is how it starts. [*pause*] And then it escalates. It gets on the telly. And in the press. And then other fans from other clubs start trying to out-do each other. And then it becomes about hate. And then it's nothing to do with football any more. It's about gangs. And scumbags like you, roaming the country, seeing who can cause the most trouble. And then we over-react. And we have to put up perimeter fences. And we treat the fans like animals. Forty, fifty thousand people, herded into pens.
   [*pause*]
   And then how long before something happens? Eh? How long before something terrible happens and we are dragging bodies out?

(Season 1, episode 5, written by Tony Jordan)

Blame is being meted out by Sam. He condemns supporters like Pete for instigating "punch-ups" and trying to justify this. He also criticizes the police. They overreacted in their approaches to crowd control and crowd violence. The endpoint of the story, as Sam and the audience know, is the real-life tragedy that occurred at Hillsborough Stadium, when these same crowd control methods, poorly applied, did in fact produce the effect that Pete can hear only as prediction.[7]

The situation is highly charged, and this is an issue on which Sam feels strongly, himself in mourning for a happier, safer era of football spectatorship that he remembers from his childhood. Is it enough, though, to rescue this exchange from a charge of didacticism? Dialogue here mediates thematic discourse through character situated within particular narrative circumstance. *Dixon of Dock Green*, by contrast, mediated comparable discourse retrospectively as regards the narrative, and in such a way as to elevate the character, Dixon, to unambiguous "spokesman" status. It is less easy—though not impossible—to read Sam in this scene as the spokesman for *Life on Mars*, not only because Sam and Pete's conversation takes place behind the fourth wall, but also because of other flaws in the "Sam Tyler" character which undercut his heroic role in this drama.

On the other hand, the writers have gone to some trouble to get this discourse on the record. They have constructed Pete as a character who is willing to explain what he has done and why, though not in a position rationally to challenge Sam's analysis. At the same time, the scene itself has been contrived as one in which Sam and Pete are alone together for long enough for Sam to say what needs to be said. Dialogue is liable to come across as heavy handed if characters themselves reach beyond the circumstances of their own lives, to make general points about society, particularly, as here, if they seem to do so as the mouthpiece for the dramatist's own views.

Was this speech successful? What did it mean to its viewers? Among all the ideas and pleasures offered by this episode, did they even notice it? Did they object to the homiletic address? My findings indicate that mostly they did not find this particular element significant enough to warrant a comment, but the few who did were appreciative. My suspicion that it might be found unjustifiably didactic was not borne out. I could find no negative references to the speech online, only the following positive ones:

> The police raided a secluded gang fight on the day of the match and Sam caught the killer—the local he'd befriended while working undercover in the bar.
>
> For me, this was where the nerve hit; when Sam remonstrated with the killer over the motives for soccer hooliganism, he reminded everyone in the audience who ever attended a U.K. soccer match in the 1970s of where it all started—and where it all ended—with the police pulling bodies from the terracing when the measures designed to segregate rival fans went too far. (Martin Conaghan on *TV Squad*, http://www.tvsquad.com/2006/02/06/life-on-mars-part-five-soccer-hooliganism/, posted February 6, 2006, retrieved April 16, 2009)

> There was an outstanding scene in episode five, when the murder of a Manchester United fan seems to point to an upswing in football hooliganism, and Sam knowing what is to come has a fantastic speech about how minor disturbances may be "part of the fun" to the lads, but that escalation is just around the corner. (Susan Hated Literature, http://www.susanhatedliterature.net/2006/02/27/life-on-mars-season-1/, blog entry for February 27, 2006, retrieved April 16, 2009)

> I loved that speech, it was so well done. He is an excellent actor. (Forum comment on Television without Pity, http://forums.televisionwithoutpity.com/index.php?showtopic=3134475&st=30, posted February 8, 2006)

> The heart of the story, however, was a poignant message—a tad heavily delivered—about football hooliganism. "A good punch-up is all part of the game," said the killer, Pete (Anthony Flanagan). Sam, coming from the future where he had witnessed Hillsborough, talked of the escalation of violence that simply breeds more violence, resulting in fans being herded into pens, and then: "How long before something terrible happens and we are dragging bodies out?" (*Mail on Sunday* TV reviews, Jaci Stephen, *The Mourning After*, February 12, 2006, page 75.)

> I really enjoyed LOM last night too, with the car chase at the start and thought the storyline had a moral message hidden inside too, with Sam's Reganesque lecture

(except without the Reganesque 70's dialogue) to the football violence ring leader. (*The Sweeney* forum, at http://www.thetvlounge.com, posted Febrary 7, 2006, retrieved April 17, 2009)

The football violence speech was a great piece of writing and everybody over 20 should have known exactly what he was referring to, speaking of which I will never forget the story of the couple who lost both their teenage daughters. You don't need to be a lover of the "beautiful game" to be moved by such events. (*The Sweeney* forum, at http://www.thetvlounge.com, posted February 8, 2006, retrieved April 17, 2009)

The writers here are broadly in sympathy with Tyler's sentiments. They like the speech because they *agree* with it. Its dramatic effectiveness would almost certainly have been weaker if Sam had been saying something that these viewers personally disagreed with. Conaghan, the writer of the first extract above, seems to appreciate that it is intended as part of a discourse that is beyond character. It is not possible to say whether the other commentators also hear it that way.

DISCUSSION

This chapter has ventured further away from the sociolinguistics of dialogue than most others in this book. In particular, it has had nothing to say about the micromanagement of characters' speech exchanges in relation to turn taking, inferences and implicatures, adjacency pairs, overlapping speech, hesitation phenomena, or misunderstanding. These are all interesting areas for exploration, and the second of my two case studies will return to this general territory.

The influence of sociolinguistics here is broadly that of the ethnography of communication (see chapter 6 in this volume, especially the section "Communication Ethnography and the Dramatization of Communicative Events"). When any TV drama is broadcast, it opens up a social interaction between dramatist and audience. This, rather than the character-to-character exchanges (though subsuming them), is the primary object of study. Dialogue, along with narrative structure, and all of the nonverbal aspects of performance and production, is a resource for achieving higher level dramatic objectives. In this perspective, the micro-sociolinguistics of character-to-character speech is communicatively relevant, (for example, it contributes to characterization), but this is only one factor among many others. The content of the talk has to be considered, as well as its styling—as I have attempted in the section "Valuable Dialogue" above.

The specific sources I have drawn on in this chapter come from film studies (Kozloff) and from the media studies literature on contemporary TV drama (Nelson), and not from the sociolinguistics of talk, or even from the cognate field of stylistics. Yet I have attempted throughout to add to a primarily textual approach, by taking seriously the suggestion in stylistics of drama's double articulation. (See the discussion in chapter 3, with reference to the work of Short and Bubel in particular). In construing TV drama as social interaction between dramatist and audience, it was necessary to look at both sides of that interaction. This is why the foregoing account quotes as much from the reviews and viewer commentary on the series as it does from the text itself.

Life on Mars, the series, has content as well as form. It relates to subjects that viewers should care about, as members of society, policing, political correctness, football hooliganism. The sociolinguistics of talk, as such, does not usually concern itself with the subject matter (see Cameron 1997 for a critique of this limitation). But anyone interested in debates about policing and other social issues, who also believes that the *how* and the *what* of expression and representation are closely connected, will want to understand how different kinds of interactions operate in their varying cultural conditions. Some things that can be said about these important subjects under the aegis of *television drama* might be harder to say in other communicative modes and contexts. Drama is fictional, so is not beholden to particular histories in its narratives. This allows the play of imagination, even, as in *Life on Mars*, at the expense of epistemological realism. It personalizes the issues and draws up possible lines of identification and repulsion across its range of characters. *Television* drama on these subjects—even in the era of niche marketing—can be addressed to very large audiences (six to seven million for episodes of *Life on Mars*, counting only the first-run British broadcasts, not repeats, DVD sales, international sales, or downloads). All of this seems to me congruent with Hymesian principles of communication ethnography—to which I would want to add a more developed awareness of the economic and industrial factors that shape the contexts of communicative practice.

Notwithstanding these theoretical points, the primary interest of this chapter is not theoretical, but in what it contributes to discussion of contemporary television drama in general and *Life on Mars* in particular, using dialogue as a point of entry into this area. The approach I have adopted requires some caution in matters of textual interpretation; otherwise it risks making unwarranted presumptions about the audience's contribution to the interaction. That contribution certainly requires more systematic enquiry, going beyond the opportunistic use of online commentaries adopted here. Nevertheless, the reviews and comments were extensive enough to point to some important lines for further research, in which dialogue would still be important, along with other textual and contextual factors. These inquiries would need to focus especially on (a) the relative significance of the *quality* and the *value* (in my terms) elements in audiences' appreciation of the series and (b) the question of how to *read* Gene Hunt, and, beyond this, the implications to be drawn from the cultural currency of an apparently *likable* character with some particular *unlikable* attitudes.

9

House and Snark

The previous chapter focused on the social interaction between dramatist and audience. In doing so, it discussed screen dialogue from a functional perspective, largely playing down the micromanagement of talk exchanges, but playing up the content of the talk. This chapter reverses the priorities. Its particular focus is on strategies of impoliteness in the American medical series *House* (Fox 2004–present). It makes a case that these strategies are interesting from an interactional sociolinguistic perspective. They demonstrate ways of being impolite that have not so far been addressed by the available theoretical accounts, and, more generally, add to the sheer *complication* of trying to theorize impoliteness.

It need not be regarded as a problem that the instances of impoliteness discussed here are drawn not from real life but from pre-scripted materials performed by actors. If the interactional moments make sense, if they *come across* in the ways I shall describe, it is because they rely on *general* principles of interpretation, not principles of interpretation that are exclusive to expressive culture and crafted texts. Theories of impoliteness and conflict talk need to be elaborate enough to cope with the kinds of material found in this TV show. Research is still coming to terms with its complexity (see Bousfield 2008; Bousfield and Loucher 2008).

Although the primary focus is on impoliteness, the chapter has a secondary interest in the project of the series as drama, and the function of the impoliteness in this particular text as a contribution to series branding. The writers and producers intend this characteristic as one of its selling points: in the DVD collection for season 1, there is a bonus feature of "House-isms"—a selection of one-liners extracted from context for the discrete pleasure that they afford collectively, separated from their narrative context.

As one viewer put it,

> I managed to get my hand on a screener of the pilot episode and watched it yesterday. And I loved it. Which came as a total surprise since I don't like shows about Doctors and CSI bores me half to death. And this show is a bit a mix of both. But: it has a non-PC main character. It has Hugh Laurie and it has the snark. Lots and lots of snark. (posted July 1, 2004, on Television without Pity, http://www. forums.televisionwithoutpity.com/, retrieved April 20, 2009)

Snark and snarky have become popular terms in cyberspace, though they seem to vary in meaning. For some they suggest criticism that is condescending and mean-spirited (Denby 2009), and snark certainly need not be witty and entertaining—though the kind that House engages in often is so, and this viewer is certainly responding to the pleasure of snark. To contextualize the examples and to enable the wider discussion, it is useful to begin with a general account of the show itself.

HOUSE

House is a medical drama series set in a large New Jersey teaching hospital, the fictional "Princeton–Plainsboro." It has a set of six principal characters, and Gregory House (Hugh Laurie) is the central one. The other characters (in the first three seasons, though with changes in the fourth and fifth) are the three junior doctors who work for him, Alison Cameron, a white American (Jennifer Morrison), Eric Foreman, an African American (Omar Epps), Robert Chase, a white Australian (Jesse Spencer), House's boss, the hospital administrator Lisa Cuddy (Lisa Edelstein), and his friend and colleague James Wilson (Robert Sean Leonard), who is head of oncology in the hospital. I will follow the usage of the characters among themselves, and refer to main characters by their surnames only, unless there is reason to do otherwise.

House is a series that has run for more than one season. In the United States it is one of the flagship series of the Fox network. In the United Kingdom its first-run broadcasts are on Five, the newest of the terrestrial (analogue) channels, free-to-air on all services and platforms. According to the Internet Movie Database, http://www.imdb.com, it is distributed worldwide to countries including, at least, France, Canada, Australia, Bulgaria, Czech Republic, Hungary, Slovakia, Singapore, Poland, Romania, Scandinavia, Spain, Japan, Germany, and Estonia. IMDb also credits the series with 22 industry awards, including one People's Choice, two Golden Globes, and two Emmys, along with countless nominations.

Although medical drama is a staple of the British and American television drama diet, this show represents a departure from recent convention in certain respects (Hallam 2009). It certainly represents a departure from the pattern followed by such shows as Chicago Hope (CBS 1994–2000) and, especially, ER (NBC 1994–2009). This pattern has been very well explored by Jason Jacobs (2003), who focuses on depictions of the hospital workplace, drawing attention to its fascination with the damaged human body, as well as aspects of the workplace as a bureaucratically governed environment that frustrates personal and professional relationships as much as it encourages them.

A key difference between *ER* et al. and *House*, for the purposes of this chapter, is that the former are constructed as *ensemble* pieces, focusing on the life of the ward or department and the social interactions of the characters. *House* represents a return to the hero-based format of, for instance, Dr. Kildare in the series of that name (CBS 1961–1966). However, the attractive, caring Kildare has been replaced by an altogether more abrasive variant of the hero-doctor.

A significant aspect of *House* is its approach to narrative. It has been described as a medical mystery series, inasmuch as the weekly episode plots center on single patients who present with unusual symptoms that do not easily fit with known conditions. A typical episode opens with scenes presenting the prehospitalization health emergency of the "patient of the week." It moves through sequences in which possibilities are explored, brings the patient to a new crisis (often when the wrong condition has been treated, so that the "remedy" has made the patient worse), and concludes when the correct diagnosis is discovered, the therapy begun, and the patient set on the road to recovery. To this extent the series has as much in common with *CSI* (CBS 2000–present) as it does with *ER*. The comparison with *CSI* is further reinforced, visually, in the similar-but-different use that each makes of the cinematographic technique "endoscopic gaze"—of which more below.

The intensity of the single-patient drama is broken up by including within episodes one or more *clinic* scenes. The device that makes this possible is the idea that House, besides being a specialist diagnostician with patients of his own, also works on a rotation in the hospital drop-in clinic, where patients might appear with any condition from the mildest sore throat to advanced cancer. These scenes serve several functions, according to context. Sometimes it is light relief, sometimes there are thematic resonances, and occasionally a patient will migrate from the clinic to the ward. The series also has some story and character arcs (developments occurring over more than one episode).

Contemporary TV audiences expect their hospital dramas to be medically realistic, and *House* certainly displays a satisfactory quota of bodily excretions from usual and unusual places, not to mention fits, seizures, and screaming agonies. The series deals with *extreme medicine*—outrageous therapies for often extraordinary conditions. It is only proper that this should call for some correspondingly excessive imagery of medical procedures, though no doubt it "pulls its punches" to some extent in recognition that this is meant for a television and not a cinema audience. A key visual trope is the suspenseful moment when the patient's body glides into the womb-like confines of an MRI machine. *House* also makes use of the endoscopic gaze (van Dijck 2001)— moving image sequences that appear to come from *within* a human body, first popularized in the visualization of forensic detective work in the series *CSI*.

CONFLICT AND IMPOLITENESS IN TALK:
THEORETICAL ISSUES

An interdisciplinary collection on conflict talk of the early 1990s (Grimshaw 1990a) paved the way for subsequent work under this general heading. The following very selective survey of the now extensive literature pays particular attention to work involving either mass media texts (e.g., interaction in docu-soaps or on talk radio) or in drama. It is interesting to find a considerable number of such publications, suggesting perhaps not only practical difficulties in obtaining appropriate data from primary interaction contexts, but also, as Culpeper et al. (1998, 2005) suggests, the importance of conflict as a source of dramatic and entertainment value.

Conflict talk in TV drama has been scripted by screenwriters, directed by producers, and performed by actors. It is thus highly contrived in comparison with what occurs in less prearranged material. The contrivance in the case of this series is in the service of not just one but two of the functions of dialogue in audiovisual drama identified by Kozloff (2000). It is, most obviously, in the service of characterization, but in terms of Kozloff's scheme it also comes under the heading "exploiting the resources of language"—here, for the sake of the pleasure that the wit of indirect face attacks provides in the context of a dramatic entertainment.

One of the contributions to the Grimshaw collection (Tannen 1990) looked at conflict in literary texts, and thus explored represented rather than naturally occurring conflict talk. Tannen's article, focused in part on Harold Pinter's play *Betrayal*, used the written text, not a performance of that text, as its data. However, Tannen wrote about the functions of pauses and silences in this play. As is well known, Pinter was very specific in his indications of such between-turn nonlinguistic *expression*, and all faithful performances would be expected to respect his specifications. Tannen's argument here is that the pauses in this play are inserted as markers of unspoken tension in the relationship (a love triangle), whereas silences, intended as longer than pauses, are inserted to mark the climactic moments of these tensions.

Not speaking can, of course, be conflictual in different ways. It can indicate a kind of silencing—a speaker who has been cowed into silence, who can say nothing because all alternatives are equally destructive/impossible. It can also indicate a more active kind of refusal—a gesture of noncooperation in the talk and/or in the project constituted or represented by the talk.

When conflict is not pre-scripted, it may nevertheless be formulaic, especially when participants orient to an overarching institutional context. The conflict, displayed in certain kinds of talk radio shows, for instance, has been studied from this conversation-analytic perspective (Hutchby 1996). The raison d'être of the genre is the displaying of personal opinions about public issues and the challenging of those opinions by the host. Hutchby shows how hosts introduce callers, how callers display a personal opinion on some topic of public interest, and how hosts retrospectively construct that position as arguable by challenging it (cf. Maynard 1985). Callers are, from that point onward, structurally on the defensive, unless they find a way to take the initiative and push the host into clarifying his own position. If the host is left to specify his position more spontaneously, he may, when he does so, move directly without a pause into a termination of the call, ending the caller's access to the airwaves.

The performance of conflict requires attention to talk as interaction, not to isolated utterances. In Tannen's material, pauses and silences are responses to what has gone before, and in turn they influence what comes next. In Hutchby's material, it is the host's opposing of an opinion that constitutes a caller's prior utterance as an *arguable*, in conversation-analytic terms—just as happens in nonbroadcast argument sequences.

The concept of conflict in discourse has also fed into the related research field, the study of impoliteness (Bousfield 2008; Bousfield and Loucher 2008), in which attention to discourse sequencing has been less evident until recently. Impoliteness relates to the intentional expression of hostility in talk, and this does not necessarily occur as part of the study of argument. Insults, for instance, "You moron," "You're being an idiot," and so forth, are overtly hostile in intent, but can be issued outside of argumentative contexts, or they can constitute *banter* (see below). The converse is also true. Arguments, even when understood as dialogic and emergent, rather than as monologic and crafted to establish a point, can be conducted in emotionally cool, interactively cooperative, and thus nonhostile ways.

Early work on impoliteness (see Culpeper 1996) addressed a theoretical and empirical problem inherited from the pioneering work of Brown and Levinson (1978). Brown and Levinson's politeness theory introduced a model for the classification of different types of politeness. Central to their model was the idea of *face*, meaning a sense of identity and self-respect common to all normal humans, though with differences as to what constituted any specific identity. This concept, introduced to the social sciences by Erving Goffman (1967) was elaborated by Brown and Levinson into two facets: *negative face* (the desire not to be imposed upon) and *positive face* (the desire to be valued for who and what you are).[1] Face-threatening acts, behaviors that risked damage to the face of self or other in this sense, could be managed in different ways as follows: *FTA* stands for "face-threatening act." Numbers indicate each superstrategy and mark it for degree of politeness, with 1 indicating the least face-threatening option and 5 indicating the most.

As others have pointed out, this model accounts for impoliteness only as the absence of politeness. It further suggests perhaps that the basic orientation of all talk is toward politeness in the sense of interpersonal supportiveness and social

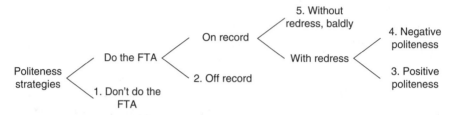

Figure 9.1 Politeness options

harmony.[2] Culpeper is one of several writers who have sought to develop a complementary account of *im*politeness in discourse (cf. Craig, Tracy, and Spisak 1986, Tracy 1990). His approach is a valuable one for my purposes, because "Gregory House" can in part be understood as a virtuoso player of the discourse instruments of impoliteness.

Culpeper's "anatomy of impoliteness" in its original guise looked as follows. The impoliteness superstrategies as presented here seem to mirror the politeness superstrategies of the Brown and Levinson model:

> Instead of enhancing or supporting face, impoliteness superstrategies are a means of attacking face:
>
> 1. Bald on record impoliteness—the FTA is performed in a direct, clear, unambiguous and concise way in circumstances where face is not irrelevant or minimized.
> 2. Positive impoliteness—the use of strategies designed to damage the addressee's positive face wants.
> 3. Negative impoliteness—the use of strategies designed to damage the speaker's negative face wants.
> 4. Sarcasm or mock politeness—the FTA is performed with the use of politeness strategies that are obviously insincere, and thus remain surface realizations [...]
> 5. Withhold politeness—the absence of politeness work where it would be expected. (Culpeper 1996: 356)

Superstrategies 2 and 3 lead to various *output strategies*. Positive politeness output strategies include "ignore, snub the other" and "use inappropriate identity markers." Negative politeness output strategies include "frighten" and "condescend, scorn, or ridicule."

This general model has been revised and developed in later work (Culpeper 1998, 2005, Culpeper et al. 2002, Bousfield 2007a, 2007b). Culpeper et al. (2002: 1576) conclude that the five superstrategy model should not be viewed as a mirror image of the politeness model—that no hierarchy of politeness could be attributed to the superstrategies. Another conclusion takes the form of a suggestion that, in actual usage, mixtures of superstrategies are more common than singular occurrence. Culpeper concludes that intentionality, although important, is not enough. He offers a definition of impoliteness, one that encompasses the perspective of the hearer as well as that of the speaker:

> Impoliteness comes about when: (1) the speaker communicates face-attack inten-tionally, or (2) the hearer perceives and/or constructs behavior as intentionally face-attacking, or a combination of (1) and (2). (Culpeper 2005: 38)

This in itself suggests that the behavior that follows the supposedly impolite act must be analytically attended to in assessing the import of that prior act, in the absence of any other information regarding the hearer's state of mind. This is consistent with the work developed in Culpeper et al. (2002), and pursued by Bousfield (2007a) and others, that explores the sequencing of conversational moves in the conduct of impolite exchanges, with reference to the options available to speakers at different stages of such episodes. It is also suggested by the definition that although a speaker may not have intended to be im-polite, impoliteness has occurred if a hearer believes that he or she did so intend when using the offending form. Intentionality, real or attributed, is key, in a way that is consistent with pragmatic approaches to talk, but inconsis-tent with theoretical positions that reject claims by analysts to be able to "see inside" the black box of someone's head. One line of defense in favor of intentionality claims is that inferring intention and motive is exactly what ordinary language users do:

> ... the availability of ethnographic context *and* of an optimally complete behavior record permits analysts to make such inferences and attributions which are "for-most-practical-purposes" (paraphrasing Garfinkel) no less plausible than those of actual participants. This claim is subject to qualification but the disambiguation process is that which we ourselves employ in interaction—where, it must be conceded, we sometimes err. (Grimshaw 1990b: 281)

Culpeper's data for the 2005 paper comprised exchanges from the "exploitative" quiz show *The Weakest Link* (BBC 2000–present), and he recognizes the importance of this mediated environment as part of the ethnographic con-text. Specifically, part of the paper discusses whether this context provides voyeuristic pleasure (note the visual metaphor) and neutralizes or sanctions the impoliteness:

> If we also take on board the fact that Anne Robinson's persona is a fiction then genuine impoliteness should not occur. However [...] evidence that the targets of the impoliteness take it as genuine is present in the form of their counter-strategies and non-verbal reactions. If the hearer "takes" a behavior as intentional face-attack, then that counts as impoliteness according to my definition. (2005: 69)

Culpeper argues that the insulted *WL* contestants do take offense, and that this can be accounted for by reference to findings in social psychology that behavior tends to be more salient than situational factors—it "engulfs the field" in Heider's (1958) terms. This must be true for some contestants—those whose response is one of embarrassment and whose communicative "presence" diminishes as a result of the attack. There is another possibility—that some of the targets are themselves performing "offense taken" for the benefit of the television audience—that, like the host Anne Robinson, they, too, are capable of presenting a constructed persona in this context. There are also issues to consider about the circumstances in which a character-to-character insult on television might also be a show-to-audience insult. This can happen in cases in which members of the audience are in a position to identify with one of the characters via attribution of category membership. An insult to one fat person is potentially an insult to all, and fat audience members could take offense—but so, too, could skinny audience members on behalf of their fat fellow citizens. Weight is safe territory for *The Weakest Link*, but race is unsafe, and Welsh nationality (following a notorious, arguably *real* insult by Robinson to the Welsh on a different program, on account of which she had to undertake remedial work in the real world)[3] has become an area of "play" for the show (in the articulation sense as well as the pleasure sense). Mediation changes things for impoliteness theory in more complex ways than have yet been examined. At the same time, it provides an important arena for examining the interface between micro and macro social variables: the conduct of insults as a form of interpersonal behavior on the one hand and their content on the other.

Another advancement in Culpeper's (2005) work from the 1996 account is that it introduces a distinction between sarcasm and off-record impoliteness. In 2005 the concept of sarcasm is explicitly restricted to superficial politeness, of the kind illustrated by Leech's original 1983 example, "DO help yourself" (falling tone on "self") can be sarcastic in the right context. This formulation has a straightforward, nonsarcastic, overtly polite use, by a host to a guest: someone who is, as English middle-class manners require, civilly refraining from eating and drinking until permission is granted to begin the feast. The sarcastic use plays with this polite use: it is addressed by a host to the guest who could *not* wait. Sarcasm, thus understood, is not an impoliteness strategy or superstrategy at all but a *meta*strategy and thus outside the basic framework (Culpeper 2005: 42). *Off-record impoliteness* takes its place in the model. An off-record insult does not have to display politeness: sarcasm does. "The FTA is performed by means of an implicature but in such a way that one attributable intention clearly outweighs any other" (Culpeper 2005: 44).

Speakers do not have to make a face-threatening act explicit if they want to be impolite. They can implicate it, by flouting a Gricean maxim. In Culpeper's own example this is managed by having a character ask a question to which he knows the answer (i.e., it is a rhetorical question) and in which the answer is insulting to the other character: "What are you—dying of some wasting disease?" The point of the distinction between strategies and metastrategies may be more important for the theoretical apparatus than for explicating actual examples. I will return to this later in discussing an example of indirect impoliteness/sarcasm on the part of Doctor House.

Culpeper follows Leech (1983) in recognizing that, if speakers can insult one another through mock politeness, they can also do the reverse—enhance face by *seeming* to be insulting. *Banter* can thus be defined as mock *im*politeness. The expression of impolite beliefs becomes banter if the beliefs in question are blatantly in violation of Grice's quality maxim, in other words, blatantly untrue: "In order to show solidarity with h, say something which is (i) obviously untrue, and (ii) obviously impolite to h [and this will give rise to an interpretation such that] what s says is impolite to h and is clearly untrue. Therefore what s means is polite to h and true" (Leech 1983: 144).

The principle whereby banter in this sense can be seen as positively polite rests on the logic that only people on close terms can afford to take risks in their interpersonal strategies—therefore, in taking such a risk, someone shows that they are, or would like to be, on intimate terms. Intimations of intimacy are a form of positive politeness. The banter principle covers, among other things, ritual insults, as studied by Labov (1972). However, it is not easy to find examples of banter in *House* that meet the requirement that the beliefs expressed should be obviously, blatantly false. This is consistent with the construction of the House character as someone who has *intimacy issues*, to use the contemporary folk-psychology idiom. I will return to this point in due course.

Recent research on impoliteness in interaction draws its data from a variety of domains, including online communication (Graham 2007), parliamentary discourse (Harris 2001), and secondary texts in the form of court reports (Kryk-Kastovsky 2006). Publicly accessible sources (i.e., mass media texts) have often been used (e.g., in Culpeper et al. 2003, Culpeper 2005, Bousfield 2007a, 2007b). Impoliteness theory has also been applied to drama dialogue (Tannen 1990, Culpeper 1996, 1998, Rudanko 2005). What is missing in this range is research in which the data take the form of represented talk (as in drama dialogue) and are mediated (as in broadcasting). Gregory House is neither Timon of Athens nor Gordon Ramsay of *Boiling Point* (London Weekend Television 1998) and other reality TV programs, though there may be traces of both in his makeup.

THE RUDENESS OF DOCTORS

Whether or not real-life doctors are habitually rude to patients (and/or to junior doctors and nursing staff) or interpreted as rude by those they interact with, it is undoubtedly true that fictional doctors (especially those deployed for comic purposes) are often rude, to the point that this could be seen as a stereotype in its own right. Because *stereotype* is such a pejorative term, however, I will refer instead to the *rude doctor schema* (cf. chapter 7 in this volume), while recognizing that even schematic rude doctors have some individuality. British film/TV characters consistent with this general schema include James Robertson Justice as Sir Lancelot Spratt in the *Doctor* film series of the 1950s and 1960s (e.g., *Doctor in the House*, 1954), Martin Clunes as Martin Ellingham (*Doc Martin*, ITV 2004–present), and Keith Allen as Tony Whitman (*Bodies*, BBC 2004–2005). This is in contrast to the Dr. Kildare/Dr. Finlay type—in hospitals or in the community, the doctors who combine professional skills with the great bedside manner (*Dr. Kildare*, NBC 1961–1966, *Dr Finlay's Casebook*, BBC 1962–1971).

Among the rude doctors, Ellingham, for instance, is styled as someone who is lacking in normal social skills. He ruins his own "first kiss" with the local schoolteacher by pointing out to her, in her own best health interests, and in the series' cliffhanger, that she has bad breath. With patients, Ellingham's rudeness can be often be a display of impatience with the demands of patients, in which viewers can hear and see that he has some justification:

> *Context.* Overweight mother wants a prescription of Ritalin or similar for her similarly proportioned daughter. Doctor thinks a better therapy for the child would be an improved diet.

1 ELLINGHAM: I have patients to see. This consultation's over.
2 MOTHER: But you haven't told me what's wrong with her yet.
3 ELLINGHAM: She's very annoying.
   [...]
4 MOTHER: I have not come here to talk about my cooking.
5 ELLINGHAM: No, you have come here to ask me to sedate your child so that
      you can pretend she's a good little girl.
6 MOTHER: She *is* a good little girl.
7 ELLINGHAM: There's nothing "little" about her.

The peremptory closing of the consultation in line 1 is blatantly impolite in Culpeper's terms, as is his description of the patient as "annoying" (line 3), his formulation of the mother's intentions (line 5), and his comment on the child's size (line 7—the wordplay perhaps giving him some personal satisfaction, too). Line 3 can be seen as the most overtly impolite if we base this judgment on literal meaning, but it is line 5 that involves the most wounding insults—the adult's motherhood and her integrity are impugned, damaging her positive face wants to be seen as a good mother.

Similar kinds of examples can be found in *House*. But the form, purpose, and range of the impolite behavior in this drama seem to take Gregory House beyond the reach of the schematic rude doctor. In the case of House, the rudeness is presented as part of a deliberate self-fashioning on his part, a manifestation of contemporary culture's interest in ironic and other "insincere" modes of speech. In relation to form, for instance, a case can be made for an interactional impoliteness resource not hitherto discussed in the sociolinguistic literature—*fake banter*. In relation to purpose, the point will be that, as in the Santa Claus example, House takes pleasure in the insults he disburses at other people's expense and does not need them to share the joke with him.

Fake Banter

Banter, as discussed by Leech and endorsed by Culpeper, already involves second-order presentation of self—the interpersonal significance of an *obvious* first-order sense is discounted by the context, and a different, opposite, interpersonal significance is rationally calculated: For Leech (see above) it is when utterances are obviously untrue *and* obviously impolite that they can function as demonstrations of solidarity. Banter asks hearers not to take the impoliteness at face value, just as sarcasm asks them not to take the politeness at face value. In *House* there is an extraordinary amount of material indicating the possibility of another metastrategy—*fake banter*, a form of speech that could, like real banter, be asking a hearer to discount the impoliteness and hear it instead as solidarity or intimacy, but which, on the other hand, and unlike real banter, bases itself on beliefs that are *not* obviously untrue, but about which there is some doubt or some problem. There may be—and in *House* there certainly are—additional doubts about the speaker's appeal to relations of intimacy with the targets of his fake banter.

Banter in Leech's sense would seem to be more appropriate for personal relationships than for workplace relationships. In real-life workplaces, professionalism puts certain normative constraints on expressions of intimacy/solidarity, although professional colleagues and coworkers do, of course, enter into personal relationships, whether officially prohibited, frowned upon, or permitted—normative rules may not be respected in practice. This has been the standard territory of medical drama, not to mention the basis of many real-life friendships, love affairs, and marriages. *De facto* workplace power relations also interfere with the possibilities for genuine intimacy. House is not the kind of character to let the demands of professionalism alone stand in the way of anything he intended to do. On the other hand, he positively enjoys the official power he has over Chase, Foreman, and Cameron, as well as the hold he exercises over his boss by virtue of being the hospital's best (though most exasperating) doctor. House gets to produce considerable quantities of "banter-like" dialogue, but there is (a) no possibility of appealing to a justification of intimacy between him and his interlocutor and (b) provocative content.

House occasionally purports to tease Foreman, a black doctor, by attributing specific characteristics to him on the basis of his racial identity. Foreman is imagined as having lived in a "bad," drug-infested neighborhood, to be familiar with recreational drug use and the kind of crime popularly associated with such areas, as in the following examples from the first and second seasons:

> *Context*: House and the junior doctors are discussing the possibility that their latest patient has taken an overdose of something to make him high:

1 HOUSE: Copy machine toner. Same punch as GHB. A little pricier, way more dangerous. On the other hand, it is legal. [*To Foreman*] I want you to go to his house and find his stash. Betcha know all the good hiding spots.
2 FOREMAN: Actually, I never did drugs. [Leaves]

(Season 1, episode 8, "Poison," written by Matt Witten)

> *Context*: Cuddy, Foreman, and House are discussing a destitute patient—they need to find out more about her, before they can make progress with her treatment.

1 CUDDY: Fine. But nothing more until you find out who she is.
2 FOREMAN: How are we supposed to—?
3 HOUSE: Hey! He knows more homeless people than any of us. Go check out the 'hood, dawg.
(*Foreman expresses exasperation nonverbally, but does not speak.*)

(Season 1, episode 10, "Histories," written by Joel Anderson Thompson)

> *Context*: House and the junior doctors are discussing the symptoms of a patient on death row.

1 FOREMAN: The guy's probably a heroin addict, which explains the tachycardia, which caused the pulmonary edema.
2 CHASE: How does an inmate on Death Row get his hands on heroin?
3 FOREMAN: Are you serious?
4 HOUSE: The man knows prisons. When we've got a yachting question, we'll come to you.

(Season 2, episode 1, "Acceptance," written by Russel Friend and Garrett Lerner)

Note that the last of these also teases Chase on the grounds of his family wealth and the kinds of recreational activity stereotypically associated with that. Because Foreman did once serve time as a juvenile for breaking-and-entering (a biographical fact that has actually secured him his position on the staff, as evidence of his *street smarts*, valued by House), the image House deploys is not wholly inappropriate. Hence the *jokes* do not fit Leech's definition of banter, which specifies that the impolite propositions need to be obviously untrue.

As indirect face attack, "I see you as a (former) homeless, drug-using prison habitué" is hearable as something that House enjoys saying (implying) to the less powerful, younger man, bracketing off as irrelevant both its truth (is/was Foreman ever really like that? Is that what black people in general are like?) and/or its sincerity (does House really believe that this is what Foreman is like or what black people in general are like?)—challenging Foreman not to do likewise. If Foreman does not bracket off these issues (as in the first of the exchanges above), then he has fallen into the strategic trap that House has laid for him. If he does, then he has allowed the taunt to pass as banter, even though it has failed to fulfill the strict criteria.[4] The face attack here therefore lies not in the content so much as in the challenge it represents—to bite back or shrug it off. Given the social relations of senior to junior here, such challenges can be regarded as House's power plays. The fact that these attacks relate specifically to *race*, in the American context, may also give them the status of face attacks directed at the attitudes of the liberal audience. House is presenting a non-PC persona: audiences do not have to take that seriously, any more than Foreman does, but they do have to hear it, as part of how he chooses to present himself. Based on what they have heard, they have to evaluate the character, or the show, or both: "But I do think Foreman needed to call House on his racist-sounding remarks at some point. They are rather bad, even though I don't believe House is really racist. He's too smart for that. He just demeans everyone" (posted September 28, 2005, on Television without Pity, http://www.forums. televisionwithoutpity.com/, retrieved April 21, 2009).

Impoliteness as Self-Gratification

If House's rudeness is partly in his use of the *fake banter* strategy, then another aspect is the personal pleasure he takes from being smarter than the people he insults. A three-line extract will serve as my illustration here, though I want to stage the presentation of this example and examine its first two lines before considering the meaning and significance of the third. Theoretically speaking, the initial issue is whether this should be classified as the use of a strategy of indirect impoliteness or a metastrategy of sarcasm, or as something indeterminate, between these two categories of impoliteness. Beyond this, a larger force field of indeterminacies makes this a recalcitrant example, hard to bring within the constructs of the theoretical apparatus.

> *Context*: House enters the examination room in the clinic where he routinely treats walk-in patients. He perceives his latest patient, in full Santa Claus costume. House ostentatiously sniffs the air, and then takes the first speaking turn:

1 HOUSE: Let me guess. Inflammatory bowel?
2 SANTA CLAUS: Wow, yeah. Is it that bad?

(Season 1, episode 5, "Damned If You Do," written by Sara B. Cooper)

Regular viewers of the show come to appreciate that House, as an essentially melancholic individual, survives emotionally by having fun at the expense of other people, including patients. This example is a minor, short-lived, and inconsequential instance of the trait, tucked away in an incidental scene of no relevance to the episode story line or any story arc. At best, this very unsatisfactory Santa Claus has thematic relevance in an episode presenting a downbeat view of Christmas, resonant with House's own Eeyore-like gloom—as well as displaying "House-as-normal," away from the more high-pressure environment of his own department in which patients are suffering from life-or-death diseases.

House indirectly conveys his belief that the patient is the cause of a bad smell in the room. Culpeper (1996: 351) claims that acts that draw attention to the fact that the target is engaged in some antisocial activity are inherently impolite, irrespective of context—arguing that such inherent impoliteness is the exception rather than the rule and that most impoliteness is context dependent. Causing a bad smell is certainly antisocial, though not deliberate on the part of the patient who is engaged in remedying the fault by attending the clinic. House is not afraid of offending Santa Claus by drawing attention to the smell: indeed, he does this kind of thing so often that audiences hear it as something that gives him pleasure (as mild compensation for essential misery). He draws attention to the smell indirectly: the more overt meaning of the act is a diagnosis of the patient's medical condition. Is he also sarcastic here? In Culpeper's terms, a sarcastic interpretation is appropriate if this utterance is overtly polite but rude by implicature. If it has any claim to politeness, that would rest on its function as a diagnosis of a medical condition, in a setting in which diagnosis is one of the requirements of the doctor.

The intention to convey the impolite belief certainly outweighs any other significance for the patient, whose response orients to House's presentation of the smell as a particularly noticeable one, as well as acknowledging the accuracy of the diagnosis. Of course House is less than polite here in other ways, too. He withholds any kind of greeting, and he offers a diagnosis prior to any talk with the patient about his symptoms and medical history. Both of these could be regarded as snubs to positive face. The absence of a greeting treats the patient as someone who does not merit even this very basic courtesy. The instant diagnosis treats him as someone whose own verbal information is of no value. House denies the patient an opportunity to produce any talk of his own until *after* the diagnosis has been made.

On the other hand, it is not impossible to hear "Let me guess. Inflammatory bowel" as House producing the *second* act of this exchange. He constructs the patient as having already performed its first act, in making the consulting room smell bad. As a response to that prior act, the move into instant diagnosis has a *remedial*, rather than a face-threatening, character, because it treats the patient's smell as a medical, not an interpersonal, fact. It might be expected that the interpretation of *artificial* examples of impoliteness, such as those found in drama, would be simpler, more straightforward, and more determinate than those found in the messiness of everyday encounters. But this example has its own complexity, and it is not unusual in that respect.

Here now is the expanded version of the extract with its third line restored:

1 HOUSE: (Sniff) Let me guess. Inflammatory bowel.
2 SANTA CLAUS: Wow, yeah. Is it that bad?
3 HOUSE: Yes. It's also written on your chart.

(Season 1, episode 4, "Damned If You Do," written by Sara B Cooper)

The chart that House refers to here is a piece of paper inside the patient's file of notes, recording previous symptoms and diagnoses. It appears now that the doctor has only *pretended* to be an instant diagnostician, though he very quickly owns up to the pretense. The chart is the true source of his information. The patient has not read the chart and does not know that House has read it. Only in these circumstances could the temporary deception work. House saw an opportunity for some fun at the patient's expense and took it. But the quick admission offers partial mitigation for the joke's bad form. Although House enjoys the moment, his character is not utterly exploitative. The off-record impoliteness strategy does not compromise medical treatment, and is subsequently redressed.[5]

At the risk of extending speculation about communicative intentionality well beyond what these imaginative constructs "House" and "Santa Claus" can really carry, I want to develop the account even further, in line with the research discussed earlier in this chapter. The purpose of the following discussion will be to press home the point that with a framework like Culpeper's, which allows for a hearer's interpretation to become decisive in the classifying of behavior as *impolite*, along with speaker intentions, the levels of indeterminacy increase to an almost unmanageable extent.

The original interpretation, and my starting point, was that House here insults the patient for causing a bad smell in the room. He does this by offering, as the direct meaning, a diagnosis of the patient's underlying condition—inflammatory bowel disease. Offering a diagnosis is not at all a rude thing to do in a clinical context—quite the opposite. It is exactly what a doctor is supposed to do, and is therefore polite (or perhaps just politic, in Watts's 2003 terms).[6] On that interpretation, it is just the *timing* of the diagnosis that is impolite, and not even that if we read it as the second rather than the first move in the exchange. Possibly, House is hedging his bets. He does intend to insult the patient with the *bad smell* (indirect) meaning. But he also intends to fall back on the *diagnosis* (direct) meaning if the patient should have the wit and will to challenge his impoliteness, perhaps by countering the attack offensively: "Who do you think you are, talking to me like that?" (cf. Culpeper et al. 2002, Bousfield 2007a, on responses to impolite acts). The interests of truth telling (i.e., the accuracy of House's diagnosis) are arguably more important than politeness in a clinical context, if the circumstances are serious. But that does not really apply here either: Santa Claus is manifestly not *seriously* ill, judging from his posture, demeanor, and mode of engagement with the doctor; and it is treatment, not a diagnosis, that he needs—he already has the latter.

Alternatively, the insulting, bad smell meaning, despite being readily retrieved by the patient, is not an impolite *implicature* but has a different theoretical status here. An implicature is meant to be recognized by a hearer as being intended by the speaker. Santa Claus *takes* the insult, recognizing its basis in the (now) mutually manifest truth of the bad smell and the explanation of this. But acceptance was never his only option. According to Culpeper et al. (2002) and Bousfield (2007a), the other main alternatives would have been a nonresponse, a counteroffensive, or a defensive countering move. Nonresponse could take the form of silence, but it could also mean refusing to acknowledge the face attack content, and responding to the direct meaning instead: "My last doctor said the problem was in my stomach, not my guts." A response of this last kind would have let the bad smell meaning pass unchallenged, unrecognized, unofficial, whatever House's intentions may have been. Culpeper et al. (2002) suggest that such responses (i.e., ones that ignore obvious but indirect face attacks) can themselves be offensive as well as defensive, because they so blatantly refuse to recognize a meaning that the speaker clearly intended (*offensive* here has the sense of "provoking," in other words, "going on the offensive," as in a battle or sport contest, rather than that of "insulting," "causing distress," though the two meanings are connected).

However, in the case I have been examining, the *offensiveness* of the patient's response is not inherent in its wording, and would have to be brought out in performance through kinesic, prosodic, and paralinguistic expression if that were the directorial decision (actually the actor embodies his line rather deferentially). It seems to me that in not orienting to the *bad smell* meaning, in refusing to be thus baited, the indirect meaning arguably gets demoted from implicature to something more like a presupposition, in pragmatic terms.

House and the patient possess only *virtual* communicative intentions. Our familiarity with one character (House) and our lack of familiarity with the other (the patient) should lead us, as regular viewers, to interpretations that are most congruent with what we already know in this situation. Although this is an early episode, it is sufficiently far into the season for us to believe him more than capable of gratuitous, face-threatening acts to patients. Whatever the theoretical status of the *bad smell* meaning, House has successfully brought it into their mutual universe of discourse. Truthfulness is well served by doing so, though politeness is not. For House, truth, along with speed and accuracy of diagnosis, with remedy the ultimate goal, are more important considerations than politeness here. There is also pleasure to be gained from the indirect manner in which House does acknowledge the smell and oblige his patient to do likewise. The indirect approach is witty, even if the wit is lost on the victim and only the offense is registered.

In the same scene House goes on to recommend that the Santa Claus patient smoke two cigarettes each day as a remedy for his condition. But tobacco in this world (as in our own) has become identified as the cause of disease to such an extent that any notion of it having therapeutic properties has become publicly unspeakable. House thereby adds to his performance of personal affront with an affront to the professional face of the institution, and colleagues will later take him to task for this. Beyond the confines of House's world, another level of face attack is in play—an attack on the face of the liberal audience whose taboo this is.

DISCUSSION

As indicated at the start of the chapter, its purpose was (by contrast with the previous chapter) to highlight the forms and functions of impoliteness in relation to the theoretical literature on this subject, and not to focus on the contribution of dialogue, impolite or otherwise, to the meaning and value of the show as drama. This is, of course, a matter of emphasis in both cases. The previous chapter did not entirely ignore the interactional details (though it did not theorize them, and it discussed content as well as form); the present chapter has not ignored the dramatic context within which the interactions take place. I do want to say just a little more about this context here.

The characteristics of snark in *House* have two functions in relation to the dramatic project: building and sustaining the character of House in his social relationships with colleagues and patients (the characterization function) and entertaining the audience (by exploiting the resources of language). To avoid any misunderstanding, I would want to add here that House is not limited to snark-like discourse in his conversation and is morally more complex than my discussion above is likely to have suggested. He is not a flat or schematic character, and the long-form dramatic structure also allows for story arcs in which he is able to change and develop. As for showcasing language play of this particular form, to appreciate this as something separate from the characterization could be seen as indicative of something related to the "aesthetic disposition" in Bourdieu's terms (1980, 1984)—enjoyment of something in formal terms, without requiring the referentiality of narrative. Compared to the previous chapter, this one has had much less to say about the audience's responses to the drama, but forum discussions do indicate that use of language is something that parts of the audience notice and appreciate. I have not explored the possibility that language-as-snark is a turnoff for other parts of the potential audience, but that seems to me quite a strong possibility: however witty it may be, it gives rein to a decidedly *unpleasant* dimension of human social relations.

Culpeper's research on impoliteness was as important for this chapter as his research on characterization in fiction was for chapter 7. His efforts to construct a theory of impoliteness that is appropriately sensitive to interactional dynamics and context are very insightful. The advice to focus on how hearers respond to impolite utterances, especially when those responses are effective determinants of whether the utterances do or do not have impolite significance, is a useful one, as is the question of whether impoliteness can be neutralized by being displayed as part of entertainment discourse. Apart from my suggestion that snark might take the form of the hitherto untheorized *fake banter*, the value of the present chapter to the ongoing study of impoliteness may lie in its attempt to reflect on the management of impoliteness across the two kinds of interpersonal relations that TV drama articulates: the one between the dramatist and the audience, and those among the characters. Impoliteness theory, even when it examines materials from mediated discourse, tends to overlook the role of insults that, in targeting socially salient aspects of *character* or identity such as weight or race, can also be heard as insulting to audience members who share those aspects and not just to the specific character in the show. Under conditions of shared viewing, audiences may respond not (just) as individuals but as part of a collectivity that includes others in the targeted categories who deserve respect. Audiences may demonstrate responses to *racism*, *sexism*, and so forth when they are exposed to talk that raises these possibilities, while varying in how they negotiate perceived offenses.

10

Conclusion

DRAMATIZATION

Raymond Williams, who was always interested in television, titled his inaugural lecture at Cambridge *Drama in a Dramatised Society* (Williams 1975). He was struck by the sheer quantity of dramatized material that people routinely encountered in the television age, and the deep normality of those encounters. Erving Goffman (1959) had a different perspective, but one in which the phrase *dramatized society* makes equally good sense. Dramatic expression is without question very much a part of everyday life, whether we take that to mean that we watch and listen to so much "official" drama, under such domesticated conditions, or to refer to the unofficial performativity of our own conduct for different *audiences* in different times and places. This insight has been around for a long time (since the 1950s, in Goffman's case), and it has not become outdated. It is still the case that *dramatization* contributes in many ways to social experience, in ways that sociolinguists (among others) have been keen to understand and explore. This interest is relevant, for instance, to the work on stylization (Rampton 1995) and other social aspects of metalanguage (Jaworski et al. 2004). It is also relevant to work on the creativities of language users (see, e.g., Carter 2004, 2007, Swann 2006). The usefully ambiguous word *play* serves as a marker for an area in which creativity (as playfulness, formal experimentation) and bracketed performance (just a play, not the real thing) come together.

Drama, as normally understood, combines the affordances of fictional narrative with those of directed and produced performance, though the officially sanctioned forms of drama, on television and elsewhere, are only the prototypical instances—much exists beyond this repertoire, and there are fuzzy boundaries between different genres and modes of fiction, different genres and modes of storytelling, and different genres and modes of performance. Specialist branches of academic study have developed around the various manifestations of each. It has been one of the challenges of this book to use *dialogue* as a means of trying to crystallize, or at least juxtapose, some of the more important approaches, albeit in a way that necessarily says something about my own intellectual formation and interests. The fictional narrative component points a direction that opens up questions around *storytelling* in specific sociocultural contexts, whereas the performance component indicates the importance of particularized human bodies and voices in sensible form.

All of this makes it important to approach the study of dialogue in TV drama so that it is congruent with trends away from narrow conceptions of *language* as a primary focus. Three important aspects of this congruence can be identified here. First, there is an acceptance that more general structures of meaning (*stories, schemata*) that language shares with other modes of representation and expression (comic book, ballet, opera) should be recognized. This is important, for example, in cognitive approaches such as those of Culpeper (2001). Second, it acknowledges that contemporary representation/expression is largely multimodal (Kress and van Leeuwen 2001). If I have not given much attention in this book to the delivery or the audiovisual staging of the dialogue lines, it is not from lack of interest in what these contribute to the overall production. There are different reasons for the neglect. One has to do with the division of labor in the production of TV drama such that within the professional community, *writing* is recognized as a specialized contribution and the writing of dialogue is understood primarily, though not exclusively, as the *wording* of that dialogue (see chapter 4, "What TV Screenwriters Know about Dialogue"). Actors and directors bring other things. Another consideration was that for much of the time (for instance, in chapter 8, "Dialogue and Dramatic Meaning: *Life on Mars*"), the focus was on the functions rather than the forms of dialogue, where it might have detracted from the analysis to give much attention to questions of delivery.

The third component here, which I will return to below, has to do with the ethnographic turn in questions of textual meaning—focusing on the communicative relationships that give rise to particular texts as part of a process. Drama, it is understood, has a double articulation of communicative relationships (Herman 1995, Short 1998, Bubel 2008). At the outer level there is a relationship between dramatist(s) and audience(s); within that are the displayed relationships between characters. A lot can be learned from using the latter to make inferences about the former. But there is value too in developing modes of research that consider the real-world dramatists and their real-world audiences, producing and consuming texts in historically specific social and cultural conditions. This need has been accommodated by including in this book a chapter that looks in particular at the writing of dialogue in TV drama and another that looks at responses to dialogue on the part of the audience.

With these three considerations in mind, I now focus more specifically on drama made for broadcast television.

TELEVISION DRAMA

Though dramatic performances of the official, *produced* kind exist in a variety of modes—street theatre, theater proper, cinema, radio, and television—it is those produced as screen fictions for film and television that get the widest exposure and contribute the most to whatever there is of *common culture*. I am obliged to fudge the issue of whose culture this might be (see Nelson 2007 for recent, relevant discussion here). At the risk of oversimplification, and from a British perspective, television drama as a mode contributes to the national culture, under varying degrees of American influence (cf. chapter 8 in this volume), and, as a channel for U.S. drama, it provides British viewers with an outside, spectator's perspective on some aspects of American culture (cf. chapter 9, "*House* and Snark"). Hollywood feature films, whether on TV or in the cinema, help cultivate an Americanized/international level of culture. Spectatorship on any other countries is marginal in the United Kingdom: the subscription services that accommodate minorities and expatriates are not accessed by consumers outside those groups. American viewers have less opportunity to be spectators on British culture via exported drama programming, though from *Monty Python* through to the new *Doctor Who*, there has always been some traffic in this direction. The reversioning of British shows as American ones is another significant trend (*The Office, Life on Mars*).

The value of television drama's contribution to culture is a separate matter. Both *popular* (Bignell and Lacey 2005) and *high-end* (Nelson 2007) or *quality* (McCabe and Akass 2007a) drama have their defenders, and it is not possible to do justice in a paragraph to the play of intellectual forces that have structured research in this area. Feminism has certainly made an important contribution (for instance, in the evaluation of soap opera genres), as has an overarching debate about cultural value more generally, with Adorno's attack on popular culture as a seminal text. Within the industry in recent years the economic, technological, and social conditions have been good for high-end drama in particular, and Nelson (2007) is among those who have welcomed this trend:

> [T]he argument is that, led by key subscription channels making expensive—and at times "edgy"—drama for selected target audiences, contemporary TV drama has both license and aspirations. In some quarters it aspires to the production values of cinema and is liberated from the LOP [least offensive programming] industrial context and regulatory constraints to be creative in drama production. Where HBO Premium and Fox television have led, the American networks—and, in a slightly different context, the UK terrestrial channels—are bound in a competitive global marketplace to follow. (Nelson 2007: 161)

Quality in relation to TV drama is of course a contested term—possibly a genre label, possibly something more (see also Thompson 1996, Hammond and

Mazdon 2005, McCabe and Akass 2007a, and chapter 8 in this volume). It is worth underlining the fact that Nelson is offering a *positive* evaluation of media texts (of a certain kind) in his book, and being clear about the terms of the evaluation. In some areas of media-related research it is much more common to find *negative* evaluations. Critical discourse analysis (CDA) is a case in point. CDA, in studying media texts with a specific interest in the reproduction of ideologies, has tended to focus on written genres more than television, and, within television, on news and current affairs more than drama; it has not developed an empirical audience research strand (see Jones 2007 for an elaborated critique). In drama, the play of imagination offers greater freedoms for both dramatists and their audiences. It is desirable on these grounds alone to remain open to the possibility of *good* media texts, in dramatic form, as well as *bad* ones—and ones in which any value is subject to contestation. This would, of course, include particular kinds of television advertisements (cf. Cook 1992).

The specific evaluative term I will want to return to in this quotation is not *quality* but *creativity*—one possible yardstick for the determination of value. I will make use of this concept as a bridge between the linguistic and the televisual aspects of the study. Before that, I will position *dialogue* within the matrix so far developed.

DIALOGUE IN TELEVISION DRAMA

At one level, dialogue in TV drama is just one element within a much more complex compositional mix, and not necessarily the most important component in the dramatic whole. At another level, it acts as a focus for thinking about dramatization and social relationships, along the lines indicated above. It also provides a context for further interrogation of the *creativity* concept in ways that provide a bridge between media interest in the quality of drama output, on the one hand, and applied linguistic interest in the uses of language, on the other.

Dialogue and Social Relationships

The primary social relationship is between dramatist and audience: those among the characters are secondary and, by design, supportive of that primary interaction. This is one way of thinking about drama's double articulation as characterized by Herman (1995) and others. Obviously the term *dramatist* here is intentionally ambiguous. In this area, design and production duties are very much shared across different contributors to a developmental process, though the publisher (broadcaster) must take final responsibility for what is transmitted. In respect of *dialogue, dramatist* here often really does mean *writer*—not producer, not director, not actor, not publisher. At other times it is shorthand for *authorial* contributions, irrespective of type or origin. This emphasis on writers is not meant as an unquestioning endorsement of the position that writers are the primary authors of TV drama, or that they make a *greater* contribution to TV drama than they do to film (though this is the case in certain respects and for certain kinds of TV drama). It is simply because the focus is on *dialogue*, the area in which the writers' contribution is the most necessary. This point is relevant even in relation to productions in which the *quality* resides more in visual characteristics than verbal ones (certain kinds of thrillers, for instance).

Dramatist to Audience

To contribute dialogue to a TV drama is to engage in an activity of public storytelling. Dramatists seek the attention of the audience for their stories, and they do so by controlling the behavior and actions (including the verbal behavior) of their characters. That verbal behavior *must* service the narrative, as it does in feature films (Kozloff 2000). It *may* go beyond this purely functional role. In Kozloff's framework, the scope for *linguistic* creativity was restricted to one specific value-added function: "exploiting the resources of language." Obviously when drama is concerned, linguistic playfulness is not the only way in which dramatists can seek to be creative in the sense of *original, different*. A new *high concept* is a more obvious way to attract attention (*Heroes, Lost*).

The dramatist-audience relationship is contextualized by the socioeconomic conditions of production. Those conditions include considerations of national versus international marketing, and dialogue is relevant to these considerations. Chapter 7 ("Dialogue, Character, and Social Cognition") uses schema theory to account for the construction of characters in various TV productions. Most of the shows referred to in this chapter are British ones, and serve to demonstrate that writers of shows for primarily British distribution can rely on its audience's access to schemata with a distinctively "British" content. The British version of *Life on Mars*, with its allusions to power cuts, the Open University, the BBC2 test card, and other very homely points of reference, was broadcast in the United States, but on a subscription channel with a British brand identity (BBC America). For mainstream television, a specifically American remake was offered (*Life on Mars*, ABC 2008). Not all recent U.S. shows have been easy for non-American audiences. *The Wire* (HBO 2002–present), when broadcast in the United Kingdom on mainstream television rather than on a subscription service, came with advice to viewers to watch the show with its written subtitles, on the grounds that this would make it easier to follow the dialogue. This sentiment is echoed by reviewers of the DVD release:

Who'd have thought that a TV show about cops and gangs would be so subtle,
3-dimensional, funny, moving and intelligent? Everybody who wants to understand
drugs, crime or America should watch it!
　　[...]
[Y]es, the DVDs of all three seasons have subtitles, and you will probably need
them, unless you are a Baltimore drug dealer. (posted March 27, 2007, on the
Amazon.co.uk website, retrieved April 23, 2009)

The linguistic aspects of this comprehension of vocabulary are a matter of
register, dictated in part by the show's focus on the Baltimore drug scene, with
which, as the review hints, even Americans need help. The *Wall Street Journal*
published a jargon guide on December 29, 2007.[1] Realism in respect of this
world has come at some cost in respect of conditions of reception overseas—but
also with a surrounding "difficult is good" discourse that may have enhanced its
brand. It would be interesting to explore the conversion of *The Wire* into a series
for non-Anglophone countries where dialogue is routinely dubbed (Hungary
and Germany have apparently both screened the series).[2]

Character to Character

It is in studying the character-to-character social relationships that the tool kit of
sociolinguistics comes into its own, whether derived from pragmatics, interactional sociolinguistics, conversational analysis or some eclectic combination of
these (this was the topic of chapter 6, "Dialogue as Social Interaction"). However
limited their speaking parts are, and even when they are realized on screen
as animals, glove puppets, and graphic shapes, these characters are imaginative exemplars of us—people in the real world—projected into ordinary and
extraordinary circumstances. That they can talk at all is one of the signs of
their existence, but their particularity comes partly from specific interactional
characteristics of the dialogue, as well as from what other characters (variously
trustworthy in this respect) say about them. The recognitions, and the lines
of affiliation and disaffiliation that any drama's design requires, depend on
the dramatist's ability to deploy appropriate dialogue and the actors' abilities to
embody the language as meaningful, contextually generated utterances to which
audiences have access only as eavesdroppers.

　　The dramatic functions of dialogic exchanges are mostly more important than
surface verisimilitude in relation to naturally occurring speech in equivalent
situations. Screenwriters appreciate that the minutiae of real-life models have
to be sacrificed for the sake of the storytelling. The comparability of *real* and
scripted interactions is at the deeper level of the constructional principles that
make speech intelligible. Its intelligibility includes its presuppositions, implicatures, hints, misdirections, and other properties that are signs of an inner,

mental life for *characters* as people, like us. Assumed possession of such an inner life complements the *backstories* of characters' previous experience that dramatists may construct. It helps when characters, also like us, have voices we can hear and faces we can see.

On the other hand, screenwriters can, if they want to, make some of the minutiae of naturally occurring speech—overlapping utterances, filled and unfilled pauses, self-corrections, silences, and so forth—really *count* in the storytelling (cf. Tannen 1980) in ways that have an oblique relationship to their use in everyday talk. In the latter, they are ubiquitous, constructionally significant and, at the least, available as resources for person inferences as well as for inferences in respect of communicative purpose. In the former, the inferences they facilitate are textual design features, engineered to contribute to the audience's understanding of purpose and character as part of the higher order semiotics of narrative. Of course, participants in everyday talk can also seek to control such expressive resources as part of their own self-fashioning performativity. However, in the absence of an overarching, authored story, only some of what is manifest to others will be under the individual's strategic control. The *through line* of a scripted conversation is determined in advance by a dramatist; in spontaneous talk, it is contingent and emergent. Person inferences are regarded as optional in everyday talk, but are part of the business of their dramatic analogues, as chapter 7 sought to explore.

Language, Creativity, and the Mass Media

Carter's (2004) publication was the first in what has become a series of contributions to research on *everyday* linguistic creativity (see Maybin and Swann 2006, and the special 2007 issue of *Applied Linguistics*, 28[4]). Carter was specifically concerned to locate, describe, and contextualize creativity in the absence of any traditionally literary/aesthetic ambition and, furthermore, to focus on spoken interaction, not written materials. This included, for instance, attention to the creation of *new* words by the extension of *old*, familiar morphological patterns, specifically the use of -*y* and -*ish* as suffixes (bluey, cubey, teatimeish, seventeenish). Mandala (2007a) is also interested in the -*y* usage as it is expressively displayed in *Buffy the Vampire Slayer*. A decision is made to identify as *creative* (and therefore good) usages that in other contexts (written language in a context governed by schooled norms) would be deemed incorrect (and therefore bad), thus providing a practical demonstration of the point that evaluations can be contextually variable. As with language, so with television drama. *Upstairs, Downstairs* (ITV 1971–1975) was received as a kind of period soap opera in the United Kingdom, but marketed as "Masterpiece Theatre" when it was first broadcast in the United States.

When I originally decided to write a book about TV drama dialogue, one of the reasons was the thought that this particular form of language use might be even more likely than Carter's *everyday* language to escape critical attention. It would not be judged good or bad, creative or familiar, because it would never be thought interesting enough, socially or aesthetically, to be worth examining. The redemptive inspiration of Carter's project is not his interest in everyday language use *per se*, because this is common ground in sociolinguistics and applied linguistics. It is specifically the discovery and characterization of *creativity* in everyday language, in which creativity is construed as a good thing, that Carter is concerned with. Conversely, because the literary language of plays, poems, and prose fiction is intended to be special, artful, and valuable, no special pleading is necessary to justify studying that. What *was* necessary, as Burton (1980) first realized, was a justification for using approaches derived from what was then called *discourse analysis*, in other words, the study of naturally occurring spoken interaction in linguistic terms. The specific creative merits of particular, contemporary, dramatic works became more apparent when approached in this way.

But where in this is there a space to position the study of dialogue in television? Most TV drama productions would lack the *literary* qualities that justified studying Pinter plays; yet they would never offer language that was *ordinary* enough for traditional sociolinguistic purposes and would always be inauthentic in relation to *real* speech. As scripted material, dialogue is also the poor relation in the *media talk* literature, which prefers to focus on unscripted interactions (interviews, reality show exchanges, call-in discussions on the radio; see chapter 3, "What Is TV dialogue Like?").

The one obvious way into an appropriately critical perspective on this was via the discourse of the industry itself (cf. Brody's definition of good television dialogue cited in two of the foregoing chapters). The industrial view is useful, and establishes that writers do have guidelines within which to work, as well as a professional working environment structured to manage the *quality control* of written inputs. However, the danger with this as the *only* frame of reference is one of conformity to a set of entertainment values that should also, when appropriate, be interrogated and challenged. In chapter 8 there is a provisional attempt to address this problem via a distinction between *quality* and *value*, aligning *quality* to formal properties of drama texts, including formal properties of dialogue, and aligning *value* to the management of content—where, also, dialogue has a part to play.

On the formal side, a possibility exists that dramatic dialogue, approached in the right way, might provide access to patterns of language behavior not (yet) discovered or fully explored in naturally occurring spontaneous interaction— might, indeed, be manifesting its creativity by expressively displaying those patterns. The *fake banter* exchanges in *House* (see chapter 9) are an instance of this. On the substantive side, dialogue is also a resource for the display of attitudes and opinions across characters offering different alignment possibilities for the viewing audience: this was explored in relation to *Life on Mars* in chapter 8. The new genre hybridities that *Shameless, House*, and *Life on Mars* all demonstrate are adaptations that accommodate variations in the viewing public by providing different pleasures for different audience segments, and openness around culturally sensitive or politically controversial topics. But the pleasures of these dramas include the display through dialogue of manifestly uncivil forms of behavior. Traditional television had only a limited license to challenge culturally accepted norms. These new hybrids and the technical-economic system that supports them have found ways to resist the restrictions. This invites discussion of why these forms of incivility should have proved such a profitable way of using creative resources.

Creativity, as used thus far, is framed within a traditional discourse of individual imagination, while reaching out to include institutionalized forms of cultural production. But as Schlesinger (2007) observes, the concept of creativity has also become a highly significant, market-oriented one in policy discourses about national economic renewal, not just restricted to the role of the *creative industries* (including the mass media) as agents of that renewal but, in intention, reaching deeply into social and cultural life at home and, especially, at work. "A concerted effort is underway to shape a wide range of working practices by invoking creativity and innovation. These attributes are supposed to make our societies and economies grow in a fiercely competitive world" (Schlesinger 2007: 377). The expression "knowledge economy" has become very familiar in recent years, and a Google search on April 29, 2009, produced over 1 million hits for this phrase. But a much less familiar combination, "imagination economy," produced around 700 hits. The policy discourse that Schlesinger describes can be regarded critically, as the co-opting of the space of the imagination into utilitarianism and the power relations of the work environment. Or it could be envisaged more positively as a source of opportunities: the new discourse may anticipate changes in the world of work itself, offering more a satisfactory accommodation with our imaginative selves than has previously been possible. In relation to the present research, consider that although the production of fan fiction inspired by TV drama (see chapter 5, "What Audiences Know about Dialogue") is currently economically marginal and mostly undertaken for personal satisfaction, not money, there may be ways to marketize the creativity it represents. It is important to think about the interests at stake in such potential marketization.

Whatever view we take on these large, structural questions, there is still value in the kind of ethnographic research offered in this book, investigating how the imaginations of cultural producers and consumers actually operate, and to what effect, in the world as it currently exists. On the basis of such research, we may be better prepared either to criticize and resist, or to welcome, top-down initiatives from the private and public sectors.

The Ethnographic Turn

Language creativity research is now set to embark down a road previously trodden in media research, and with a similar redemptive impulse:

> A clear requirement now is to embrace not simply the producer but the receiver of creative processes and to shift the analytical attention towards greater assessment and appraisal of creative outputs, with the aim of gaining enriched understanding of processes of reception on the part of different socially positioned readers or viewers of or participants in creative performances. (Carter 2007: 600)

The article from which this quotation is taken appeared in a special issue of *Applied Linguistics*, "Language Creativity in Everyday Contexts." There is nothing in this perspective that excludes the reception of television shows. Watching and listening to television is an everyday context, as Raymond Williams recognized, even if writing and producing television still remains a specialist one, in which considerable financial investment is at stake.

Carter points out that a shift in attention from producers to receivers "would parallel the shift in literary criticism since the 1960s from author centered accounts and studies to arguments for more empirical reader response studies in which definitions of literature were seen to be in the reader as much as if not more so than in the author" (2007: 600). The sense of déjà vu for literary critics is stronger still for anyone who has worked in or near the media studies field. The audience had never been neglected in media research (e.g., in effects research and the "uses and gratifications" tradition), but the specific "audience turn," which corresponds to what Carter is concerned with here, related to the repro-duction of meaning through textual production and consumption. It is often traced back to Stuart Hall's 1973 encoding/decoding paper (Hall 1980). Unlike in literary criticism, the audience turn in media studies led to specific strands of empirical research, starting with the work of David Morley (1980). Such research still continues, though much has changed since the early days, both in terms of theoretical concerns (the question of ideology is much less central) and changes in the modes of mediated communication (including the development and growth of the Internet).

The arguments for this shift were so convincing that advocacy for text-based research now often agrees that such research should be more conscious of its vulnerability (Creeber 2006). Variability of reception for mass media texts and productions is not disputed theoretically (though there is still scope to finesse, conceptually, the contours of this reception—for instance, in respect of how cognitive and affective responses might be articulated) and is supported empirically. Nor is there any longer a need to argue that reception is active, not passive. What can be acknowledged is that the *activeness* of audiences needs something on which to work, and that the characteristics of that something make a contribution to their cultural experience and social understanding—even if empirical audience research is then necessary to determine the exact nature of that contribution.

It is also important to acknowledge the polysemy of the word *active*. It is *active*, in one sense, as an audience member to supply an interpretative schema that fills out and makes sense of perfunctory details in a text. The schema is in the brain of the consumer, not in the text. Cognitive work on the part of the latter is required to bring the schema to bear on the text. But the result of this *activity* is, thus far, in conformity with what the text itself has appeared to require. So basic is this aspect of the textual encounter that one might want to call it *comprehension*, not *interpretation*. At the other end of the scale, there is no disputing the *activeness* of audience members whose affiliation to a particular TV series is sufficiently strong that it motivates them to create additional and alternative story lines and scenes (including dialogue), borrowing and appropriating, for their own purposes, the characters developed for the official version of the series (see chapter 5) in the production of fan fiction. Sociolinguists reading this book should also be interested to note the return, at this point, from multimodal textuality to the monomodal form of (written) language. Economic and legal considerations may rule out anything more ambitious, notwithstanding the opportunities that relatively inexpensive recording devices and YouTube provide for democratizing audiovisual creativity. Nevertheless, it is worth drawing attention to the affordances of old-fashioned writing, with publication enabled by twenty-first-century technology, for the liberation of the imagination—along with the fact that it is products of the mass communication industry that have activated that imagination.

Between the two poles of active comprehension and active textual production is the work of active textual criticism—voices that say to the dramatist "You could do better." Thanks to the Internet, confidence and opportunity to say that *publicly* is more widespread than it has ever been, providing a basis for future interactions among dramatists, reviewers, fans, and other viewers about the merits of TV drama—and an arena for future research.

Appendix

List of Television Shows

This list comprises an index of shows and series referred to in the book, offering dates and company credits, with brief indications of show content. Readers seeking further information are referred to the Internet Movie Database, http://www.imdb.com, which I have relied on extensively here. Specific episode screenwriters are not identified in this table but can be found in the chapter in which their material is cited. "Creator, not known" is used when the details on the Internet Movie Database are unclear as to what particular individual(s) should take principal creative credit.

24

2001–present. Creators, Robert Cochran and Joel Surnow. Production company and broadcaster, Fox/Imagine Entertainment. American thriller series starring Kiefer Sutherland as Jack Bauer, based on the idea that each of 24 episodes represents an hour of time in the fictional world and that the time is continuous from episode to episode. Chapters 3 and 6.

All My Children

1970–present. Creator, Agnes Nixon. Production company and broadcaster, ABC. American daytime soap. "Erica Kane" (Susan Lucci) is its best-known character. Chapter 2.

Ally McBeal

1997–2002. Creator, David E. Kelley. Production company and broadcaster, 20th Century Fox and David E. Kelly/Fox. American dramedy. Calista Flockhart played the eponymous central character. Chapter 2.

The Amazing Mrs. Pritchard

2006. Creator, Sally Wainwright. Production company and broadcaster, Kudos/ BBC. A 6-episode British political drama starring Jane Horrocks as Ros

Pritchard, a supermarket manager who launches a political party, becomes the leader of the British government, and wrestles with the dilemmas of high office. Chapter 3.

America's Most Wanted

1988–present. Creator, not known. Production company and broadcaster, 20th Century Fox/Fox. True-crime dramatizations—the nearest U.S. equivalent to *Crimewatch* in the United Kingdom, both attempting to recruit the audience into crime solving. Chapters 3 and 7.

The Archers

1950–present. Creator, Godfrey Baseley. Production company and broadcaster, BBC/BBC Light Programme/Home Service/Radio 4. British radio soap opera, with daily episodes on weekdays. A cornerstone of British media history. Chapter 4.

Armchair Theatre

1956–1974. Creator, not known. Production company and broadcaster, ABC Weekend and Thames Television/ITV. Influential British anthology drama series, especially under Sydney Newman. Chapter 3.

Ashes to Ashes

2008–present. Creators, Mathew Graham and Ashley Pharaoh. Production company and broadcaster, Kudos and BBC Wales/BBC. British crime drama on fantasy premises. Central characters Alex Drake (Keely Hawes) and Gene Hunt (Philip Glenister). A follow-up to *Life on Mars*, set mostly in the 1980s. Chapters 4 and 8.

An Audience with Dame Edna Everage

1980. Creator, Barry Humphries. Production company and broadcaster, London Weekend Television/ITV. British-made comedy series with Australian Barry Humphries as "celebrity" Dame Edna performing to an invited audience. Chapter 3.

Battlestar Galactica

2003–present. Creator, Ronald D. Moore. Production company and broadcaster, British Sky Broadcasting and NBC/Sky One and Sci-Fi Channel. Science fiction series with American ensemble cast. A reworked version of an older series with the same name. Chapter 4.

Between the Lines

1992–1994. Creator, J. C. Wilsher. Production company and broadcaster, BBC. British crime drama, focusing on police corruption, starring Neil Pearson as Detective Superintendent Tony Clark. Chapter 8.

The Bill

1984–present. Creator, Geoff McQueen. Production company and broadcaster, Thames/ITV. British continuing police series (soap) set in a borough of London. "The Old Bill" is a traditional expression referring to the police. Chapter 8.

Bleak House

2005. Creator, Andrew Davies. Production company and broadcaster, BBC and WGBH/BBC. A 14-episode adaptation of Charles Dickens's novel, starring Anna Maxwell Martin as Esther Summerson and Gillian Anderson as Lady Dedlock. Chapter 8.

Bob the Builder

1999. Creator, Keith Chapman. Production company and broadcaster, HIT entertainment/BBC. British animated series for children. Chapter 5.

Bodies

2004–2006. Creator, Jed Mercurio. Production company and broadcaster, Hat Trick Productions/BBC. Chapter 9.

Boys from the Blackstuff

1982. Creator, Alan Bleasdale. Production company and broadcaster, BBC. Miniseries about the experiences of five unemployed tarmac layers (the "blackstuff") on Merseyside, screened at a low point in the country's economic fortunes and during Margaret Thatcher's premiership. Chapter 4.

Brothers and Sisters

2006–present. Creator, Jon Robin Baitz. Production company and broadcaster, Ken Olin/ABC. American ensemble drama with, among others, Sally Field, Calista Flockhart, Rob Lowe, and Rachel Griffiths. Chapter 7.

Buffy the Vampire Slayer

1997–2003. Creator, Joss Wheedon. Production company and broadcaster, 20th Century Fox/WB Network and UPN. Influential American science fiction series starring Sarah Michelle Gellar as Buffy Summers. Chapter 2 and 4.

Casualty

1986–present. Creators, Jeremy Brock and Paul Unwin. Production company and broadcaster, BBC. Long-running British ensemble medical drama series set in an emergency ward. Chapter 9.

Charlie Jade

2005–present. Creators, Chris Roland and Robert Wertheimer. Production company and broadcaster, Jonsworth Productions, The Imaginarium, 4142276, CinéGroupe. Canadian/South African coproduction set mainly in South Africa. Chapter 4.

Chicago Hope

1994–2000. Creator, David E. Kelley. Production company and broadcaster, 20th Century Fox Television; David E. Kelley Productions/CBS. American ensemble medical drama series. Chapter 9.

Columbo

1971–2008. Creator, Richard Levinson. Production company and broadcaster, Universal TV/NBC. Until 2003, Peter Falk played the role of Lieutenant Columbo in this inverted detective story format in which each episode reveals the crime and its perpetrator before the detection work. Chapter 7.

The Cops

1998–2000. Creator, Anita J. Pandolfo. Jimmy Gardner. Robert Jones. Production company and broadcaster, BBC. British crime series. Chapter 8.

Coronation Street

1960–present. Creator, Tony Warren. Production company and broadcaster, Granada Television/ITV. British urban soap opera set in the northwest of England. Chapters 4, 6, 7, and 8.

Crimewatch UK

1984–present. Creator, not known. Production company and broadcaster, BBC. True crime dramatizations and reportage: the nearest British equivalent to *America's Most Wanted*, both attempting to recruit the audience into crime solving. Chapters 3 and 7.

CSI: Crime Scene Investigation

2000–present. Creator, Ann Donahue, Carol Mendelsohn, and Anthony E Zuiker. Production company and broadcaster, Jerry Bruckheimer Television, CBS Productions, Alliance Atlantis Communications, Arc Entertainment/CBS. American forensic crime series starring William Petersen as Gil Grissom and set in Las Vegas. Chapters 1, 6, 7, and 9.

CSI Miami

2002–present. Creators, Ann Donahue, Carol Mendelsohn, and Anthony E Zuiker. Production company and broadcaster, CBS Productions, Jerry Bruckheimer Television, Touchstone Television, Alliance Atlantis Communications, The American Travelers/CBS. Spin-off from *CSI: Crime Scene Investigation*, but with a different setting and a different cast. Chapters 4 and 9.

CSI New York

2004–present. Creator, Ann Donahue, Carol Mendelsohn, and Anthony E Zuiker. Production company and broadcaster, Alliance Atlantis Communications, Alliance Atlantis Motion Picture Production, Jerry Bruckheimer Television, CBS Productions, Alliance Atlantis Productions, Clayton Entertainment/CBS. Spin-off from *CSI: Crime Scene Investigation*, but with a different setting and a different cast. Chapter 9.

Dallas

1978–1991. Creator, David Jacobs. Production company and broadcaster, Lorimar Television/CBS. The lives and loves of a wealthy Texas family in the oil industry. This series was extremely successful internationally. Chapter 7.

The Dame Edna Experience

1987–1989. Creator, Barry Humphries. Production company and broadcaster, London Weekend Television/ITV. Comedy/entertainment: celebrity interviews conducted by Barry Humphries in his "Dame Edna" persona. Chapter 3.

Days of Our Lives

1965–present. Creator, Allan Chase, Ted Corday, and Irna Phillips. Production company and broadcaster, Corday Productions, Cutter Productions, David E. Kelley Productions, Sony Pictures Television, Columbia Pictures Television, Columbia TriStar Television, National Broadcasting Company, Screen Gems/NBC. American daytime soap. Chapter 4.

Dead Ringers

2002–present. Creators, Simon Blackwell and Rupert Russell. Production company and broadcaster, BBC. Impressionists performing sketches. Chapter 3.

The Deal

2003. Creators, Stephen Frears and Peter Morgan. Production company and broadcaster, Granada Television/ITV. Dramatic reconstruction of the relationship between Tony Blair and Gordon Brown up to and including the point at which Blair took on the leadership of the Labour Party. Chapter 1.

Desperate Housewives

2004–present. Creator, Marc Cherry. Production company and broadcaster, Cherry Alley productions, Touchstone Television, ABC Studios, Cherry Productions/ABC. American dramedy working through melodramatic and mundane story lines about the lives of various women living on fictional Wisteria Lane. Chapters 1, 3, and 7.

Dexter

2006–present. Creator, Michael Cuesta. Production company and broadcaster, John Goldwyn/Showtime Networks. Thriller. Chapter 7.

Diagnosis Murder

1993–2001. Creator, Joyce Burditt. Production company and broadcaster, Dean Hargrove Productions, Fred Silverman Company, Viacom Productions. American crime series showcasing Dick van Dyke as a hospital doctor with a sideline in detection. Chapter 4.

Dinnerladies

1998–2000. Creator, Victoria Wood. Production company and broadcaster, BBC. British situation comedy about the relations among a group of women in a factory staff canteen. Written by stand-up comedian Victoria Wood. Chapter 7.

Dixon of Dock Green

1955–1976. Creator, not known. Production company and broadcaster, BBC. Classic early British police series. Chapters 7 and 8.

Doc Martin

2004–present. Creator, Mark Crowdy, Craig Ferguson, and Dominic Minghella. Production company and broadcaster, Buffalo Pictures, Homerun Productions/ITV. British dramedy about the life of a general practitioner in a rural Cornish community. Chapter 9.

Doctor Who

1963–1989 and 2005–present. Creator, Russell T. Davies. Production company and broadcaster, BBC Wales/BBC. British science fiction series. Cancelled in 1989 but revived to huge acclaim in 2005. Chapters 4, 5, 7, and 8.

Doctor Who Confidential

2005–present. Creator, not known. Production company and broadcaster, BBC Wales/BBC. Behind-the-scenes exploration of the making of *Doctor Who*. Chapter 8.

Dr. Finlay's Casebook

1962–1971. Creator, A. J. Cronin. Production company and broadcaster, BBC. British medical drama set in a rural Scottish community. Chapter 9.

Dr. Kildare

1961–1966. Creator, not known. Production company and broadcaster, Arena Productions/NBC. Classic American medical series with a hero-doctor. Chapter 9.

Dragnet

1951–1959. Creators, Dan Aykroyd, Alan Zweibel, and Tom Mankiewicz. Production company and broadcaster, Mark VII Ltd./NBC. Classic American crime series. Chapter 8.

Eastenders

1985–present. Creator, not known. Production company and broadcaster, BBC. British evening soap opera set in the East End of London—in competition with the "northern" *Coronation Street*. Chapters 3, 4, and 7.

ER

1994–2009. Creator, Michael Crichton. Production company and broadcaster, Constant C Productions, John Wells Productions, Amblin Entertainment, Warner Bros. Television, Amblin Television, Hands Down Entertainment/ NBC. Groundbreaking American medical drama set in Chicago. George Clooney was a star of the early seasons. Chapter 5.

The Fall and Rise of Reginald Perrin

1976–1979. Creator, John Howard Davies. Production company and broadcaster, BBC. British situation comedy set in an office, with "misfit" staff. A remake with Martin Clunes was launched in 2009. Chapter 5.

Fawlty Towers

1975–1979. Creators, John Cleese and Connie Booth. Production company and broadcaster, BBC. British situation comedy set in a small seaside hotel. John Cleese and Prunella Scales played the proprietors. Chapter 2.

Fighting for Gemma

1993. Creator, not known. Production company and broadcaster, Granada Television/ITV. Documentary about a young girl's health problems and the possible link to the local nuclear power plant. Chapter 2.

Frasier

1993–2004. Creator, David Angell, Peter Casey, and David Lee. Production company and broadcaster, Grub Street Productions, Paramount Network Television Productions, Paramount Television/NBC. American situation comedy about a psychologist with a job as a radio talk show host. Starring Kelsey Grammer as Frasier Crane. Chapter 2.

Friends

1994–2004. Creators, David Crane and Marta Kauffman. Production company and broadcaster, Warner Bros. Television, Bright-Kauffman-Crane Productions/NBC. American situation comedy about a group of friends aged 20-something (rising to early 30s over the length of the series) living in Manhattan. Chapters 5, 6, 7, and 8.

GBH

1991. Creator, Alan Bleasdale. Production company and broadcaster, GBH Films/Channel 4. British comedy drama series about local politics, starring Robert Lindsay as a local politician, initially blustering but ultimately neurotic. Chapter 4.

God on Trial

2008. Creator, Frank Cottrell Boyce. Production company and broadcaster, BBC Scotland/BBC. Single TV play by Frank Cottrell Boyce about a group of Jewish prisoners in a death camp putting God on trial for breach of his covenant with them. Chapter 4.

The Golden Girls

1985–1992. Creator, Susan Harris. Production company and broadcaster, Touchstone Television/NBC. American situation comedy about a group of older women living in Florida. Chapter 2.

Guiding Light

1952–2009 (from 1937 on radio). Creator, Irna Phillips. Production company and broadcaster, Procter & Gamble Productions/CBS. Longest running soap opera, cancelled in 2009, but with the company pursuing options that would keep it on air. Chapter 3.

Heartbeat

1992–present. Creator, not known. Production company and broadcaster, Yorkshire Television/ITV. British dramedy about a rural Yorkshire community in the 1960s/1970s (albeit vaguely), with particular emphasis on the local police. Chapter 8.

Heroes

2006–present. Creator, Tim Kring. Production company and broadcaster, NBC Universal Television, Tailwind Productions, UMS/Sci-Fi Channel. American science fiction series in which a wide range of ordinary people discover their varied superpowers and try to put them to good use in apocalyptic storylines. Chapters 1, 3, 7, and 8.

Heroes and Villains: Spartacus

2004. Creators, Colin Heber-Percy and Lyall B. Watson. Production company and broadcaster, BBC. Dramatization of the life of rebel Roman slave Spartacus. Chapter 1.

Hill Street Blues

1981–1987. Creators, Steven Bochco and Michael Kozoll. Production company and broadcaster, MTM Enterprises/NBC. Groundbreaking American police series set in a hard urban environment. Chapter 8.

Holby City

1999–present. Creator, not known. Production company and broadcaster, BBC. British ensemble series set in the medical wards of a regional hospital. Made out to be the same as the hospital in *Casualty*. Chapters 2 and 9.

Home and Away

1988–present. Creator, Alan Bateman. Production company and broadcaster, 7 Network. Australian soap opera set in a seaside town. Also broadcast in the United Kingdom over many years in a teatime slot for a school-age audience and lead-in to the early news. Chapter 8.

Homicide: Life on the Street

1993–1999. Creator, Paul Attanasio. Production company and broadcaster, Baltimore Pictures, Fatima Productions, MCEG/Sterling Entertainment, NBC Studios, Reeves Entertainment Group, Thames Television/NBC. Classic American crime series. Chapter 8.

House

2004–present. Creator, David Shore. Production company and broadcaster, Heel & Toe Films, NBC Universal Television, Bad Hat Harry Productions, Shore Z Productions, Moratim Produktions/Fox. American medical drama with a cantankerous doctor-hero who is an excellent diagnostician of extraordinary cases despite his unfortunate personality. Chapters 1, 7, 8, and 9.

House of Cards

1990. Creators, Andrew Davies and Michael Dobbs. Production company and broadcaster, BBC. British political series with a conspiratorial plot about the will to power. Two follow-up series were made. Chapter 3.

Inspector Morse

1987–2000. Creator, Colin Dexter. Production company and broadcaster, Carlton UK Productions/ITV. British crime series set in Oxford with John Thaw as the eponymous detective. Chapter 8.

Jackanory

1965–2003? Creators, Alfred Bestall, Mary Tourtel, and Joy Whitby. Production company and broadcaster, BBC. Children's series involving the reading aloud of stories from books. Chapter 1.

The Jerry Springer Show

1991–present. Creator, production company, and broadcaster, Multimedia Entertainment, NBC Universal Television, Universal TV/NBC. Talk show, hosted by Jerry Springer, that frequently leads to confrontation among the guests who are noncelebrities with difficult domestic issues. Chapter 3.

Jerry Springer: The Opera

2005. Creator, not known. Production company and broadcaster, Avalon Productions/BBC. A staged *operatic* treatment of the world of Jerry Springer, filmed and broadcast in Britain. Chapters 3 and 6.

Judge John Deed

2001–present. Creator, G. F. Newman. Production company and broadcaster, BBC. Courtroom series featuring a maverick judge with love interest. Chapter 1.

Juliet Bravo

1980–1985. Creator, Ian Kennedy Martin. Production company and broadcaster, BBC. A British series set in a small northern English town with a female chief constable. Chapter 8.

Kath and Kim

2002–present. Creators, Gina Riley and Jane Turner. Production company and broadcaster, Riley Turner Productions/ABC. An Australian domestic situation comedy set in suburbia. Chapter 8.

Kojak

1973–1978. Creator, Abby Mann. Production company and broadcaster, Universal TV/CBS. American crime series centered on a particular detective played by Telly Savalas. Chapter 8.

Law and Order

1990–present. Creator, Dick Wolf. Production company and broadcaster, Studios USA Television, NBC Universal Television, Universal Network Television/NBC. American crime series in which a court case follows from a criminal investigation. Chapters 6 and 8.

League of Gentlemen

1999–2002. Creator, Mark Gatis. Production company and broadcaster, BBC. A British situation comedy with a cast of grotesque characters set in a small provincial town close to the countryside. Chapter 3.

Life on Mars

2006–2007. Creator, Mathew Graham, Tony Jordan, and Ashley Pharaoh. Production company and broadcaster, Kudos Film and Television/BBC. A British crime series in which the hero is transported from 2006 back to 1973 and has to deal with the very different social mores of the earlier time. Chapter 1.

Little Britain

2003–present. Creators, Matt Lucas and David Walliams. Production company and broadcaster, BBC. A British sketch show featuring various caricature creations. Chapters 2 and 7.

Look in on London: Streetcleaners

1956. Creator, not known. Production company and broadcaster, Associated Rediffusion/ITV. A social documentary about life in Britain from the 1950s. Chapter 2.

Lost

2004–present. Creators, J. J. Abrams, Jeffrey Lieber, and Damon Lindelof. Production company and broadcaster, ABC, Touchstone Television, Bad Robot/ABC. Survivors of a plane crash have mysterious experiences on a deserted island. Chapters 3 and 10.

Mad Men

2007–present. Creator, Matthew Weiner. Production company and broadcaster, American movie classics, AMC. A drama about the life of successful advertising executives on Madison Avenue in the early 1960s. Chapter 4.

Mastermind

1972–present. Creator, not known. Production company and broadcaster, BBC. British quiz show at the more serious end of the intellectual spectrum. Chapter 6.

Mission: Impossible

1966–1973. Creator, Bruce Geller. Production company and broadcaster, Desilu productions, Paramount Television/CBS. American crime series. Chapter 5.

Mister Ed

1961–1966. Creator, Walter Brooks. Production company and broadcaster, CBS, Filmways Pictures, The Mister Ed Company/CBS. American situation comedy with a talking horse. Chapter 7.

Monty Python's Flying Circus

1969–1974. Creators, Graham Chapman, Eric Idle, Terry Jones, Michael Palin, Terry Gilliam, and John Cleese. Production company and broadcaster, BBC. British experimental sketch comedy series. Chapter 2.

The Mrs. Merton Show

1994–1998. Creators, Caroline Aherne, Dave Gorman, and Henry Normal. Production company and broadcaster, Granada Television/ITV. Celebrity talk show in which the guests are interviewed by Caroline Aherne in her middle-aged Mrs. Merton persona. Chapter 3.

Neighbours

1985–present. Creator, Reg Watson. Production company and broadcaster, Grundy Television Australia/Network 10. Australian soap opera popular with teenagers and children in the United Kingdom as well as Australia. Chapters 2, 7, and 8.

NYPD Blue

1993–2005. Creators, Steven Bochco and David Milch. Production company and broadcaster, 20th Century Fox Television/Fox. American police series. Chapter 8.

The Office

2001–2003. Creators, Ricky Gervais and Steven Merchant. Production company and broadcaster, BBC. British mockumentary situation comedy set in the offices of a paper supply company. Chapter 8.

The Office: An American Workplace

2005–present. Creators, Greg Daniels, Ricky Gervais, and Stephen Merchant. Production company and broadcaster, Reveille Productions/NBC. American version of *The Office*. Chapters 8 and 10.

One Foot in the Grave

1990–2000. Creator, David Renwick. Production company and broadcaster, BBC. British situation comedy about a retired couple in suburbia. Chapters 2 and 5.

Outnumbered

2007–present. Creators, Andy Hamilton and Guy Jenkin. Production company and broadcaster, Hat Trick Productions/BBC. Part-improvised British situation comedy about life in a family with small children. Chapter 3.

Pennies from Heaven

1978. Creator, Dennis Potter. Production company and broadcaster, BBC. Drama about the fantasy life and the real life of a man selling sheet music for a living in the 1930s, constructed as a musical with the characters periodically miming to American popular songs of the period. Chapter 3.

Perfect Strangers

2001. Creator, Stephen Poliakoff. Production company and broadcaster, TalkBack Productions/BBC. Drama about a family reunion, occasioning the telling of poignant stories with photographic memorabilia. Chapter 8.

Play for Today

1970–1984. Creator, not known. Production company and broadcaster, BBC. British anthology drama series. Chapter 3.

Pride and Prejudice

1995. Creator, Andrew Davies. Production company and broadcaster, BBC. Classic adaptation of the Jane Austen novel. Chapters 3 and 8.

Prime Suspect

1991 (sequels until 2006). Creator, Lynda La Plante. Production company and broadcaster, Granada Television/ITV. British crime drama series with a senior female officer and significant social themes as well as a strong story line. Chapter 8.

Pushing Daisies

2007–present. Creator, Bryan Fuller. Production company and broadcaster, Jinks/Cohen Company, Living Dead Guy Productions, Warner Bros. TV/ABC. American fantasy drama. Chapters 3 and 7.

Queer as Folk

1999. Creator, Russell T. Davies. Production company and broadcaster, Red Production Company/Channel 4. British drama about the lives of young gay males in Manchester. Chapter 7.

Ramsay's Boiling Point

1998. Creator, James Allen. Production company and broadcaster, London Weekend/ITV. Reality show about the life of a professional celebrity chef. Chapter 9.

Rome

2005. Creators, Bruno Heller, William J. MacDonald, and John Milius. Production company and broadcaster HD Vision Studio/HBO. Historical series. Chapter 1.

The Royal

2003–present. Creator, Ken Horn. Production company and broadcaster, Yorkshire Television/ITV. British hospital series, spin-off from *Heartbeat* and set in the same generic 1960s/1970s imagined world. Chapter 8.

The Royle Family

1998–present. Creators, Caroline Aherne and Craig Cash. Production company and broadcaster, Granada Television/BBC. British situation comedy about the lives of a northern working-class family, focusing on their living room and kitchen interactions to the exclusion of nearly everything else. Chapters 3 and 4.

Saturday Night Live

1975–present. Creator, not known. Production company and broadcaster, NBC Studios/NBC. American variety series with performing guests (e.g., musicians) as well as a permanent cast who provide comedy material. Chapter 4.

Scenes from a Marriage

1973. Creator, Ingmar Bergman. Production company and broadcaster, Cinematograph AB. Ingmar Bergman's reflections on marital relations. Chapter 2.

Secrets and Lies

1996. Creator, Mike Leigh. Production company and broadcaster, Channel 4 Films. Mike Leigh's reflections on family life. Chapter 2.

Sergeant Bilko/The Phil Silvers Show

1955–1959. Creator, Nat Hiken. Production company and broadcaster, CBS/CBS. Situation comedy about military life for disaffected conscripts. Chapter 2.

Shameless

2004–present. Creator, Paul Abbott. Production company and broadcaster, Company Pictures/Channel 4. Comedy drama about Northern working class life in England. Chapter 7.

The Simpsons

1989–present. Creator, Matt Groening. Production company and broadcaster, 20th Century Fox Television/Fox. Very significant American animated series with Homer Simpson as its most famous character. Many celebrities have been featured during the course of the series. Chapter 7.

Soldiering On. See Talking Heads.

The Sooty Show

1968–1992. Creator, not known. Production company and broadcaster, Thames Television/ITV. The antics of a set of glove puppets. Chapter 7.

The Sopranos

1999–2007. Creator, David Chase. Production company and broadcaster, HBO. The antics of a Mafia family in New Jersey. Chapters 1, 3, 7, and 8.

Spooks

2002–present. Creator, David Wolstencroft. Production company and broadcaster, Kudos/BBC. The espionage services (MI5) in the United Kingdom. Chapter 2.

Star Trek Enterprise

2001–2005. Creators, Gene Roddenberry, Rick Beman, and Brannon Braga. Production company and broadcaster, Braga Productions, Paramount Television Network Productions, Paramount Television, Rick Berman Productions/UPN. Final series of the *Star Trek* chronicles, constructed as a prequel to the original *Star Trek* series. Chapter 4.

Starsky and Hutch

1975–1979. Creator, not known. Production company and broadcaster, Spelling-Goldberg Productions/ABC. American crime series. Chapter 8.

The State Within

2006. Creators, Lizzie Mickery and Daniel Percival. Production company and broadcaster, BBC and BBC America. British thriller set in Washington and international locations. Jason Isaacs stars, and Sharon Gless (of *Cagney and Lacey* fame) has a major role. Chapter 3.

Steptoe and Son

1962–1974. Creators, Ray Galton and Alan Simpson. Production company and broadcaster, BBC. Situation comedy about the dysfunctional relationship between father and son rag-and-bone men in London. Chapter 7.

Studio 60 on the Sunset Strip

2006–2007. Creator, Aaron Sorkin. Production company and broadcaster, Warner Brothers Television/NBC. Dramedy set backstage of a live American variety show. Written by Aaron Sorkin, who was also responsible for seasons 1–4 of *The West Wing*. Chapter 4.

Summer Heights High

2007. Creator, Chris Lilley. Production company and broadcaster, Princess Pictures/ABC. Australian school-based situation comedy in mockumentary mode. Chapter 8.

The Sweeney

1975–1978. Creator, Ian Kennedy Martin. Production company and broadcaster, Euston Films/ITV. British crime series. Chapter 8.

Talking Heads: Soldiering On

1987. Creator, Allan Bennett. Production company and broadcaster, BBC. In this particular *Talking Heads* monologue, Stephanie Cole plays a military widow whose life deteriorates and whose son deceives her for the sake of money. Chapter 1.

The Thick of It

2005–present. Creator, Armando Iannucci. Production company and broadcaster, BBC. British political situation comedy. Chapter 3.

Thunderbirds

1965–1966. Creators, Gerry Anderson and Sylvia Anderson. Production company and broadcaster, AP Films/ITV. Science fiction with string puppets. Chapter 7.

Tom and Jerry

1965–1972. Creators, William Hanna and Joseph Barbera. Production company and broadcaster, MGM Television/CBS. Animated series that followed the antics of a predator cat and a canny mouse. Chapter 7.

The Two Ronnies

1971–1987. Creator, not known. Production company and broadcaster, BBC, ITV. British comedy show with sketches and musical numbers. Chapters 5 and 6.

Vote, Vote, Vote for Nigel Barton

1965. Creator, Dennis Potter. Production company and broadcaster, BBC. In the episode "The Wednesday Play," a follow-up to "Stand Up Nigel Barton," Barton is a working-class youth who rises to the middle classes via Oxford University and then runs for parliament but loses respect for the system and himself and pulls out. Chapter 3.

Waking the Dead

2000–present. Creator, Barbara Machin. Production company and broadcaster, BBC Drama Group/BBC. British crime series. Chapter 3.

The Weakest Link

2000–present. Creator, not known. Production company and broadcaster, BBC. Entertaining quiz show in which the celebrity host Anne Robinson makes fun of contestants. An American version with the same host was also made. Chapter 9.

The Wednesday Play

1964–1970. Creator, not known. Production company and broadcaster, BBC. Classic British anthology drama series (see *Vote, Vote, Vote for Nigel Barton*, above). Chapter 3.

The West Wing

1999–2006. Creator, Aaron Sorkin. Production company and broadcaster, John Wells Productions/NBC. American political drama series written by Aaron Sorkin (seasons 1–4). Chapters 1, 2, 6, and 8.

Whose Line Is It Anyway?

1988–1998. Creator, not known. Production company and broadcaster, Hat Trick/ Channel 4. Improvisational comedy sketches to order. An American version was also made. Chapter 1.

Z Cars

1962–1978. Creator, Troy Kennedy Martin. Production company and broadcaster, BBC. British police series set in a northern England town. For its time, a venture in the direction of greater realism, including more location shooting. Chapters 7 and 8.

Notes

CHAPTER I

1. Here and throughout this book I will use the term *sociolinguistic* inclusively, although the emphasis will mainly be at the *micro* rather than the *macro* end of the sociolinguistic spectrum of concerns. This reaches out to all research on the study of language in use, irrespective of subdisciplinary origins—pragmatics at its more social end; conversation analysis, critical discourse analysis, applied linguistics, stylistics, as well as core sociolinguistic territory, including interactional sociolinguistics, the ethnography of speaking, and the study of linguistic variation. It is important for the study that it should be data driven, not theory driven, but the terminology used is intended without prejudice to the integrity of specific approaches.

2. In principle, this list ought to include the dialogue of feature films, because they are so often experienced in a domestic context via a TV set or home computer, just like television drama, whether they are broadcast, on DVD/VHS, or downloaded. However, there will be little direct discussion of dialogue in feature films here. Readers are invited to determine for themselves where the account fits the case of films and where it does not.

3. From here on, the first reference to any TV show or series in each chapter will supply the name of the channel on which the show was first broadcast and the year(s) of broadcasting. Subsequent references to the same show in the same chapter will not supply this information. There is a full list of shows and series referred to with brief descriptions at the end of this book. When the information is available, quotations such as this will be accompanied by the correct episode writing credits, including those that are reproduced from other sources rather than my transcriptions from recordings and DVDs. Series creators, who have more status than the writers of particular episodes, are not necessarily credited in the text, but this information is provided in the appendix.

4. Sociolinguistically trained readers will recognize this allusion to the truth, relevance, sincerity, and informational adequacy of Carmela's line here as a reference to the four maxims of Gricean pragmatics. According to this approach, indirect meaning is potentially created whenever an utterance is in breach of one of these maxims.

5. For an overview of storytelling on television, and the relevance of narrative research to this, see Kozloff (1992).

6. The relevant code of practice for British broadcasters on access is available online: http://www.ofcom.org.uk/tv/ifi/codes/ctas/ (accessed May 3, 2009).

7. Chatman acknowledges that he is following the path set by the Russian formalists as well as the Prague School and French structuralists. He cites in particular the work of Claude Bremont.

8. In narratology, terminology varies when it comes to distinguishing between chronological elements of a narrative and their textual arrangement. I will refer to *narratives* when it is not important to make this distinction, to *story* when the focus is on the chronological sequence of actions/events within a narrative, and *plot* for the sequential organization of those actions/events in a text, which may or may not be in chronological order. A *flashback* can therefore occur only in a plot, not in a story—though a story can have backward or forward time travel.

CHAPTER 2

1. In the current decade, books on contemporary TV drama include Bignell, Lacey, and MacMurraugh-Kavanagh (2000), Caughie 2000, Jancovich and Lyons (2003), Creeber (2004), Thornham and Purvis (2004), Hammond and Mazdon (2005), Bignell and Lacey (2005), Nelson (2007), McCabe and Akass (2007a). This list can be extended by including books about the history of TV drama (Jacobs 2000), Cooke 2003), books that focus on single series or single individuals (Lavery 2002 on *The Sopranos*, Peacock 2007 on *24*, Cardwell 2005 on Andrew Davies, Hallam 2005 on Lynda LaPlante), and those that consider adaptations of literary works (Cardwell 2002), not to mention edited collections in which drama is addressed alongside other genres (Davin and Jackson 2008). Formal concerns of the kind indicated by Geraghty are variably addressed within this literature.

2. Cardwell is willing to declare her own criteria for the determination of value: shows are good, for her, when they can sustain repeated viewings because they have either stylistic integrity or thematic importance or both (2007: 30). These are ultimately arguments about the cognitive-affective-cultural effects of texts, giving rise to familiar social scientific difficulties: some people watch programs with all of the requisite formal qualities without being affected in the ways that textual analysis has envisaged. If the texts are good in such cases, the obvious inference is that the audiences must be bad. The quality debate is revisited in chapter 8 and in the conclusion; see also Brundson (1990), Corner (1994), and Nelson (1997).

3. In date order, some key landmarks here are Modleski (1982), Hobson (1982), Ang (1985), Livingstone (1991), and Geraghty (1991).

4. *Age markers* are spoken references that a person makes related to his or her own age. In the case of older adults, such a person might reveal his or her age, call him- or herself a retiree, refer to grandchildren, or talk about age-related health complaints, for instance. See Coupland, Coupland, Giles, and Henwood (1988).

CHAPTER 3

1. For example, "Caroline Ahearne's [sic] and Craig Cash's sit-com is even more perfectly reflective at Christmas when the levels of drunkenness, indigestion and banal conversation standard on the Royles' sofa are matched in most homes." *Guardian*, December 22, 2000. Retrieved May 3, 2009, from http://www.guardian.co.uk/christmas2000/story/0,414515,00.html

"*The Royle Family* is an intricate study in banality, preserving a snapshot of British working-class culture nearing the turn of the millennium. Chronicling six evenings in the lives of the Royles, the mundane conversations captured within the confines of the family's sitting room provide a voyeuristic odyssey worthy of so-called reality television, but is all the more impressive because it's a scripted program with a fidelity to reality that suggests a hidden-camera documentary rather than a filmed sitcom." Jason Davies, "Imitation of Life," February 23, 2006. Retrieved April 11, 2008, from http://www.creativescreenwriting.com/csdaily/dvds/02_23_06_RoyleFamilyS1.html

2. *America's Most Wanted* (Fox 1988–present) is a close U.S. equivalent.

3. Shows with these characters include *An Audience with Dame Edna Everage* (ITV 1980), *The Dame Edna Experience* (ITV 1987–1989), and *The Mrs Merton Show* (ITV 1994–1998).

CHAPTER 4

1. A complementary ethnographic approach from within media studies, though without a specific focus on dialogue, is offered by Messenger Davies (2007), who interviews two of the writers on *Star Trek: Enterprise* (UPN 2001–2005).

2. *Eastenders* (BBC 1985–present) is a British soap opera set in the working-class East End of London. It is generally compared with the even more venerable *Coronation Street* (ITV 1960–present).

3. To get a feeling for the writers' room experience, *Studio 60 on the Sunset Strip* (NBC 2007–2008) is well worth watching—it made a point of incorporating "room culture" into its diegesis. The imaginary show being produced in this case was not a drama but a live sketch show with musical guests, on the model of the real *Saturday Night Live* (NBC 1975–present). Nevertheless, the function of its writing team, to come up with ideas, is not unlike the function of a drama/comedy writing team. In Britain, the "room" experience is less common (Batty and Waldeback 2008).

4. A *spec script* is a script, for a movie or a television show, that is written without expectation that it will ever be produced, to convince gatekeepers that the writer deserves a commission, a staff post, and representation by an agency or a fellowship (*spec* being short for "speculative"). A *slug line* is a line in a script that indicates where the action takes place, whether outside or inside, during the day or at night. A *parenthetical* is a stage direction.

5. For *theme*, read also *moral, point, evaluation*, and *message*, according to genre and/ or analytic tradition. Such terms are not synonymous, but they do all point to more abstract meanings than those present in the story at the literal level.

6. This generalization would not be true for TV dramatization understood inclusively, because this would encompass TV advertising in its dramatic forms, where thematic content (of a particular kind) is primary.

7. Brody acknowledges Harlan Ellison as the originator of the story on which this material is based but does not specify the particular story.

CHAPTER 5

1. Useful discussion of these differentiations can be found in Livingstone (2007), who traces the trajectory of theoretical discussion from Stuart Hall, through David Morley to John Corner and Justin Wren-Lewis, taking in relevant research by Celeste Condit and by Umberto Eco. The following selective list of sources, which focuses mainly on the theoretical and not the applied contributions to the field, should provide a starting point for readers wishing to explore this trajectory: Hall (1980, 1994), Morley (1980, 1992), Wren-Lewis (1983, 1991), Lewis (1991), Corner (1991b), Eco (1979), and Condit (1989).

2. BBC News, "Doctor Who Attracts 8.4m Viewers." Retrieved May 3, 2009, from http://news.bbc.co.uk/1/hi/entertainment/7333321.stm

3. Andrew Billen, Doctor Who; Louis Theroux's African Hunting Holiday. The Times, April 7 2008. retrieved 6th August 2009 from http://entertainment.timesonline.co.uk/tol/arts_and_entertainment/tv_and_radio/article3684082.ece, *Guardian*, "Doctor Who—Partners in Crime Was a Good Start to Season Four." Retrieved May 3, 2009, from   http://www.guardian.co.uk/media/organgrinder/2008/apr/07/doctorwhopartner-sincrimew

5. TV.com, "Doctor Who: Partners in Crime, Episode recap." Retrieved May 3, 2009, from http://www.tv.com/Doctor+Who+%282005%29/Partners+in+Crime/episode/1166297/recaphtml

6. Jonathan Tilove, "Something Borrowed, Nothing New in Politics." Retrieved May 3, 2009, from http://www.freerepublic.com/focus/f-news/1973378/posts

7. Richard Grigonis, "This Instant Message Will Self-Destruct in Five Seconds." Retrieved May 3, 2009, from http://mobile-voip.tmcnet.com/topics/mobile-communications/articles/25512-this-instant-message-will-self-destruct-five-seconds.htm

CHAPTER 6

1. This problem, extended beyond the communicative acts of characters to encompass all description of fictional works, has been addressed by Wikipedia under the heading "The Problem with In-Universe Perspective":

> An in-universe perspective describes the narrative from the perspective of charac-ters within the fictional universe, treating it as if it were real and ignoring real-world context and sourced analysis. The threshold of what constitutes in-universe writing is making *any* effort to re-create or uphold the illusion of the original fiction by omitting real-world info.

For Wikipedia, seeking to be an authoritative source of reference, in-universe perspec-tives on fictional works potentially blur the boundary between real and fictional to an unacceptable extent:

> For example, if a fictional TV detective loses a partner in the line of duty, taking an in-universe perspective will obscure whether this occurred in the backstory, the pilot or the main series. If the partner died in the pilot, but is the subject of little-known prequel novels, then an in-universe perspective may describe the partner in exces-sive detail. If later episodes have events which suggest the dead partner never existed, this is impossible to describe from an in-universe perspective, and editors [i.e., Wikipedia contributors] will have to try to explain away such continuity errors themselves, leading to original research [i.e., speculation by Wikipedia contributors] and inaccuracy.

Retrieved May 3, 2009, from http://en.wikipedia.org/wiki/Wikipedia:Manual_of_ Style (writing_about_fiction)#The_problem_with_in-universe_perspective.

2. A *transition relevance place* is understood as a structurally projected boundary in the flow of a single speaker's talk, such as the end of a grammatical clause, which participants agree to treat as an opportunity for another speaker to take the floor. An *adjacency pair* is a

bounded set of utterances such that the former, from one speaker, projects the other, from another speaker. If someone asks a question, an answer is then expected, and its absence will be notable for participants. *Preference organization* refers to the fact that in some adjacency pairs there may be more than one possible second part (an offer, for example, may be either accepted or refused). In such circumstances it is often the case that one of the two possibilities will be delivered with extra features, such as hesitation, hedging, or delaying prefaces, which mark it as the "dispreferred" response.

3. Accent convergence and divergence are not much in evidence as resources in the performance of television dramatic dialogue. We can explain this by reference to the public character of this particular kind of communication, specifically to the fact that its audience is construed as geographically heterogeneous. Such a mixed audience could not be relied upon to register as meaningful the subtleties of convergence and divergence in pronunciation. If convergence was rendered "obvious" enough to be thus registered, it would cease to be faithful to the realities of real-life linguistic accommodation and become caricature convergence. I have not, in my own research, come across any examples of this, though I can imagine it being made to work in a comedic production. Accent mimicry (by characters of one another) is a different matter, and not uncommon, especially in Britain. Caricature performance is perfectly acceptable in that context.

CHAPTER 7

1. There is more about the responses of fans/audiences to dialogue in chapter 5 in this volume.

2. At the time of writing, about a dozen of these commercial were available online at: http://www.tellyads.com/show

3. The sponsor of *House* at the time was Spontex Comfy Gloves.

4. My use of the adjective *prototypical* here is meant to evoke another relevant concept from cognitive science that has influenced language theory. Eleanor Rosch's work in the 1970s (see, e.g., Rosch 1973) offered a way out of the difficulty of assigning phenomena to categories based on necessary and sufficient conditions, by proposing that human cognition works on the basis of core and peripheral category membership. Other things being equal, a robin is a *better* (more central) bird than an ostrich, because an ostrich cannot fly. Category membership is clear in the center of the category but fuzzy at the boundaries. As a consequence, a set of people with the *same* concepts can agree about the categorization as *red* of, say, a color that is near the center of the *reds* section on a decorator's paint sample sheet, but there will be understandable/legitimate disagreement about a swatch that falls in the range between red and orange.

5. I am using the concept of *referential reading* here in the sense similar to that of Liebes and Katz (1990). Referential readings in this research were those that interpreted characters in the American soap *Dallas* (CBS 1978–1991) as people, and treated the show as if it were a kind of documentary about those people. Liebes and Katz contrasted such readings with *critical readings* that maintained some distance from the representations. In Richardson and Corner (1986) the notion of *transparency reading* is used in a similar way, emphasizing a predilection to ignore the work of mediation and regard on-screen persons as if they were being encountered directly. Both of these studies focus on actual audience uptake of particular shows.

6. Readers not familiar with *Little Britain* may find clips and other related material via the BBC website at http://www.bbc.co.uk/comedy/littlebritain (accessed June 9, 2008).

7. The BBC's website currently offers the opportunity to view various crime reconstructions online at http://www.bbc.co.uk/crimewatch/ (accessed June 9, 2008). A comparable show on American television is *America's Most Wanted* (Fox 1988–present), which I have not seen.

8. The work of Schank and Abelson (1977) is generally cited as the inspiration for much of what developed when the theory moved beyond its origins in artificial intelligence. It has of course been a huge influence on research in discourse analysis, sociolinguistics, and social psychology. See Cook (1994) for a detailed, critical review of the relevant sources written expressly as part of an exploration of the relevance of schema theory for literary research.

For my purposes, it is important to note that schemata, in this approach (as well as the related concepts of scripts and frames), are higher order cognitive structures, in other words, more abstract than the medium (language, image) from which they are derived. *Schemata*, according to the theory, are mental structures that represent knowledge in the brain. Cook himself disputes the claims of total separation between linguistic and mental representations.

9. There was a subsequent American version of this series that initially aired on a U.S. cable network 2000–2005 and has been seen in some other countries, including Spain and Germany, but not the United Kingdom.

10. It would be wrong to use this argument to oversimplify what television has offered audiences over the years in terms of *images of policing*. O'Sullivan (2005) surveyed existing research in this area with respect to the United Kingdom's crime drama series from *Dixon of Dock Green* (BBC 1955–1972) onward, and found considerable variation. The general point still holds, however, because dramas that *focus* on the police are more readily available to expand on the characteristics of individual police officers than those in which police officers are incidental to the plotline. These are the ones in which default, schematic "police officer" assumptions will be in play.

11. Review at http://libcom.org/library/shameless-paul-abbott-series-1–2-channel-4–20034-television-review-%E2%80%93-tom-jennings (accessed May 9, 2009).

12. At the time of writing, this episode was available online to institutional subscribers via the British Film Institute—sponsored website, at http://www.screenonline.org.uk/media/stream.jsp?id=1234745 (accessed June 9, 2008).

13. *Claptraps* are rhetorical devices (such as the three-part list) used in formal speeches, for example, by politicians, to provoke applause "on cue" (see Atkinson 1984). I am suggesting that there are equivalent cues for laughter in comic genres.

14. Sperber and Wilson (1986) is the main work in the relevance theory literature.

15. See, for example, Jakobson (1960).

16. See Kress and van Leeuwen (2001).

CHAPTER 8

1. This raises issues about national versus international audiences, which this chapter does not have scope to address. Comprehensibility of language is one of the issues, even when the trade is between one Anglophone country and another, as with American imports to the United Kingdom and vice versa. Cultural references both unite and divide:

"Wild West" analogies may achieve the former, but the period character of this show introduces a specifically British frame of reference (power cuts, *The Sweeney*, Open University TV broadcasts). Of course, these characteristics can contribute an exotic flavor for international audiences (or British viewers too young to access their substantive content). The same applies to American cultural references in shows exported to the United Kingdom and elsewhere, though in this case it may also be that sufficient exposure to the same references in a range of such programming makes them familiar internationally as well as nationally. (See chapter 10 for further discussion.)

2. The American equivalent of this caution is referred to as reading someone their Miranda rights.

3. Sam Wollaston, "Last Night's TV," *Guardian*, January 10, 2006. Retrieved May 3, 2009, from http://www.guardian.co.uk/media/2006/jan/10/broadcasting.tvandradio

4. Ray King, "Life on Mars Writers on Another Planet—Top Cop," *Manchester Evening News*, February 21, 2006. Retrieved May 9, 2009, from http://www.manchestereveningnews.co.uk/entertainment/film_and_tv/s/205/205246_life_on_mars_writers_on_another_planet__top_cop.html

5. David Smith, "£1,500 in a Carrier Bag? What Planet Are You On?" *Observer*, April 8, 2007. Retrieved May 9, 2009, from http://www.guardian.co.uk/media/2007/apr/08/broadcasting.uknews

6. James Rampton, "It's an Unfair Cop: Gene, the Most Defiantly Un-PC Cop on the Block, Is Back," *Independent*, April 13, 2009. Retrieved May 3, 2009, from http://www.independent.co.uk/arts-entertainment/tv/features/its-an-unfair-cop-gene-hunt-the-most-defiantly-unpc-pc-on-the-block-is-back-1667712.html

7. Hillsborough is a football ground in the city of Sheffield. On April 15, 1989, the match to be played was between Liverpool and Nottingham Forest. Ninety-six Liverpool supporters eventually died of asphyxiation in the crush of bodies after entering the ground. A subsequent official report laid responsibility at the door of the police, while also recognizing that the spectators would not have died if they had been able to get on to the field. This was not possible because of the hooligan-proof fencing that kept the fans in separate "pens."

CHAPTER 9

1. The concept of *face* in Brown and Levinson's original 1978 account has been criticized for being spuriously universalistic when in fact restricted to Western cultures (see, e.g., Matsumoto 1989, Gu 1990). The binary distinction between positive and negative face has been subjected to conceptual critique and revision (see, e.g., Spencer-Oatey 2002, Tracy and Tracy 1998). The concept of *politeness* continues to be contested (Eelen 2001; Watts 2003; Mills 2003). In the absence of theoretical consensus, and with no theoretical axes of my own to grind, I have related my account of the aggressive facework in *House M.D.* to the Brown and Levinson model on the grounds (a) that it is the one that is most familiar to all researchers in this area, and (b) that Culpeper's influential account of impoliteness in discourse is itself derived from this approach, albeit with critique and revisions.

2. An opposite case can, in fact, be made: that Brown and Levinson have made all talk, all interaction, and all human proximity inherently hostile or at least dangerous, by putting face threatening acts at the core of any encounter, with politeness strategies as

an optional extra. This representation is then compounded by setting up several different kinds of no-win situations for would-be speakers. A compliment, for example, counts as positive politeness in their schema, a kind of redressive action. But it can also count as a negative, face-threatening act in its own right—an intrusion into the personal space of an addressee who would rather be left alone than have to find a way of responding to the unsought and unwelcome attention. In practice, perhaps, contexts will contribute in assigning just the right kind of interpersonal meaning to any specific compliment, but the general issue of the ubiquity of "face danger" still remains. As an image of human social relations, it has a decidedly neurotic flavor.

3. See Sarah Womack and Thomas Penny, "Robinson Tells Welsh: You Are Weakest Link," *Daily Telegraph*, March 5, 2003. Retrieved April 21, 2009, from http://www.telegraph. co.uk/news/uknews/1325280/Robinson-tells-Welsh-you-are-weakest-link.html

4. See also Kochman (1983) and Eder (1990) for more evidence that banter-like talk is possible even if the offensive content is not obviously untrue.

5. Martin Ellingham in the series *Doc Martin* also has to contend with a smelly patient in one episode, and the contrast is striking. It actually turns out that the smell is not from the patient at all, but from his dead pet goldfinch, rotting away into a bag that the patient has been carrying around with him. Whereas House takes pleasure in drawing attention to the smell, Ellingham and his receptionist are depicted as being forced into doing so by its insuperable potency. Ellingham's patient, an elderly, frail, rather timid man, treats his own smell as a face-threatening act for which he is obliged to apologize. The doctor accepts the apology ("It's all right," in a matter-of-fact, rather than sympathetic, tone), and obliges himself to examine the patient despite the smell. Other things being equal, House would have delegated such a repellent task to a junior, or found some other way of sidestepping his duties while ensuring the patient got medical care.

6. Watts (2003) draws a distinction between *politic behavior* and *polite behavior*. The former refers to behavior that is conventionally expected, such as greetings, "please" and "thank you," and so forth; the latter goes beyond conventionality, such as compliments. Although this works well enough in relation to politeness phenomena, it is awkward in relation to impoliteness, because the deliberate, intentionally rude, withholding of greetings, as in this example, is just as strategic as paying a compliment.

CHAPTER 10

1. *Wall Street Journal*, "Talk the Talk: A 'Wire' Insider's Guide to the Show's Street Slang," December 28, 2007. Retrieved May 3, 2009, from http://online.wsj.com/article/ SB119888101122256433.html

2. Questions about the cultural grounding of interpretation are not unique to the understanding of drama. The production of intelligible talk in any context requires the use of both general and culture-specific interpretative resources. In the case of schema theory, the point of division would be between schema-based understanding as such, and the content of particular schemata, in which the latter is understood to be culture specific, whereas the general principle is universal. Theoretical difficulties occur when purportedly general universal principles are themselves discovered to be culture specific, as has happened in the case of politeness theory (see chapter 9, "*House* and Snark").

References

Abercrombie, David. 1963. Conversation and spoken prose. *ELT Journal*, 18(1), 10–16.

Akass, Kim, and Janet McCabe. 2002. Beyond the Bada Bing!: Negotiating female narrative authority in *The Sopranos*. In *This thing of ours: Investigating "The Sopranos,"* ed. David Lavery, 146–161. London: Wallflower Press.

Altman, Rick. 1986. Television/sound. In *Studies in entertainment: Critical approaches to mass culture*, ed. Tania Modleski, 39–52. Bloomington: Indiana University Press.

Ang, Ien. 1985. *Watching "Dallas": Soap opera and the melodramatic imagination*. London: Methuen.

Atkinson, Max. 1984. *Our masters' voices: The language and body language of politics*. London: Methuen.

Austin, John L. 1962. *How to do things with words*. Oxford: Clarendon Press.

Barthes, Roland. 1974. *S/Z: An essay*. Trans. Richard Miller. New York: Hill and Wang.

Barthes, Roland. 1977. The death of the author. In *Image, music, text*, trans. S. Heath, 142–148. London: Fontana Press.

Basso, Keith. 1974. The ethnography of writing. In *Explorations in the ethnography of speaking*, ed. Richard Bauman and Joel Scherzer, 425–432. London: Cambridge University Press.

Batty, Craig, and Zara Waldeback. 2008. *Writing for the screen*. Basingstoke: Palgrave Macmillan.

Baym, Nancy. 2000. *Tune in, log on: Soaps, fandom, and online community*. Thousand Oaks, CA: Sage.

Biber, Douglas. 1988. *Variation across speech and writing*. Cambridge: Cambridge University Press.

Bignell, Jonathan, and Stephen Lacey, eds. 2005. *Popular television drama: Critical perspectives*. Manchester: Manchester University Press.

Bignell, Jonathan, Stephen Lacey, and Madeleine MacMurraugh-Kavanagh. 2000. *British television history: Past, present and future*. London: Palgrave Macmillan.

Blum, David. 2001. Television/radio, tired joke, or cultural touchstone: The sitcom clam. *New York Times*, December 9, 2001.

Bordwell, David, and Kristin Thompson. 2006. *Film art: An introduction*. New York: McGraw-Hill.

Bourdieu, P. 1980. The aristocracy of culture. *Media, Culture and Society*, 2, 225–254.

Bourdieu, P. 1984. *Distinction: A social critique of the judgment of taste*. Trans. Richard Nice. Boston, Mass.: Harvard University Press.

Bousfield, Derek. 2007a. Beginnings, middles and ends: A biopsy of the dynamics of impolite exchanges. *Journal of Pragmatics*, 39, 2185–2216.

Bousfield, Derek. 2007b. Impoliteness, preference organization and conducivity. *Multilingua*, 26, 1–33.

Bousfield, Derek. 2008. *Impoliteness in interaction*. Amsterdam: John Benjamins.

Bousfield, Derek, and Miriam Loucher, eds. 2008. *Impoliteness in language: Studies in its interplay with power in theory and practice*. Berlin: Mouton de Gruyter.

Bouton, L. 1998. Formulaic implicatures as conversational routines. Paper presented at the 6th International Pragmatics Conference, Reims, France, July 1998.

Brody, Larry. 2003. *Television writing from the inside out: Your channel to success*. New York: Applause Cinema and Theatre Books.

Broe, Dennis. 2004. Fox and its friends: Global commodification and the new cold war. *Cinema Journal*, 43(4), 96–102.

Brookes, Ian, ed. 2005. *TV talk: A dictionary of words and phrases popularized by television*. Edinburgh: Chambers.

Brown, Penelope, and Stephen Levinson. 1978. Universals in language usage: Politeness phenomena. In *Questions and politeness*, ed. Esther Goody, 56–324. Cambridge: Cambridge University Press.

Brunsdon, Charlotte. 1990. Problems with quality. *Screen*, 31(1), 67–91.

Bubel, Claudia. 2005. "I'm on total ovary overload": The linguistic representation of women in "Sex and the City." In *Dialogue analysis ix: Dialogue in literature and the media. Part 2: media. Selected papers from the 9th IADA conference, Salzburg 2003*, ed. Anne Betten and Monika Dannerer, 205–214. Tübingen: Niemeyer.

Bubel, Claudia. 2008. Film audiences as overhearers. *Journal of Pragmatics*, 40, 55–71.

Bubel, Claudia, and Alice Spitz. 2006. "One of the last vestiges of gender bias": The characterization of women through the telling of dirty jokes in "Ally McBeal." *Humor: International Journal of Humor Research*, 19(1), 71–104.

Burton, Deirdre. 1980. *Dialogue and discourse: A sociolinguistic approach to modern drama dialogue and naturally occurring conversation*. London: Routledge.

Cameron, Deborah. 1997. Performing gender identity: Young men's talk and the construction of heterosexual masculinity. In *Language and masculinity*, ed. Ulrike Meinhof and Sally Johnson, 47–64. London: Blackwell.

Cameron, Deborah. 2001. *Working with spoken discourse*. London: Sage.

Cameron, Deborah. 2004. "Out of the bottle: The social life of metalanguage." In *Metalanguage: Social and ideological perspectives*, ed. Adam Jaworski, Nik Coupland, and Dariusz Galasinski, 311–321. Berlin: Mouton de Gruyter.

Cardwell, Sarah. 2002 *Adaptation revisited: Television and the classic novel*. Manchester: Manchester University Press.

Cardwell, Sarah. 2005. *Andrew Davies*. Manchester: Manchester University Press.

Cardwell, Sarah. 2007. "Is quality television any good? Generic distinctions, evaluations and the troubling matter of critical judgment." In *Quality TV: Contemporary American television and beyond*, ed. Janet McCabe and Kim Akass, 19–34. London: I.B. Tauris.

Carter, Ron. 2004. *Language and creativity: The art of common talk*. London: Routledge.

Carter, Ron. 2007. Response to special issue of *Applied Linguistics* devoted to language creativity in everyday contexts. *Applied Linguistics*, 28(4), 597–607.

Caughie, John. 2000. *Television drama: Realism, modernism, and British culture*. Oxford: Oxford Television Studies.

Chatman, Seymour. 1978. *Story and discourse*. Ithaca, N.Y.: Cornell University Press.

Chatman, Seymour. 1990. *Coming to terms: The rhetoric of narrative in fiction and film.* Ithaca, N.Y.: Cornell University Press.

Chiarella, Tom. 1998. *Writing dialogue: How to create memorable voices and fictional conversations that crackle with wit, tension and nuance.* Cincinnati, Ohio: Story Press Books.

Condit, Celeste. 1989. The rhetorical limits of polysemy. *Critical Studies in Mass Communications,* 6(2), 103–122.

Cook, Guy. 1992. *The discourse of advertising.* London: Routledge.

Cook, Guy. 1994. *Discourse and literature.* Oxford: Oxford University Press.

Cooke, Lez. 2003. *British television drama: A history.* London: BFI.

Corner, John. 1991a. Media, genre and context: The problematics of "public knowledge" in the new audience studies. In *Mass media and society,* ed. James Curran and Michael Gurevitch, 287–264. London: Methuen.

Corner, John. 1991b. The interview as social encounter. In *Broadcast talk,* ed. Paddy Scannell, 31–47. London: Sage.

Corner, John. 1994. Debating culture: Quality and inequality. *Media, Culture and Society,* 16, 141–148.

Corner, John. 2006. Documentary. In *Encyclopaedia of language and linguistics,* vol. 3, 2nd ed., ed. K. Brown, 755–758. Oxford: Elsevier.

Corner, John, and Kay Richardson. 2008. Political culture and television fiction: "The Amazing Mrs. Pritchard." *European Journal of Cultural Studies,* 11(4), 387–403.

Coupland, Nik. 2004. Stylized deception. In *Metalanguage: Social and ideological perspectives,* ed. Adam Jaworski, Nik Coupland, and Galasinski Dariusz, 259–274. Berlin: Mouton de Gruyter.

Coupland, Nik, Justine Coupland, Howard Giles, and Karen Henwood. 1988. Accommodating the elderly: Invoking and extending a theory. *Language in Society,* 17, 1–41.

Craig, Robert, Karen Tracy, and Frances Spisak. 1986. The discourse of requests: Assessment of a politeness approach. *Human Communication Research,* 12, 437–468.

Creeber, Glen. 2004. *Serial television: Big drama on the small screen.* London: BFI.

Creeber, Glen. 2006. The joy of text. *Critical Studies in Television,* 1(1), 81–88.

Culpeper, Jonathan. 1996. Towards an anatomy of impoliteness. *Journal of Pragmatics,* 25, 349–367.

Culpeper, Jonathan. 2001. *Language and characterization.* Harlow, U.K.: Longman.

Culpeper, Jonathan. 2005. Impoliteness and entertainment in the television quiz show: *The Weakest Link. Journal of Politeness Research,* 1(1), 35–72.

Culpeper, Jonathan, Derek Bousfield, and Anne Wichmann. 2002. Impoliteness revisited: With special reference to dynamic and prosodic aspects. *Journal of Pragmatics,* 35, 1545–1579.

Culpeper, Jonathan, Mick Short, and Peter Verdonk. 1998. *Exploring the language of drama: From text to context.* London: Routledge.

Davin, Solange, and Rhona Jackson. 2008. *Television and criticism.* Bristol, U.K.: Intellect Books.

Davis, Rib. 2008. *Writing dialogue for scripts,* 3rd ed. London: A and C Black.

Denby, David. 2009. *Snark.* New York: Simon and Schuster.

Eco, Umberto. 1979. *The role of the reader: Explorations in the semiotics of texts.* Bloomington: Indiana University Press.

Eder, Donna. 1990. Serious and playful disputes: Variation in conflict talk among female adolescents. In: *Conflict talk: Sociolinguistic investigations of arguments and conversations,* ed. Allen D. Grimshaw, 67–84. Cambridge: Cambridge University Press.

Eelen, Gino. 2001. *A critique of politeness theories.* Manchester: St. Jerome.

Ellis, John. 1983. *Visible fictions.* London: Routledge and Kegan Paul.

Emmott, Catherine. 1997. *Narrative comprehension: A discourse perspective.* Oxford: Oxford University Press.

Epstein, Alex. 2006. *Crafty TV writing: Thinking inside the box.* New York: Holt Paperbacks.

Feuer, Jane. 2005. The lack of influence of *thirtysomething.* In *The contemporary television series,* ed. Michael Hammond, and Lucy Mazdon, 27–36. Edinburgh: Edinburgh University Press.

Field, Syd. 2005. *Screenplay: The foundations of screenwriting.* New York: Delta Trade Paperbacks.

Fine, Marlene 1981. Soap opera conversations: The talk that binds. *Journal of Communication,* 31(3), 97–107.

Flinn, Denny Martin. 1999. *How not to write a screenplay: 101 common mistakes most screenwriters make.* New York: Watson-Guptill.

Fricker, Karen. 2007. "Quality TV" on show. In *Quality TV: Contemporary American television and beyond,* ed. Janet McCabe and Kim Akass. London: I. B. Tauris.

Geraghty, Christine. 1991. *Women and soap opera.* London: Polity.

Geraghty, Christine. 2003. Aesthetics and quality in popular television drama. *International Journal of Cultural Studies,* 6(1), 25–45.

Goffman, Erving. 1959. *The presentation of self in everyday life.* Garden City, N.Y.: Doubleday.

Goffman, Erving. 1967. Interaction ritual: Essays on face-to-face behavior. Garden City, N.Y.: Anchor Books.

Goffman, Erving. 1978. Response cries. *Language,* 54 (4), 787–815.

Goffman, Erving. 1979. Footing. *Semiotica,* 25, 1–29.

Graham, Sage Lambert. 2007. Disagreeing to agree: Conflict, (im)politeness and identity in a computer-mediated community. *Journal of Pragmatics,* 39(4), 742–759.

Gray, Jonathan, Cornel Sandvoss, and C. Lee Harrington 2007. *Fandom: Identities and communities in a mediated world.* New York: New York University Press.

Grice, H. Paul. 1975. Logic and conversation. In *Syntax and Semantics,* vol. 3, ed. Peter Cole, 41–58. New York: Academic Press.

Grimshaw, Allen, ed. 1990a. *Conflict talk: Sociolinguistic investigations of arguments in conversation.* Cambridge: Cambridge University Press.

Grimshaw, Allen, 1990b. Research on conflict talk: Antecedents, resources, findings, directions. In *Conflict talk: Sociolinguistic investigations of arguments in conversation,* ed. Allen Grimshaw, 280–324. Cambridge: Cambridge University Press.

Gu, Yueguo, 1990. Politeness phenomena in modern Chinese. *Journal of Pragmatics,* 14, 237–257.

Hall, Stuart. [1973] 1980. Encoding/decoding. In *Culture, media, language: Working papers in cultural studies, 1972–79,* ed. Stuart Hall, Dorothy Hobson, Andrew Lowe, and Paul Willis, 128–138. London: Hutchinson.

Hall, Stuart. 1994. Reflections on the encoding/decoding model. In *Viewing, reading, listening: audiences and cultural reception,* ed. Jon Cruz and Justin Lewis, 253–274. Boulder: Westview Press.

Hallam, Julia. 2005. *Lynda La Plante.* Manchester: Manchester University Press.

Hallam, Julia. 2009, April. Playing doctor in the USA today. Retrieved April 20, 2009, from http://www.criticalstudiesintelevision.com/index.php?siid=10173

Hamilton, David Lewis. 2005. *Social cognition.* New York: Psychology Press.

Hammond, Michael, and Lucy Mazdon, eds. 2005. *The contemporary television series.* Edinburgh: Edinburgh University Press.

Harris, Sandra. 2001. Being politically impolite: Extending politeness theory to adversarial political discourse. *Discourse and Society,* 12, 451–472.

Harwood, Jake. 2000. "Sharp!": Lurking incoherence in a television portrayal of an older adult. *Journal of Language and Social Psychology,* 110–140.

Harwood, Jake, and Howard Giles. 1992. "Don't make me laugh": Age representations in a humorous context. *Discourse and Society,* 3, 403–436.

Heider, Fritz 1958. *The psychology of interpersonal relations.* Hillsdale, N.J.: Erlbaum.

Herman, Vimala. 1995. *Dramatic discourse: Dialogue as interaction in plays.* London: Routledge.

Hobson, Hobson 1982. *Crossroads: The drama of a soap.* London: Methuen.

Horton, Donald, and Richard Wohl. 1956. Mass communication as para-social interaction: observations on intimacy at a distance. *Psychiatry,* 19(3), 215–229.

Hutchby, Ian. 1996. *Confrontation talk: Arguments, asymmetries and power on talk radio.* Mahwah, N.J.: Erlbaum.

Hutchby, Ian. 2006. *Media talk: Conversation analysis and the study of broadcasting* Maidenhead: Open University Press.

Hymes, Dell. 1972. Models of the interaction of language and social life. In *Directions in sociolinguistics: The ethnography of communication* ed. John Gumperz and Dell Hymes, 35–71. New York: Holt, Rinehart and Winston.Inbau, Fred, John Reid, Joseph Buckley, and Brian Jayne, eds. 2004. *Criminal interrogation and confessions.* Boston: Jones and Bartlett.

Jacobs, Jason. 2000. *The intimate screen: Early British TV drama.* Oxford: Oxford University Press.

Jacobs, Jason. 2003. *Body trauma TV: The new hospital dramas.* London: BFI.

Jakobson, Roland. 1960. Closing statement: Linguistics and poetics. In *Style and language* ed. Thomas Sebeok, 350–377. Cambridge, Mass.: MIT Press.

Jancovich, Mark, and James Lyons, eds. 2003. *Quality popular television: Cult TV, the industry and fans.* London: BFI.

Jaworski, Adam, Nik Coupland, and Dariusz Galasinski. 2004. *Metalanguage: Social and ideological perspectives.* Berlin: Mouton de Gruyter.

Jones, Peter E. 2007. Why there is no such thing as "critical discourse analysis." *Language and Communication,* 27, 337–368.

Keane, Christopher. 1998. *How to write a selling screenplay.* New York: Broadway Books.

Kempton, Gloria. 2004. *Dialogue: Techniques and exercises for crafting effective dialogue* (Write Great Fiction). Cincinnati, Ohio: Writers' Digest Books.

Kochman, Thomas. 1983. The boundary between play and nonplay in Black verbal dueling. *Language in Society,* 12 (3), 329–337.

Kozloff, Sarah. 1992. Narrative theory and television. In *Channels of discourse, reassembled,* ed. R. C. Allen, 67–100. Chapel Hill: University of North Carolina Press.

Kozloff, Sarah. 2000. *Overhearing film dialogue.* Berkeley, Calif.: University of California Press.

Kress, Gunther, and Theo van Leeuwen. 2001. *Multimodal discourse: The modes and meanings of contemporary discourse.* London: Arnold.

Kryk-Kastovsky, Barbara. 2006. Impoliteness in early modern English courtroom discourse. *Journal of Historical Pragmatics,* 7(2), 213–243.

Labov, William. 1972. Rules for ritual insults. In *Language in the inner city: Studies in the Black English vernacular*, ed. W. Labov. Philadelphia: University of Pennsylvania Press, 297–353.

Labov, William, and Joshua Waletzky. 1967. Narrative analysis. In *Essays on the verbal and visual arts*, ed. June Helm, 12–44. Seattle: University of Washington Press.

Lavery, David, ed. 2002. *This thing of ours: Investigating the Sopranos*. New York: Columbia University Press.

Leech, Geoffrey. 1983. *Principles of pragmatics*. London: Longmans.

Leishman, Frank, and Paul Mason. 2003. *Policing the media: Facts, fictions and factions*. Cullompton, U.K.: Willan.

Lewis, Justin. 1991. *The ideological octopus: An exploration of television and its audience*. London: Routledge.

Liebes, Tamar, and Elihu Katz. 1990. *The export of meaning: Cross-cultural readings of Dallas*. New York: Oxford University Press.

Littwin, Susan. 2004. In the company of women: Five who run hit shows at CBS. *Written By*, November 2004.

Livingstone, Sonia. 1987. The implicit representation of characters in Dallas: A multidimensional scaling approach. *Human Communication Research*, 13(3), 339–420.

Livingstone, Sonia. 1989. Interpretive viewers and structured programs: The implicit representation of soap opera characters. *Communication Research*, 16, 25–57.

Livingstone, Sonia. 1990. *Making sense of television: The psychology of audience interpretation*. Oxford: Pergamon Press.

Livingstone, Sonia. 1991. Audience reception: The role of the viewer in retelling romantic drama. In *Mass media and society*, ed. James Curran and Michael Gurevitch, 285–306. London: Edward Arnold.

Livingstone, Sonia. 1998. Audience research at the crossroads: The "implied audience" in media and cultural theory. *European Journal of Cultural Studies*, 1(2), 193–217.

Livingstone, Sonia. 2007. *Audiences and interpretations*. Retrieved July 1, 2009, from http://www.compos.org.br/files/01_Livingstone.pdf

Lury, Karen. 2007. CSI and sound. In *Reading CSI: Crime TV under the microscope* (Reading Contemporary Television), ed. Michael Allen, 107–121. London: I. B. Tauris.

Mamet, David. 1991. *On directing film*. London: Penguin.

Mandala, Susan. 2007a. Solidarity and the Scoobies: An analysis of the -*y* suffix in the television series Buffy the Vampire Slayer. *Language and Literature*, 16(1), 53–73.

Mandala, Susan. 2007b. *Twentieth-century drama dialogue as ordinary talk*. Aldershot, U.K.: Ashgate.

Maras, Steven. 2009. *Screenwriting: History, theory, practice*. London: Wallflower Press.

Matsumoto, Yoshiko. 1989. Politeness and conversational universals: Observations from Japanese. *Multilingua*, 8, 207–221.

Maybin, Janet, and Joan Swann. 2006. *The art of English: Everyday creativity*. London: Palgrave Macmillan.

Maybin, Janet, and Joan Swann. 2007. Introduction: Language creativity in everyday contexts. Special issue, *Applied Linguistics*, 28(4), 491–496.

McCabe, Colin. 1974. Realism and the cinema: Notes on some Brechtian theses. *Screen* 15 (2), 7–27.

McCabe, Janet, and Kim Akass, eds. 2007a. *Quality TV: Contemporary American television and beyond*. London: I. B. Tauris.

McCabe, Janet, and Kim Akass. 2007b. Introduction: Debating quality. In *Quality TV: Contemporary American television and beyond*, ed. Janet McCabe and Kim Akass, 1–12. London: I. B. Tauris.

McCabe, Janet, and Kim Akass. 2007c. Sex, swearing and respectability: Courting controversy, HBO s original programming and producing quality TV. In *Quality TV: Contemporary American television and beyond*, ed. Janet McCabe and Kim Akass, 62–76. London: I. B. Tauris.

McIntyre, Dan. 2006. *Point of view in plays: A cognitive stylistic approach to viewpoint in drama and other text-types*. Amsterdam: John Benjamins.

McIntyre, Dan. 2008. Integrating multimodal analysis and the stylistics of drama: A multimodal perspective on Ian McKellen's Richard III. *Language and Literature*, 17, 309–334.

McKee, Robert. 1999. *Story: Substance, structure, style and the principles of screenwriting*. London: Methuen.

Messenger Davies, Maire. 2007. Quality and creativity in TV: The work of television storytellers. In *Quality TV: Contemporary American television and beyond*, ed. Janet McCabe and Kim Akass, 171–184. London: I. B. Tauris.

Mills, Sara. 2003. *Gender and politeness*. Cambridge: Cambridge University Press.

Modleski, Tania. 1982. *Loving with a vengeance: Mass produced fantasies for women*. Hamden, Conn.: Archon.

Montgomery, Martin. 1999. Talk as entertainment: The case of the Mrs Merton Show. In *Talk about shows: La parola e lo spettacolo*, ed. L. Haarman, 101–105. Bologna: CLUEB.

Montgomery, Martin. 2006. Broadcast news, the live "two-way" and the case of Andrew Gilligan. *Media, Culture and Society*, 28, 233–259.

Morley, David. 1980. *The "nationwide" audience*. London: BFI.

Morley, David. 1992. *Television, audiences and cultural studies*. London: Routledge.

Naremore, James. 1988. *Acting in the cinema*. Berkeley: University of California Press.

Nelson, Robin. 1997. *TV drama in transition: Forms, values and cultural change*. London: Palgrave Macmillan.

Nelson, Robin. 2006. "Quality Television": "*The Sopranos* is the best television drama ever . . . in my humble opinion. . . ." *Critical Studies in Television* 1(1), 60–71.

Nelson, Robin. 2007. *State of play: Contemporary "high-end" TV drama*. Manchester: Manchester University Press.

O'Sullivan, Sean. 2005. UK policing and its television portrayal: "Law and Order" ideology or modernising agenda? *The Howard Journal of Criminal Justice*, 44(5), 1468–2311.

Page, Norman. 1973. *Speech in the English novel*. London: Longman.

Paget, Derek. 1998. *No other way to tell it: Dramadoc/docudrama on television*. Manchester: Manchester University Press.

Peacock, Steven. 2007. *Reading 24: TV against the clock*. London: I. B. Tauris.

Prodromou, Luke. 2007. Bumping into creative idiomaticity. *English Today*, 23(1), 14–25.

Quaglio, Paul. 2009. *Television dialogue: The sitcom Friends vs. natural conversation*. Studies in corpus linguistics 36. Amsterdam: John Benjamins.

Quigley, A. E. 1975. *The Pinter problem*. Princeton, N.J.: Princeton University Press.

Rampton, Ben. 1995. *Crossing: Language and ethnicity among adolescents*. London: Longman.

Richardson, Kay. 2006. The dark arts of good people: How popular culture negotiates "spin" in NBC's *The West Wing*. *Journal of Sociolinguistics*, 52–69.

Richardson, Kay, and John Corner. 1986. Reading reception: Mediation and transparency in viewers accounts of a TV programme. *Media, Culture and Society*, 8, 485–508.

Rosch, Eleanor. 1973. Principles of categorization. In *Cognition and categorization*, ed. Eleanor Rosch and Barbara Lloyd, 27–48. Hillsdale, N.J.: Erlbaum.

Rudanko, Juhani. 2005. Aggravated impoliteness and two types of speaker intention in an episode in Shakespeare's *Timon of Athens*. *Journal of Pragmatics*, 38(6), 829–841.

Sacks, Harvey. 1972. On the analyzability of stories by children. In *Directions in sociolinguistics: The ethnography of communication*, ed. John Gumperz and Dell Hymes, 325–345. Oxford: Basil Blackwell.

Sanger, Keith. 2001. *The language of drama*. London: Routledge.

Scannell, Paddy. 1991. *Broadcast talk*. London: Sage.

Schank, Roger, and Robert Abelson. 1977. *Scripts, plans, goals and understanding*. Hillsdale, N.J.: Erlbaum.

Schlesinger, Philip. 2007. Creativity: From discourse to doctrine. *Screen*, 48(3), 377–387.

Schmitt, Norbert, and Ron Carter. 2004. Formulaic sequences in action. In *Formulaic sequences: Acquisition, processing and use*, ed. Norbert Schmitt, 1–22. Amsterdam: John Benjamins.

Searle, John. 1969. *Speech acts: An essay in the philosophy of language*. Cambridge: Cambridge University Press.

Short, Mick. 1996. *Exploring the language of poems, plays and prose*. London: Longman.

Short, Mick. 1998. From dramatic text to dramatic performance. In *Exploring the language of drama: From text to context*, ed. Jonathan Culpeper, Peter Verdonk, and Mick Short, 6–18. London: Routledge.

Shuy, Roger. 1998. *The language of confession, interrogation and deception*. London: Sage.

Simpson, Paul. 1998. Odd talk: Studying discourses of incongruity. In *Exploring the language of drama: From text to context*, ed. Jonathan Culpeper, Peter Verdonk, and Mick Short, 34–53. London: Routledge.

Smethurst, William. 2007. *How to write for television: A guide to writing and selling successful TV scripts*, 5th ed. Oxford: How To Books.

Snell, Julia. 2006. Schema theory and the humor of Little Britain. *English Today*, 22(1), 85.

Spencer-Oatey, Helen. 2002. Managing rapport in talk: Using rapport sensitive incidents to explore the motivational concerns underlying politeness. *Journal of Pragmatics*, 34, 529–545.Sperber, Dan, and Deirdre Wilson. 1986. *Relevance: Communication and cognition*. Oxford: Basil Blackwell.

Stockwell, Peter. 2003. Schema poetics and speculative cosmology. *Language and Literature*, 12, 252–271.

Swann, Joan. 2006. Text and performance. In *The art of English: Literary creativity*, ed. Sharon Goodman and Keiron O'Halloran, 145–184. London: Palgrave Macmillan.

Sydney-Smith, S. 2002. *Beyond Dixon of Dock Green: Early British police series*. London: I. B. Tauris.

Tannen, Deborah. 1989. *Talking voices: Repetition, dialogue and imagery in conversational discourse*. Cambridge: Cambridge University Press.

Tannen, Deborah. 1990. Silence as conflict management in Pinter's *Betrayal* and a short story, "Great Wits." In *Conflict talk*, ed. Allen Grimshaw, 260–279. Cambridge: Cambridge University Press.

Tannen, Deborah, and Robin Lakoff. 1984. Conversational strategy and metastrategy in a pragmatic theory: The example of *Scenes from a Marriage*. *Semiotica*, 49(3/4), 323–346.

Thomas, Jenny. 1995. *Meaning in interaction: An introduction to pragmatics*. London: Longman.

Thompson, Robert J. 1996. *Television's second golden age: From* Hill Street Blues *to* ER. Syracuse, N.Y.: Syracuse University Press.

Thornborrow, Joanna, and Shan Wareing. 1998. *Patterns in language: An introduction to language and literary style*. London: Routledge.

Thornham, Sue, and Tony Purvis, eds. 2004. *Television drama: Theories and identities*. London: Palgrave Macmillan.

Tolson, Andrew. 1991. Televised chat and the synthetic personality. In *Broadcast talk*, ed. Paddy Scannell, 178–200. London: Sage.

Tolson, Andrew. 1996. *Mediations: Text and discourse in media studies*. London: Arnold.

Tolson, Andrew. 2006. *Media talk: Spoken discourse on TV and radio*. Edinburgh: University of Edinburgh Press.

Tracy, K., and Sarah J. Tracy. 1998. Rudeness at 911 Reconceptualizing face and face attack. *Human Communication Research*, 25, 221–251.

van Dijck, Jose. 2001. Bodies without borders: The endoscopic gaze. *International Journal of Cultural Studies*, 4(2), 219–237.

Van Leeuwen, Theo. 1999. *Speech, music, sound*. Basingstoke: Macmillan.

Van Leeuwen, Theo. 2004. *Introducing social semiotics*. London: Routledge.

Verschueren, Jeff. 1999. *Understanding pragmatics*. London: Arnold.

Walters, James. 2006. Saving face: Inflections of character role play in Shameless. *Journal of British Cinema and Television*, 3, 95–106.

Watts, Richard. 2003. *Politeness*. Cambridge: Cambridge University Press.

Williams, Raymond. 1975. *Drama in a dramatised society*. Cambridge: Cambridge University Press.

Wray, Alison, and Mick Perkins. 2000. The functions of formulaic language: An integrated model. *Language and Communication*, 20, 1–28.

Wren-Lewis, Justin. 1983. The encoding/decoding model: Criticisms and development. *Media, Culture and Society*, 5, 179–197.

Zulawski, David, and Douglas Wicklander. 2002. *Practical aspects of interview and interrogation*. London: CRC Press.

Index